# Modern Slavery

## The Margins of Freedom

Julia O'Connell Davidson
*University of Bristol, UK*

First published 2015 by
PALGRAVE MACMILLAN

Palgrave Macmillan in the UK is an imprint of Macmillan Publishers Limited, registered in England, company number 785998, of Houndmills, Basingstoke, Hampshire RG21 6XS.

Palgrave Macmillan in the US is a division of St Martin's Press LLC, 175 Fifth Avenue, New York, NY 10010.

Palgrave Macmillan is the global academic imprint of the above companies and has companies and representatives throughout the world.

Palgrave® and Macmillan® are registered trademarks in the United States, the United Kingdom, Europe and other countries.

ISBN 978-1-137-29728-0      ISBN 978-1-137-29729-7 (eBook)
DOI 10.1057/9781137297297

A catalogue record for this book is available from the British Library.

A catalog record for this book is available from the Library of Congress.

*For Django, Inez and Alfreda*
*and*
*in memory of Isabel Barroso Taylor*

# Contents

# Figures

# Acknowledgements

I am extremely grateful to the Leverhulme Trust for the award of a Major Research Fellowship (MRF-2012-085), without which it would have been impossible for me to write this book; also to the ESRC for funding research on 'trafficking' between 2002 and 2006 (R000239794), and a seminar series 'The Politics of Victimhood' (RES-451-26-0921) co-organized with Laura Brace; and to the British Academy for funding a Landmark Conference, 'Slaveries Old and New', in March 2014, jointly organized with Laura Brace, Mark Johnson and Zoe Trodd. Thanks too to Zoe for her generosity in reading and commenting on the book's manuscript, and to Philippa Grand, Harriet Barker and Amelia Derkatsch at Palgrave for supporting the book and bringing it to fruition.

One way or another, I have been thinking about phenomena that are discussed under the rubric of 'modern slavery' for a very long time. My original intellectual debt is to Theo Nichols, who supervised my doctoral research and whose work inspired my interest in capitalism and free and unfree labour, and I have an almost equally longstanding debt to Laura Brace, whose work on concepts of property, self-ownership, freedom and slavery has shaped my own thinking over the past 20 years or so. It was Ola Florin who set me off on the 'trafficking' trail in 2001, and his acuity, humour and encyclopaedic knowledge of the gaps between the rhetoric and reality of rights (as well as of more or less everything else) has sustained me on the subsequent journey. Bridget Anderson, deep mine of theory and knowledge on the tangled politics of migration, citizenship and rights, and stalwart comrade in the cocktail bar of life, has been my other constant companion on the trafficking trek, and my thanks to her and to Ola for comments on various writings that have gone into this book as well as draft chapters. I also thank Nirmal Puwar, Dimitris Papadopoulos, Maria Puig de la Bellacasa, Hannah Bradby and Srila Roy, for the many conversations over the years through which key ideas in this book were shaped, as well as for their conviviality and friendship (and additional thanks to Srila for reading and commenting on Chapter 7).

The 'Modern Slavery' module that I teach on the MA in Global Citizenship, Identities and Human Rights at the University of Nottingham has been a testing ground for ideas in this book, so thanks to all the students who have helped me refine them over the years. I am also grateful to members of the Critical Modern Slavery Studies Facebook Group, and to colleagues in the openDemocracy editorial partnership 'Beyond Trafficking and Slavery' – Prabha Kotiswaran, Genevieve LeBaron, Samuel Okyere, Joel Quirk, Cameron Thibos and above all Neil Howard, whose optimism of the will made the partnership happen. 'Trafficking' led me to work with Esther Bott, Inka Stock and Patrizia Testai, and I have benefitted from their amity as well as learning much from their subsequent research. In addition to all those mentioned above, my understanding of the matters discussed in this book has been enriched by opportunities to engage with the research and thinking of Katie Cruz, Mike Dottridge, Joe Greener, Iman Hashim, Andrew Jefferson, Kerwin Kaye, Christian Karner, Kyunghee Kook, Roda Madziva, Bronwyn Parry, Svati Shah, Nandita Sharma, May-Len Skilbrei, Dag Stenvoll and Nick Stevenson, and I am especially grateful to Nicolas Lainez, who generously supplied me with a huge number of useful references, and to Alf Gunvald Nilsen, who provided incredibly helpful comments on a draft of Chapter 3. Particular thanks also to John Holmwood, James Kincaid and Tommy Lott for their intellectual generosity and encouragement, to Samuel Okyere for his inspiring research, camaraderie and many kindnesses both to me and my dog, and to Amal Treacher Kabesh for taking the time to read draft chapters of this book (even in the midst of marking hell), for her insights into processes of Othering and for her friendship.

Finally, many thanks to Mike Patten, who referred me to several works that have proved invaluable and who read and helpfully commented on an entire draft manuscript; to Gordon and Anthea Brace for their enduring support and encouragement, and for fostering my interest in the value and limits of liberalism; to Bill, Frances and Laura Brace for the solace and confederacy of siblings; to Inez Grummitt for continuing to light up my life and for being such a true mensch; and to Django Davidson for his legendary determination, energy and generosity. I wish very much that Isabel Barroso Taylor was still here to thank for all she taught me about the heroism required to remake lives in the aftermath of political violence and dislocation, as well as the many wonderful things she gifted me. To the incomparable Jacqueline Sánchez Taylor, who not only valiantly endured my absent presence while I was writing this book, but also read innumerable drafts and alerted me to missing links and new connections, the debt is too deep for words. But in any case, the last word must go, as it always does, to Alfreda Barroso Taylor, who is a great joy to me, wise beyond her years, and who offered some excellent advice on how to write this book. Thank you Alfi!

# 1
# Imagining Modernity, Forgetting Slavery

How can we end modern slavery? In the second decade of the twenty-first century, a new brand of anti-slavery campaigners (referred to in this book as the 'new abolitionists') tell us that around 35 million people across the globe today have been trafficked into, or otherwise trapped in, slavery. Hardly a week goes by without a documentary on some aspect of the problem being aired, an international conference on the topic taking place or a fund raiser being held to support the work of one of the many non-governmental organizations (NGOs) campaigning to free the slaves and eradicate modern slavery. Since 2000, 'no fewer than thirty antislavery books and a profusion of research articles have been published' (Stewart, 2015: 127). The question of how to end slavery is routinely posed on the myriad anti-slavery websites and in other materials produced by campaigners, and answered in a variety of ways. There are, for example, calls for the United Nations to take a stronger lead in the fight against slavery; for more international aid to be targeted at countries worst affected; for governments to enact tougher and more comprehensive legislation against slavery and human trafficking; for businesses to root out slavery in their supply chains; for researchers to investigate and map the problem more thoroughly and accurately; and, above all, for individuals to act against modern slavery by learning about the problem, engaging in fund raising and awareness-raising activities, inspiring others to become involved in anti-slavery activism, keeping watch for signs of slavery in their communities and consuming slave-free products (see, for example, Free the Slaves, 2007–2014a; CNN Freedom Project, 2011a; Not for Sale, 2015).

The new abolitionism has remarkably broad appeal. Those involved in campaigns against trafficking and modern slavery include religious leaders from across faiths, trades unions and big business. The

Global Business Coalition against Human Trafficking includes Coca-Cola, ExxonMobil, Ford, Microsoft and ManpowerGroup amongst its members. As its co-founder, David Arkless, stated, 'When you get involved in something like this your employees will love it, the public will love it and your shareholders will love it' (Balch, 2013). Famous actors and pop stars are also there 'lovin' it', contributing to what Dina Haynes (2013) terms, 'the celebrification of human trafficking', and lending their support to the many NGOs campaigning to end modern slavery. And this is a fight endorsed by politicians from across the political spectrum. Certainly, the imperative to end modern slavery is very much on the contemporary political agenda in affluent, liberal states. In 2013, the British Home Secretary, Theresa May, announced her intention to introduce a Modern Slavery Bill; the US President, Barack Obama, proclaimed January 2014 as National Slavery and Human Trafficking Prevention Month; in December 2014, the Australian Justice Minister, Michael Keenan, launched a five-year national action plan to intensify efforts to combat human trafficking, slavery and forced marriages (news.com.au, 2014).

Such measures, like NGOs' exhortations to combat it, presuppose that the term 'modern slavery' names a definite and particular phenomenon. And yet closer attention to the ways in which the term is employed by the many and various actors involved in the fight against 'modern slavery' will not assist in identifying what, exactly, that phenomenon is. In fact, listening to talk of 'modern slavery', I am often reminded of Gustave Flaubert's satirical work, *The Dictionary of Accepted Ideas*, which lists the inane bromides and clichés of his time. Flaubert was prompted to compile the dictionary in the 1870s by his impatience with people's tendency to spout empty speculation and received ideas, rather than to study seriously and to think critically about the social world in which they lived: 'Instead of examining, people pontificate', he observed in a letter to George Sands (Barzun, 1954: 8). He considered including a preface stating that the book's motive was 'the desire to bring the nation back to Tradition, Order and Sound Conventions – all this so phrased that the reader would not know whether or not his leg was being pulled' (Barzun, 1954: 3). The dictionary included the following definition of 'Feudalism – No need to have one single precise notion about it: *thunder against*' (Barzun, 1954). Had he been writing such a satire today, he might be tempted to attach this same definition to the term 'modern slavery'.

For today, platitudes about the 'scourge of modern slavery' are wheeled out by politicians, media pundits and campaigners in discussions on anything from prostitution to child labour to illegal immigration to female circumcision to begging to organ-trading. And though there is no single, precise definition of 'modern slavery', a series of stock phrases and highly dubious statistics about it are circulated, repeated so often and so earnestly that they have taken on the mantle of incontrovertible truths. Speculation on the enormity of the problem is presented as 'fact', even though the next 'fact' to be unfurled is invariably that it is impossible to measure the scale of this hidden, criminal trade. And when political leaders pontificate on the topic, their thunder against 'modern slavery' is almost always redolent of an underlying desire to bring their nations back to 'Tradition, Order and Sound Conventions'.

This book, which includes discussion of what is described as 'forced labour', 'debt-bondage', 'forced marriage', 'trafficking' and 'sex trafficking', offers a critique of these received ideas. The argument is not that the world is free of oppression, domination, exploitation and suffering – far from it – but rather that the new abolitionism offers a highly selective lens through which to view restraints on human freedom. Instead of posing the question 'How can we end modern slavery?', this book asks 'What does the term modern slavery mean?', or, to paraphrase Ananya Roy's (2012) question about poverty: 'Who sees modern slavery, and what do they see?' What leads the new abolitionists to identify some, but not other, forms of injustice, violence and exploitation as 'slavery', and what traditions of thought, conceptual schema, and collective memories frame their vision? How is the figure of the 'modern slave' worked in political life (to borrow Honig's (2001) question about 'the foreigner'), as well as by those organizations campaigning for an end to 'modern slavery', and to what ends? Which problems, and *whose* problems, are addressed by professing a profound and passionate commitment to combatting the problem of 'modern slavery'?

## From state security to modern slavery: a brief history

Policy measures to address 'modern slavery' are invariably presented with much thunder about the need to protect universal human rights and freedoms. Yet current political interest in 'slavery' can be traced back to the 1990s when there was growing political anxiety about threats to state powers from what came to be termed 'transnational organized crime'. In the context of more porous borders in the post-Cold War era, state actors worried about a perceived expansion of illegal markets, both domestic and global, viewing this as a threat to the legitimate economy and to political institutions. They were also concerned about their own capacity to control immigration (including but not limited to the mobility of criminal actors across national borders), which was regarded as a threat to national sovereignty and security. 'Human trafficking' first entered into policy consciousness through the lens of these disquiets. Strongly associated with the forced movement of women and girls across borders and into prostitution, it was parcelled up with phenomena such as smuggling, money laundering and drug and gun running, as part of a problem that could only effectively be addressed through international cooperation between the states it imperilled. The United Nations Convention on Transnational Organized Crime (2000), and its three additional Protocols (the Protocol to Prevent, Suppress and Punish Trafficking in Persons, Especially Women and Children; the Protocol against the Smuggling of Migrants by Land, Sea and Air; and the Protocol against the Illicit Manufacturing of and Trafficking in Firearms, Their Parts and Components and Ammunition) sought to secure such cooperation.

The Trafficking Protocol provides a very loose definition of 'trafficking' not as a single, one-off event, but a *process* (recruitment, transportation and control) that is organized for purposes of exploitation, that takes place over time and that can be developed in a variety of different ways.[1] 'Exploitation' is not defined, but 'shall include, at a minimum, the exploitation of the prostitution of others or other forms of sexual exploitation, forced labour or services, slavery or practices similar to slavery, servitude or the removal of organs'. It is noteworthy that while in political rhetoric trafficking is said to *be* modern slavery, in international law, slavery is just one of a number of possible outcomes of what is termed trafficking. It is also important that, taken together, the trafficking and smuggling protocols reflect an assumption that migration is *either* voluntary *or* forced, and that a neat line can be drawn between the two. Where trafficking is held to be 'carried out with the use of coercion and/or deception', smuggling is described as 'a voluntary act on the part of those smuggled' (Home Office, 2013: 7). The assumed 'either/or' binary between forced and voluntary migration is reflected in the kind of obligations that states are deemed to have in relation to the two categories of migrant it produces. Though still limited, states' obligations towards Victims of Trafficking (VoTs) are more extensive than they are towards smuggled persons (Bhabha and Zard, 2006).

In the run-up to the drafting of the Convention on Transnational Organized Crime and its Protocols, and immediately thereafter, politicians and policy-makers often remarked that 'Smuggling is a crime against the state, trafficking is a crime against a person.' Then came 9/11, read as an even more direct and deathly threat to Western liberal democracy than 'organized crime', and terrorism was added to the bundle of security threats supposedly presented by or linked to trafficking. 'Human smuggling, trafficking in persons, and clandestine terrorist travel are transnational issues that threaten national security', a US Human Smuggling and Trafficking Center (HSTC) report states, and the HSTC was itself established under a section of the Intelligence Reform and Terrorism Prevention Act of 2004 (HSTC, 2005: 1). Trafficking now appeared as a simultaneous assault on the person and the state. It was increasingly represented in international and domestic policy circles as a vast and ever-growing problem affecting every corner of the earth, part of a dark underbelly of globalization that could only be tackled through tougher immigration controls, stronger law enforcement, and new and greater powers for those charged with safeguarding national security.

The response to these perceived threats to state sovereignty and national security has been extraordinarily violent. As future chapters will show, immigration policies and border controls have been pursued that have led to many thousands of deaths, and there has been a dramatic expansion of the use of immigration detention in liberal democratic states. But alongside this growing use of force, the claim that 'trafficking is nothing short of modern slavery' has been frequently and vigorously asserted. Moreover, if this is so, then any and all measures to combat it can be presented as measures to protect the human rights of its victims. Indeed, in this new double-speak, cracking down on 'illegal immigration' becomes part of a fight to secure fundamental human rights, as opposed to implying a violation of those rights (Anderson and O'Connell Davidson, 2003). The metaphor of slavery also works to obviate difficult questions about how the exploitation, 'unfreedom' and suffering of the VoT is to be disentangled from that of other groups of migrants, in particular those imagined as 'economic migrants' and those classed as 'asylum seekers', for it takes trafficking outside migration. We are no longer speaking of an ordinary, everyday phenomenon in which modern liberal states have an interest (or multiple, often conflicting interests), but of an 'old evil', as George W. Bush put it in a speech to the United Nations in 2003, an anachronistic 'slave trade' that must be abolished (Bravo, 2011).

Another effect of framing the fight against trafficking as a fight *against* modern slavery and *for* fundamental human rights has been to open the door for new alliances between governmental and non-governmental organizations in the fields of human and child rights. States, especially the United States, have been prepared to commit spectacular sums to the battle against 'illegal immigration', and within this, against 'human trafficking' (Andersson, 2014a; Dottridge, 2014). Though much of this money has gone to the countless new governmental programmes and task forces to combat 'trafficking' that have been set up around the world, international agencies and NGOs have also enjoyed a generous share of the pie. Even in the 1990s, the growing political and public interest in trafficking and associated opportunities for fund raising provided many human and child rights international organizations and NGOs with an incentive to re-badge some or all of their existing activities as 'anti-trafficking' work.

It would be wrong to present the NGOs and international agencies that campaign against 'trafficking' and 'modern slavery' as an undifferentiated group. While some, in effect, function as an arm of government (helping to sort 'deserving' VoTs from the 'undeserving' smuggled or otherwise 'illegal' migrants, for example), others attempt to hold governments to account for their lip-service approach to the issue and the rights violations associated with their anti-trafficking policies. Nonetheless, it is the case that as more and more governmental organizations, NGOs, and researchers came to view trafficking as *the* topical and 'hot' human rights issue, the term experienced what Joel Best (1993) names 'domain expansion' (see also Chuang, 2013). Where initially the focus had been on forced movement into prostitution, 'trafficking' now came to embrace a large and disparate collection of global social problems and rights violations. By the 2000s, concerns about child labour, forced labour, domestic servitude, enforced criminal activity, benefit fraud, inter-country adoption and fostering, organ trading, child soldiers, prostitution and underage, servile or forced marriage were all included under the umbrella of 'trafficking', and through this, absorbed into what is dubbed 'modern slavery'. This process of assimilation was aided by actors in the 'new abolitionist' movement, a strand of anti-slavery activism that emerged and prospered alongside the post-millennium flood of interest in trafficking.

## The new abolitionism

In 2000, the long established, British-based NGO Anti-Slavery International acquired a new, US-based sister organization, Free the Slaves (the two have since severed their links). Many other anti-slavery NGOs were subsequently founded, especially in the United States, Australia and

Western European countries, including Stop the Traffik in 2006; Not for Sale in 2007; End Slavery Now in 2008; Alliance against Modern Slavery in 2011 and Walk Free Foundation in 2012. The International Justice Mission (IJM), which had been founded in 1997, continued to focus on 'rescuing victims from slavery and sexual exploitation', and other existing human rights organizations extended the remit of their activities to include 'anti-slavery' work. Such organizations have been active in promoting the notion that 'trafficking' is a growing problem and the modern equivalent of the transatlantic slave trade, and have more generally set the agenda for talk of 'slavery' as a contemporary global problem. This they have achieved not least through their prodigious efforts to circulate certain 'global facts and figures' concerning trafficking and slavery, in particular: 'there are more people in slavery today than at any other time in human history'; 'the average cost of a slave today is less that the equivalent cost of an average slave in the American South in 1850'; 'human trafficking is the third largest global criminal industry, behind only guns and drugs, generating 32 billion US dollars annually'. And as 'the main attraction of these "facts" stems from their value as advocacy tools, there has been a widespread reluctance to ask how they have been calculated, and whether or not they are true' (Quirk and O'Connell Davidson, 2015).

These 'facts and figures', and indeed the new abolitionist movement more generally, owes much to one man, Kevin Bales, co-founder of Free the Slaves. Indeed, his influence has been so great that this book's ambition to deconstruct dominant discourse on 'modern slavery' unavoidably demands a good deal of critical attention to his work. In 1999, Bales published and then widely publicized an estimate of 27 million slaves in the contemporary world. This was a reduction to the estimate of 100 million previously bandied around by some NGOs, but an advance on the estimate of 20 million that Anti-Slavery International worked with. Anti-Slavery International (2015) remains more cautious when it comes to quantifying contemporary slavery. Bales subsequently worked with the Walk Free Foundation to produce its first *Global Slavery Index* in 2013, which enlarged the total global estimate to 29.8 million 'modern slaves'. This was then raised it to 35.8 million in its 2014 report (Walk Free, 2014). The index purports to measure the size of the modern slavery problem country by country, and provides a quantitative ranking of 162 countries around the world according to the estimated prevalence of slavery (that is to say, the estimated percentage of enslaved people in the national population at a point in time).

Since 'slave' is no longer anywhere a legally recognized status, the index relies on data on a series of proxy categories (forced labour, trafficking, forced marriage, worst forms of child labour, bonded labour and so on). As will be seen in the course of this book, each of these categories presents its own definitional problems, and the phenomena to which they refer are embedded in, or overlap with, other – often socially sanctioned – markets, institutions or practices (labour markets and marriage, for example). They also often take place in contexts where the lives of much of the population are characterized by hardship, privation and lack of citizenship, labour or human rights. Indeed, in the countries that top the *Global Slavery Index*, vast numbers of people live below the international poverty line of US$1.25 per day – 88 percent of the population in the Democratic Republic of Congo, 62 percent of the population in Haiti, around 30 percent of the population (some 360 million people) in India (UNICEF, 2014) and around 46 percent of the population in Uzbekistan (OPHI, 2010).

This particular method of measuring poverty, and the relation between the US$1.25 poverty level and vulnerability to extreme labour exploitation, are foci of academic debate (Phillips, 2015). However, it is undoubtedly the case that in such contexts, many people's lives are heavily constrained by debts they have had little choice but to take on and that they are unlikely ever to repay; many people labour for long hours for wages that do not even meet subsistence needs; and many of those defined as children by the UN Convention on the Rights of the Child (UN, 1989), (persons under the age of 18) need to work, often in poor and hazardous conditions, to survive. But they are not all 'modern slaves', according to the new abolitionists, who draw a strong distinction between *real* slavery and other, more ordinary forms of drudgery and oppression that exist in the contemporary world. As Free the Slaves (2007–2014) puts it: 'Free the Slaves believes that all labor abuses and human rights abuses are wrong. Our mission, however, is ending slavery.'

Such a mission presupposes that 'modern slavery' constitutes a uniquely intolerable moral wrong, and that it can be separated from other social and global ills for purposes of practical intervention and for purposes of quantification, something very important to their project. Walk Free, for example, was founded by Australian mining magnate Andrew Forrest, and he took advice from Microsoft founder, Bill Gates, when setting up the organization. Gates told Forrest that to end modern slavery, he must 'find a metric to quantify it' – 'Bill's a measure kind of guy,' Forrest is reported to have said – and went on to observe that in 'management speak, if you can't measure it, it doesn't exist' (Behrmann, 2013). Leaving aside concerns we may have about this as an ontological statement and its implication that all aspects of human and social experience can be translated into numbers, corporate management's pithy wisdom that you cannot control what you cannot measure deflects attention from a much more certain truism, namely that you cannot measure what you cannot define. To quantify any given social phenomenon, a precise and neutral definition that clearly separates it from other, associated or neighbouring phenomena is required. Chapter 2 will argue that the definition of 'modern slavery' offered by the new abolitionists does not fit this bill.

Notwithstanding the absence of an exact and operational definition (or perhaps precisely because of this lack), campaigns against 'trafficking' and 'modern slavery' seemingly tap directly into the current Zeitgeist. In February 2008, at a major UN conference on human trafficking in Vienna attended by A-list celebrities as well as representatives from governments, NGOs and international agencies, Antonio Maria Costa, head of the UN Office on Drugs and Crime, described the event as something between the World Economic Forum at Davos and the 1960s music festival Woodstock – 'This is not an inter-governmental conference, nor is it a talk shop', he said. 'Think of it more as a rally. We march together'. Costa continued, '200 years after the end of the trans-Atlantic slave trade, we have the obligation to fight a crime that has no place in the 21st Century. Let's call it what it is: modern slavery' (BBC, 2008). His remarks are indicative of the wider 'feel good' factor associated with the new abolitionism, the sense of solidarity and collective identity for the 'we' who come together to fight this appalling anachronism.

This 'we' is, in one sense, remarkably heterogeneous – young and old, trade unionists and business leaders, politicians of the left and the right, believers and atheists, celebrities and 'ordinary' folk. In another sense, the 'we' who are on the march are not so diverse. They are overwhelmingly drawn from the affluent Western world, or from privileged elites of the developing world, for this is very far from a grass-roots, bottom-up movement. The NGOs and activists that drum up popular support for the anti-trafficking/anti-modern-slavery project in North America, Europe and Australia closely fit the mould of their forerunners in anti-poverty campaigns such as Band Aid, Jubilee 2000, Make Poverty History (indeed, there is even some overlap in personnel). This is a mould that has been described as the 'democratization of development' (Roy, 2012, see also Krabill, 2012).

Ananya Roy observes that poverty became visible as an urgent global social problem in the final decades of the twentieth century not simply because development elites and policy experts placed it on the international political agenda, but also as a result of a form of democratization inspired and mobilized by iconic figures from Bill Gates to Bono. They helped to make poverty visible to 'the millennials', the small, privileged group with the access to leisure and resources – the 'we' who sees poverty – and also called on them to *act* upon poverty, to become part of global poverty action. 'Poverty action is a key part of how millennials create a sense of self as global citizens', Roy (2012) argues, and it embodies ethics 'not as a sense of norms' but as something more Foucauldian – 'a practice of the self'.

Viewed as such, the uplifting, Woodstock vibe that surrounds modern slavery activism becomes more explicable. As the NGO 'Free the Slaves' (FTS, 2013a) tells potential donors and volunteers, 'There is a common myth about the nature of anti-slavery work: that it's terribly depressing. Actually, fighting slavery is the most joyful experience that you can imagine.' The costs of helping 'communities in slavery become free ... can be surprisingly small', FTS (2013b) explains elsewhere, 'A few cows, goats and chickens can provide the stability of food and income that is the first step on the ladder to self-sufficiency and real freedom.' In fact, Bales (2007a) tells us, it would cost relatively little to 'eradicate slavery around the world' – only about US$15 billion over a 25-year period – and this spend is not only the right moral course, but also a great investment since:

> Freed slaves know how to work, and they will quickly begin to build assets ... They will also become what they have never been allowed to be – consumers, buying food, clothing and education for their children. In areas with extensive slavery, liberation leads to economic growth.

In short, freeing slaves is joyous, cheap, and hugely personally rewarding – 'WE CAN ALL BE HEROES', as FTS puts it (2013b, original emphasis).

One reason why such heroism is open to all and endorsed by the political leaders of the affluent world is that it is a form of action imagined as lying beyond and outwith politics. This is not least because slavery is represented as a pre-modern institution belonging to a benighted past, something we all know to be wrong and all share an interest in combatting or, as Kevin Bales (2013) has it, 'a disease of our common being' that we can wipe out 'the way we've wiped out smallpox'. The term 'modern slavery' rests upon a particular vision of modernity, as well as a particular understanding of slavery and, for this reason, while it is described as a global problem, its representation varies with its geography.

In Western media reports on 'slave trading' in contemporary Africa, for instance, the problem is presented as evidence that 'African' societies still have not yet fully joined the modern world (Woods, 2013). Similarly, when India is the focus of attention, the presence of 'slavery' appears as an indicator of how far the country has left to travel in order to become a truly modern nation. As Svati Shah (2014) notes, the trope of slavery as a timeless cultural tradition in India is especially pronounced in discussions of prostitution and 'sex trafficking'. The CNN Freedom Project (2011b), for example, provides a web page advertised as answering 'Your questions on slavery in India' where it offers commentary on a documentary film aired in 2011, tellingly titled, 'Trapped by Tradition'. Speaking of a form of prostitution it describes as slavery, the author states: 'This has been going on for generations and is a by-product of poverty and tradition'. The same tropes also appear in talk of what is termed 'debt-bondage slavery' in sectors other than prostitution. Another commentator claims, 'It is apparent that India has unique conditions that have enabled slavery to persist over a great length of time, and allowed slaves to exist in greater numbers there than in any other country on Earth' (Knight, 2012).

There is no such harking back to tradition, custom or culture in campaigning, or in popular or policy discussion of 'modern slavery' in contemporary liberal democratic societies. Abhorrence of slavery is taken to be a defining characteristic of the United States, a nation committed, in President Barack Obama's (2012) words 'to the enduring cause of freedom' and 'steadfast in [its] resolve to see that all men, women, and children have the opportunity to realize this greatest of gifts', and love of freedom is regarded as equally fundamental to Canadian, Australian, British and other Western European societies. The idea of slaves on their soil is thus, in the words of British Home Secretary Theresa May (2013), 'scarcely believable'. The new abolitionists, too, are emphatic that the anti-slavery impulse is rooted in Western liberal societies. Slavery may have *persisted* in 'traditional' societies after the nineteenth century, but when what is described as 'slavery' is found in modern liberal societies, it is held to be an unwanted import from lawless and 'uncivilized' regions of the world – it has been 'trafficked' onto the territory of the modern liberal state. David Batstone, founder of the organization Not for Sale, offers the following summary:

It certainly was a momentous day in 1833 when the British Parliament passed the Slavery Abolition Acts, which gave freedom to all slaves held captive in the British Empire. Likewise, the Thirteenth Amendment of the U.S. Constitution passed in 1865 at the end of the Civil War, left no ambiguity about the legal standing of slavery in America... The establishment of laws that criminalized the slave trade meant a major advancement in the cause for human freedom... Abolition laws eventually spread to nearly every nation of the world. In our own day, however, a thriving black market in human beings has emerged once again. It is a criminal enterprise involving both local scoundrels and sophisticated international syndicates.

(2007: 5)

In a similar vein, Jean Allain and Kevin Bales (2012) state that there are distinctive parallels between the contemporary abolitionist movement and the abolition movement of the past both in terms of the role played by Christian religious activists, and in terms of that played by liberal nations:

Just as British dominance of the seas during the Nineteenth Century allowed it to end... the slave-trade; so too has the current dominance of the United States allowed it, through legislation dealing with trafficking, to force other countries to get serious about prosecuting cases of slavery.

Though the new abolitionists tend to deliver their message with the righteously indignant fervour that is usually associated with movements of religious and political dissent, the 'truth' that they speak to power is actually very palatable to governments of affluent liberal states, and to the corporate world. They call for action against a peculiarly morally repugnant form of suffering, but since this wrong is presented as exceptional to, and incompatible with, the dominant political and economic world order, their project is readily allied to a celebration of the existing status quo. In fact, their account of slavery past and present chimes well with the version of the history of liberal societies (popularized in the nineteenth century through tomes like Thomas Babington Macaulay's 1848 *The History of England from the Accession of James II*) as 'a story to be proud of, a story of progress' (Hall, 2014: 72), and more generally underscores the rightness of the norms and values of modern liberal societies.

## Modernity and the demise of slavery: a liberal tale

W.E.B. Dubois (1966: 722) once commented on the frequent recurrence in the study of history of 'the idea that evil must be forgotten, distorted, skimmed over':

> We must forget that George Washington was a slave owner...and simply remember the things we regard as creditable and inspiring. The difficulty, of course, with this philosophy is that history loses its value as an incentive and example; it paints perfect man and noble nations, but it does not tell the truth.

His remarks remain highly pertinent to the dominant narrative of Western history in which acts of abolition and proclamations of emancipation completed a historical movement from the dark ages to Enlightenment that had been in process since the seventeenth century, dotting the 'i' and crossed the 't' of 'liberty', so to speak, and marking a conclusive transition into modernity and freedom. This narrative is at the heart of liberal understandings of liberalism, the dominant political outlook in contemporary Western societies.

Liberalism, Charles W. Mills (2008: 1380) observes, has its origins in the 'antifeudal egalitarian ideology of individual rights and freedoms that emerges in the seventeenth and eighteenth centuries to oppose absolutism and ascriptive hierarchy', and viewed through its lens, the Age of Enlightenment (roughly 1650–1800) marked a watershed in human history. 'Enlightenment', Emmanuel Kant wrote in 1784, 'is man's emergence from his self-incurred immaturity', an immaturity caused not by 'lack of understanding, but lack of resolve and courage to use it without another's guidance. *Sapere aude*! Dare to know! That is the motto of Enlightenment' (Kant, 2009: 1). Enlightenment scientists had the courage to reject the direction of religious authority, throw off the blinkers of tradition, received ideas and superstition, and instead observe, classify and theorize the natural world guided by the forces of reason alone. Similarly, Enlightenment political thinkers refused old certainties about the political and social order as preordained and God-given, and sought answers to questions about the legitimate exercise of political power and the rights of the individual through the application of reason.

Their reasoning led them to the idea of the social contract, an idea that explains political obligation as 'based on an agreement between rational and equal individuals, rather than on a natural hierarchy'

(Brace, 2007: 25). Classical social contract theory tells of individuals leaving the 'state of nature' and making a pact to surrender certain liberties in exchange for security, civil equality and freedom. Through this contract, political or civil society is born (Pateman, 1988). The novelty of classical social contract theory lay in its 'rejection of traditional patriarchy, of divine right and all forms of tradition-based, naturalised authority' (Brace, 2007: 26), and its emphasis on 'the idea of personal volition, the idea that obligation was created by free will rather than arising from relations of authority and subjection' (Stanley, 1998: 5). This emphasis on consent as necessary to the legitimate exercise of authority was extended to other aspects of social life, in particular, to relations between workers and masters.

According to John Locke, 'Every man has a property in his own person. This nobody has any right to but himself. The labour of his body, and the work of his hands, we many say, are properly his' (1993: 274). The idea of property in the person led to a view of the human capacity to labour as property that could be lent, hired out or sold as a commodity. It became possible to envisage a social order in which sovereign individuals 'were entitled to put their labor and its fruits up for sale', and to contract to exchange their labour for a wage (Stanley, 1998: 9). The people who feature in this narrative are taken to be free because, unlike slaves or serfs, they are proprietors of their own persons and capacities. Indeed freedom itself looks 'like a function of possession' as C. B. MacPherson (1962: 3) put it in his description of 'the theory of possessive individualism', and society appears as 'a lot of free equal individuals related to each other as proprietors of their own capacities and of what they have acquired by their exercise. Society consists of exchange between proprietors'.

In such a society, political and economic freedoms go hand in hand. Economic activity had been suborned to cultural and religious goals in pre-modern societies, and individuals' social status determined the role they would play in processes of production and consumption. Cut loose from traditional authority, the sovereign individuals of the modern liberal world had the political right and the capacity to make economic contracts. In the narrative of history generated by Enlightenment political thinkers, and elaborated (albeit in very different ways) by nineteenth- and early twentieth-century social and political theorists, economic and political change unfolded together in a staged procession (Steinfeld, 2001). As European societies made the transition from feudalism to mercantilist market societies to free market capitalist societies, progressively more people enjoyed progressively more political freedom, and 'Unfree serf labor gave way to regulated wage labor and finally to free wage labor' (Steinfeld, 2001: 1).

As far as slavery is concerned, different strands of liberalism offer slightly different perspectives on its demise. For some thinkers, the development of free market capitalism made slavery untenable economically. Writing in the late-eighteenth century, Adam Smith was firmly of the view that slavery and serfdom were inimical to economic growth and prosperity. Masters may have thought it cheaper to use slave labour than to pay free waged workers, but this was a false economy. Wage labour is ultimately cheaper than slave labour, first because free workers work more diligently and more innovatively, and second because wages allow workers both to maintain themselves and to procreate, thereby furnishing the economy with the next generation of workers. This latter is a task that free men can perform with more 'frugality' and 'parsimony' than any master can achieve, Smith said (1986: 184). Twentieth century 'free market' liberals similarly told a story in which slavery appeared incompatible with capitalist development. In his classic 1962 book, *Capitalism and Freedom*, Milton Friedman wrote that throughout history, tyranny, servitude and misery had been the 'typical state of mankind':

> The nineteenth and early twentieth century in the Western world stand out as striking exceptions to the general trend of historical development. Political freedom in this instance clearly came along with the free market and the development of capitalist institutions.
>
> (Friedman, 1962: 10)

Contemporary disciples of Friedman follow suit. For them, freedom is negatively constituted as 'the absence of the initiation of physical force' (Reisman, 2002), and the story of modernity is one of movement away from the dark ages in which the social order was established and maintained purely on the basis of brute violence or its threat, towards an enlightened era in which equal and sovereign individuals freely associate with each other by means of peaceable, voluntary contractual exchange. Writing on 'the benevolent nature of capitalism', Reisman (2002) states that:

> Historically, political freedom has followed the emergence of free markets and capitalist institutions... Where monopolies and trading restrictions are rife, so is special treatment of one social, racial or religious group over another; the ability to 'keep people in their place'

remains. In a genuinely free market, economic efficiency is separated from irrelevant characteristics such as skin color or faith.

Through this lens, slavery was not only 'a blatant contradiction of the principle that the individual has the right to the pursuit of his own happiness' (Reisman, 2002), but also made no economic sense.

Mainstream, liberal commentary on the actual abolition of slavery tends to switch the emphasis, focusing less on structural economic forces and more upon the role of human agency, especially that of (some) anti-slavery activists. Teaching resources such as the UK-based Understanding Slavery Initiative, for example, explain that opposition to the transatlantic slave trade was first voiced by American and English Quakers from the mid-seventeenth century, then mobilized, with support from Methodist and other Nonconformist groups in the eighteenth century to become a political movement against slavery. Singled out for attention in this narrative are George Fox, John Wesley, Granville Sharp, Thomas Clarkson, and William Wilberforce (there is no mention of slave rebellion or revolution or of anti-slavery activism on the part of freed and fugitive slaves), and their battle was against those with strong vested interests in the slave trade: 'After all, major commercial interests were determined to see the slave trade continue. Merchants, shippers, financiers, planters, colonial officials – all these and more saw their future livelihoods tied to the slave trade' (USI, 2013).

This focus on the role of individual anti-slavery activists in the abolition of the slave trade may appear to challenge the notion that the development of free market capitalism is ineluctably linked to political equality and freedom. However, even in narratives that lead with white abolitionists' activism, it is also generally assumed that slavery was discordant with the economic structures and long-term interests of modern liberal capitalist societies. Thus, Understanding Slavery Initiative's account of the campaign for abolition concludes by observing that one of anti-slavery activists' core and most powerful arguments was that:

> Africa had more to offer the outside commercial world than its enslaved humanity... Not only was the [slave] trade cruel and un-Christian, but it also blocked the development of more normal forms of trade. To those who said that abolition of the slave trade would bring about economic disaster, Clarkson (and, later, others) answered that normal trade with Africa would flourish – if only the slave trade were abolished.
>
> (USI, 2013)

The orthodox, taken-for-granted history of liberal societies thus depicts a linear progression from subjection to liberty. Modernity, political liberty, and free wage labour are fused together in this narrative, with slavery imaginatively cast as a feature of previous and pre-modern societies, societies in which people were or are 'trapped by tradition'. Struggles to abolish slavery appear as part of a modernizing effort to bring law and custom into line not simply with the declaratory ideals of liberalism concerning universal rights to life, liberty and estate, but also with the requirements of modern, capitalist economies. In this history of liberal democratic societies, modernity appears 'as the outcome of a break, as a radical contrast with what preceded it' (Caverno, 1992: 32), and modern, liberal society is imagined as defined by what is new about it. This is a vision of history that reflects and reproduces what Raia Prokhovnik (1999) terms 'binary thinking', and that relies on highly selective remembering and forgetting.

## 'Modern slavery' and binary thinking

In classical sociological theory, as well as in the mainstream liberal story of liberal societies, modernity is characterized as fundamentally new and standing in sharp contrast to the past, and 'Typologies and theories grounded in the presumed radical distinctiveness of modernity continue to be the stock-in-trade of sociological thought' (Sayer, 1991: 12, see also Bhambra, 2007). The main features of the assumed transition from past to present can be diagrammatically summarized in the following table:

| Past | Present |
|------|---------|
| Traditional | Rational |
| Tyranny | Freedom |
| Status | Contract |
| Hierarchy | Equality |
| Slavery | Free waged labour |

Such past/present contrasts reflect a more general tendency within Western post-Enlightenment thought to conceive of social and political reality in terms of a series of interlocking binaries or dualisms. The mind/body, subject/object and persons/things dualisms are of special and particular importance to the way in which both slavery and freedom are commonly pictured. In the liberal imaginary, commodity exchange and personhood (or economic and political life) are represented as both separate and mutually constitutive. They are separate in the sense that material things (objects) and rights to them are taken to 'represent the natural universe of commodities', while people (subjects) are taken to 'represent the natural universe of individuation and singularization' (Kopytoff, 1986: 64). The subject/object binary thus marks off persons (who have both the right and the capacity to make political and economic contracts) from property (in which people have rights and are free to contractually exchange). They are mutually constitutive in the sense that, in liberal thought, entering into commodity exchanges is one of the ways in which personhood is posited and confirmed. The freedom to do so is part of the equal, civil freedom that the liberal democratic state affords its citizens, and it is by entering into voluntary, peaceable acts of commodity exchange that liberal subjects recognize each other as persons (Sayer, 1991: 58–9).

This assumed split between the public world of civil and political life, and the private world of economic action generates powerful contrasts between the slave and the free person. Slavery is envisaged as reducing the human being to nothing but a body, a 'thing' to be used as the instrument of another's will, whereas the free and equal political subjects of modern liberal democracies are constructed as disembodied: they are rational, abstract, universal, *individuals* (Brace, 2014: 485). In contemporary discourse on modern slavery, this plays out in an emphasis on the treatment of human beings as disposable objects, mere commodities to be bought, used and discarded. So, for instance, John Miller (2006), who served as the director of the US State Department's Office to Monitor and Combat Trafficking in Persons from 2002, states:

> The underground market in people, termed human trafficking, functions by the benign rules of supply and demand – which makes this market particularly grotesque because the commodity is human life and the exchange results in modern-day slavery.

Anti-trafficking and new abolitionist campaign materials emphasize this stress on the reduction of victims to objects of trade. They abound with visual imagery of women and girls as slabs of meat, or packed in jam jars or sardine tins, or with bodies barcoded ready for sale, or as inanimate objects such as puppets, or as decapitated heads packaged as sex toys (Andrijasevic, 2007; Aradau, 2004). When politicians and new abolitionists state that trafficking and modern slavery involve the commodification of human beings, they mean to underline the intrinsic and absolute wrongness of these phenomena. Human beings are 'not for sale', as David Batstone's antislavery tag line has it. In the twenty-first century, slavery is presented as the *sine qua non* of unacceptable commodification because it disregards the distinction between persons and things that should be held inviolable.

And yet this supposedly inviolable distinction between persons and things has long been, and still is, routinely ignored in liberal societies. There is a gap – a vast chasm even – between the discourse surrounding what may and may not be treated properly as a commodity, and the realities of social life (Constable, 2009; Kopytoff, 1986; Radin, 1996). In actuality, human attributes and capacities – especially the capacity to labour, but also sometimes human organs, tissues and blood – have been, and are still, marked as commodities, and whole human beings have also been commodified and sold across markets as chattel slaves in modern liberal societies. Indeed, one of the most striking flaws in the narrative that casts the European Enlightenment period as the birth of freedom, the beginning of an unstoppable march from status to contract, from hierarchy to equality and so on, is its disregard for the fact that liberalism as a political ideology actually developed and thrived alongside the *expansion* of European colonialism and transatlantic slavery:

> The evolution of the modern version of the contract, characterized by an antipatriarchalist Englightenment liberalism, with its proclamations of the equal rights, autonomy and freedom for all men… took place simultaneously with the massacre, expropriation, and subjection to hereditary slavery of men at least apparently human.
>
> (Mills, 1998: 64)

Transatlantic slavery *was* modern slavery (Gilroy, 1993; Mills, 1998).

## Anti-tyranny thinking: liberty for the free, bondage for the slave

The idea that a system of chattel slavery was introduced, operated, condoned and/or tolerated by people who simultaneously voiced a passionate commitment to the ideal of freedom may today seem extraordinary. But viewed in relation to the long arc of history that preceded the Enlightenment, it is not so incomprehensible. To understand how the circle could be squared, we need to think more about the distinction imaginatively drawn between the realms of public, political life and private life, and the difference between opposition to political tyranny and opposition to private slave-holding.

As Mary Nyquist (2013: 1) notes, the term 'slavery' has long been employed as a figurative depiction of political tyranny. 'Greek, and later Roman, antityranny ideology represents the tyrant's subjects as figuratively enslaved – enslavement that seeks to dishonor and disenfranchise citizens who are meant to be "free".' This figurative, political slavery must be distinguished from the personal, or chattel slavery 'against which it asserts its claims', for the anti-tyranny ideology that condemns political slavery 'has its own unique logic and codes, none of which arise from concern for those who are actually enslaved' (Nyquist, 2013: 2). In ancient Greece, Nyquist continues, political tyranny was a matter 'of concern to the freeborn male citizens who collectively constitute the *polis*', and tyranny was a term of abuse: 'It charges a ruler with obtaining power unconstitutionally or with ruling in defiance of laws and customs over citizens who are thereby metaphorically enslaved by his behavior' (Nyquist, 2013: 5).

Anti-tyranny ideology was also a feature of Roman republicanism, and it resurfaced 'in early modern political traditions that drew on Greek and Roman literature' (Nyquist, 2013: 50). Anti-tyranny principles are apparent in the logic and codes of revolutionary thought in seventeenth-century England and also in eighteenth-century American challenges to British rule. Protesting against the taxation of Americans by the British colonial power in the late 1760s, John Dickinson (a free white man) asked whether it was 'possible to form an idea of a slavery more complete, more miserable, more disgraceful, than that of a people, where justice is administered, government exercised, and a standing army maintained, AT THE EXPENSE OF THE PEOPLE, and yet WITHOUT THE LEAST DEPENDENCE ON THEM' (Dickinson, 1767–1768). Political slavery was even invoked by white West Indian slaveholders protesting against the limits on the powers they exercised over their slave property imposed by English law (Wong, 2009: 59).

Slavery continues to be employed as a metaphor for political tyranny today. In the United States in particular, right-wing politicians and other public figures use the language of slavery in relation to what they perceive as unrepresentative taxation, as well as to describe a variety of other ills. Even President Obama's health-care law has been described as 'slavery in a way, because it is making all of us subservient to the government' (Sullivan, 2013 ). Today, as in the past, those who employ slavery as a metaphor to call attention to what they regard as unwarranted infringements on their liberties do not mean to say that they are *really* slaves. Indeed, just as Arthur Koestler (1964) argued that jokes work by bringing two mutually incompatible frames of reference into sudden collision, so the rhetorical punch of describing their own condition as 'slavery' is powered by the surprise conjunction of two otherwise irreconcilable conceptual matrices: 'the free citizen' or person on the one hand, and 'the slave' or sub-person on the other. As Nyquist (2013: 5) explains:

> In the very act of rhetorically gesturing toward its possibility, political 'slavery' constitutes a community of 'free' citizens whose direct participation in self-rule ensures they will not brook subjection. In denouncing tyranny's lawlessness, those who are threatened with 'slavery' do not call attention to the vulnerable, legally unprotected condition of chattel slaves. Rather, they polemically signal the values cherished in and by means of the political arena – in Athens, where it originates, *isonomia*, the equality associated with law's rule, together, later, with *eleutheria*, freedom.

Viewed through this lens, the challenge to tradition-based, naturalized authority articulated in classical liberal theory looks as much like a continuation of anti-tyranny thought as it does like a radical break with all political thinking that preceded it. A 'process of negative self-definition' (*we* deserve liberty because *we* are not slaves) is also there in liberal calls for 'nonmonarchical, representative, or more egalitarian, democratic government' (Nyquist, 2013: 5).

In the seventeenth and eighteenth centuries, the 'we' who would brook no subjection were white male property owners who sought emancipation from the arbitrary authority of monarch, state and/or church, and asserted their right to membership of what Domenico Losurdo (2011) terms a 'community of the free'. For them, the emergence of a modern liberal order did imply something new. It did not ring in liberty for all humanity, however, for the liberal social contract contained certain subcontracts or exclusion clauses. As famously identified by Carole Pateman (1988), there was a 'sexual contract' behind the social contract, one that afforded propertied men 'the right to rule over their women in the private, domestic sphere', even as they themselves were granted civil freedom and equality 'within the public, political sphere' (Yuval-Davis, 1997: 79). The social order of the liberal imaginary:

> contains a double separation of the private and public: the *class* division between civil society and the state (between economic man and citizen, between private enterprise and the public power); and

the patriarchal separation between the private family and the public world of civil society/state.

(Pateman, 1998: 245)

The mastery enjoyed by propertied men extended to all those incorporated into their households as dependents, which originally meant not just their children and wives, but also their servants, labourers, apprentices and slaves, should they hold them (Edwards, 1998).

The social contract was also supported by what Charles Mills describes as a 'racial contract', one that distinguished between the bodies whose owners were and were not judged capable 'of forming or fully entering into a body politic' (1998: 53, see also Parekh, 1995; Puwar, 2004). And an exclusion clause based on nationality through which liberal states grant themselves permission to distinguish between 'citizens' and 'migrants' in terms of entitlement to rights, protections and liberties has operated and continues to operate. It is only by forgetting these exclusion clauses – which is to say by forgetting, distorting or skimming over the historical experience of those racialized as 'other', migrants, the colonized, women, children and propertyless labourers – that it is possible to imagine an inviolable link between modernity and the enjoyment. Of liberal liberties, in other words, to suppose that 'the enduring cause of freedom' to which modern liberal states are committed, is necessarily an inclusive or universal one. Indeed, once the historical and on-going experience of those not imagined as 'naturally' entitled to freedom comes into view, all of the conceptual binaries that structure and support the liberal worldview begin to blur and reveal themselves as but fictional devices.

## Structure and themes of the book

Chattel slavery is an institution 'older than human records', and was, for thousands of years, across much of the world, one of the social and legal statuses that defined and structured relationships between human beings (Davis, D., 2003: 5). Some estimates suggest there are still today around 1.6 million people, mostly in Niger, Sudan and Mauritania, who are socially ascribed the status of slave despite legislation that officially outlaws slavery (Patterson, 2012). But the remaining 34 million or so who are named 'modern slaves' by organizations like Walk Free are neither socially nor legally constructed as 'slaves'. The new abolitionists describe them as such because they consider that there are certain features of these people's experience that resemble the experience of chattel slaves historically. The new abolitionist case thus rests on a set of assumptions about the historical experience of chattel slavery, as well as about the experience of those affected by the phenomena they name 'modern slavery'.

This book questions the new abolitionism's readings of both the past and the present. The second chapter offers a critique of the definition of 'slavery' offered by the new abolitionists. In the chapters that follow, historical overlaps between the experience of chattel slaves and other categories of dependants (servants, wives, children) are explored against contemporary phenomena that are dubbed 'modern slavery': bonded labour and worst forms of child labour (Chapter 3); forced labour (Chapter 6); forced marriage (Chapter 7); sex trafficking (Chapter 8). The aim is to show – among other things – that were we to apply the new abolitionists' definition of 'slavery' retrospectively, we would find eighteenth- and nineteenth-century Europe and America awash with white 'modern slaves'. This not only tells us that there is something very wrong with the definition of 'slavery' they employ, but also indicates a staggering disregard for the history of race as a system of domination, and for the afterlife of racial slavery. As Chapter 4 argues, the fiction of race worked sharply to differentiate transatlantic slaves from the dependent white wives, servants and children whose position was in some respects analogous to slavery, and race continues to have powerful significance for restraints on freedom that are *not* regarded as 'modern slavery' by the new abolitionists, for example, those implied by the Prison Industrial Complex in the United States. The idea of race is also central to the history of immigration controls, controls that have been and remain a mechanism through which some groups of human being are rendered marginal, dependent and unequal in terms of freedom, rights and protections.

The book also challenges the new abolitionists' assertion that it is possible to lose or be robbed of 'free will' and agency, and that slavery is defined by its reduction of persons to things. Chattel slaves had, as Saidiya Hartman (1997) puts it, a bifurcated existence or double character as both persons *and* things. Failure to attend to this contradiction allows slave resistance and revolution to be forgotten (the amnesia is especially acute with regard to the Haitian revolution and its pivotal role as the catalyst for 'transformations in the larger world of Atlantic slavery and anticolonial nationalism' (Brown, 2009: 1247)). As with other liberal and social scientific dichotomies, such as 'personal/political, material/symbolic, organized rebellion/everyday resistance', the persons/things binary obscures as much it reveals (Camp, 2004: 3). It also allows the freedom/slavery binary to be conceptually mapped onto the subject/object binary to produce a view of 'the slave' as the ultimate premodern Other, forever draped in the poisoned cloak of Nessus. As such, 'the slave' comes symbolically to embody more general fears of objectification, engulfment, infantalization, exclusion and dishonour (Brace, 2004), and thus works as a device to tell liberal subjects who they are by showing them what they are not.

The heavy emphasis on slaves as objects, suffering bodies, emptied of will, in the original European anti-slavery movement left a complicated legacy for humanitarian activism. Its sentimental tropes and figures produced an unstable and moveable vision of who should be the focus of humanitarian concern (Festa, 2010). Moreover, the very qualities attributed to slaves by European abolitionists to construct them as victims worthy of pity and assistance (namely, lack of agency, reduction to but a body) are precisely the qualities that are seen to degrade human beings in Western cultures. To be visible as a body, which is to say literally or metaphorically unclothed or unmasked, and to be forced to bow to the will of another, is to be stripped of dignity and honour (Greenberg, 1996; Patterson, 1982). This remains highly pertinent to the contemporary discourse of humanitarian concern about modern slavery (Trodd, 2013). People may rail against what they perceive as tyranny by claiming that they are being treated *like* slaves, but to be described by others as *actual* slaves is to be afforded a label that comes with a profound stigma. And to name as 'slaves' millions of people in the Global South who are not legally ascribed the status chattel slave is also to continue a tradition in which 'the rich nuances of human life, everyday living and socio-political complexity' are erased in favour of stereotypical representations of 'the Orientalised other and the Occidentalised subject' and simplistic binaries of 'victim/victimisers and oppressors/oppressed' (Treacher Kabesh, 2013: 4).

A further problem that arises from failure to attend to the 'double character' of the slave historically is that it prevents us from understanding slavery as a system of domination, and so from thinking about the role of the state in producing and maintaining it. If the powers of ownership exercised over slaves had literally reduced human beings to objects or things, there would have been no call for a legal and political machinery to enforce slaves' subjugation to their owners. Laws, law enforcement and guards may be necessary to prevent others from stealing one's property in gold bullion, for example, but additional legislation, patrols and sentries are not required to prevent gold bullion from running away, or to compel it to offer up its market value. Another aim of this book is to highlight the role of states in constructing the system of transatlantic slavery both as a market and a form of political domination, and to think through parallels with the role played by contemporary states in producing and often violently imposing heavy restrictions on the freedom of certain groups of people. Restraints on human mobility are of particular significance here.

Historically, to exercise mastery, slaveholders were dependent on a legal, social and physical edifice that constricted slave movement (Camp, 2004: 6). Evading such controls over free movement was a central aspect of slave resistance (whether in the form of running away permanently, 'lying out' for a period of days or weeks, or breaking curfews in order to spend time with loved ones held on other plantations), and the 'right of locomotion' was an important component of the freedom demanded by freed and fugitive slaves of the original abolitionist movement (Wong, 2009). Today, the mobility of certain populations is also heavily restricted by immigration laws and the patrols and physical boundaries (walls, razor wire fences, check points, detention centres, for example) associated with their enforcement. The new abolitionism does not challenge the right claimed by states to control and restrict freedom of movement, but limits its concern to liberating 'modern slaves' who 'cannot walk away' from an oppressive relationship with a private individual. However, as Chapters 5 and 6 will show, vulnerability to exploitation and abuse by private individuals is very often a by-product of immigration regimes, so that condemning the private violence but not the legal and institutional structure that leaves people open to it is rather like castigating individual slaveholders for the exercise of violence without questioning the broader legal, customary and physical arrangements that empowered them to do so.

The book draws on two sets of literature: first, the extraordinarily rich literature on transatlantic slavery (including the writings of freed and fugitive slaves in the eighteenth and nineteenth centuries), on the original abolitionist movement, and on slave emancipation and its aftermath, from a range of disciplines including philosophy, political theory, English literature, law, anthropology, sociology and cultural studies, as well as history. This literature complicates and challenges virtually all the ideas and beliefs about slavery that are taken for granted in contemporary liberal societies. Second, the book draws on the substantial and growing body of ethnographic and interview research that illuminates the complexity and variability of phenomena that are dubbed 'modern slavery' by new abolitionists. In a book of this length, I am only able to scratch the surface of these groups of literature, but I hope the scratch is deep enough to reveal the immense value of the works cited, and other similar research, as an aid to understanding the similarities and dissimilarities, and links and ruptures, between chattel slavery in the transatlantic world and the condition of various different groups whose rights and freedoms are most heavily restrained today.

To read and seriously engage with these works is not 'the most joyful experience that you can imagine'. It may even be 'terribly depressing'. It does not easily lend itself to the production of soundbites and catch-phrases about modern slavery, and it certainly does not encourage the idea that there are three, four, five or 12 easy steps you can take to end what the new abolitionists call 'modern slavery', or indeed, to eradicate the harsh restraints on human freedom that lie beyond the orbit or their concern. In fact, it points to the conclusion that the new abolitionists are mistaken in their insistence that the term 'modern slavery' refers to a definite and particular 'thing', a thing like a disease that we all know to be wrong, a thing that can be defined, counted and eliminated. The term 'modern slavery', I hope to show in this book, is more usefully compared to a term like 'pornography', which, as Lynne Hunt (1996: 13) notes, 'was historically shaped, and its development as a category was always one of conflict and change. Pornography was the name for a cultural battle zone'. 'Modern slavery' names not a thing, but a set of claims about what is (and what is not) morally and politically obscene. The trouble with the new abolitionists is that they do not acknowledge this. And by pretending that they are talking about a thing, not a set of political judgements, they close down rather than open up debates that I believe we ought to be having.

New abolitionism's call to end modern slavery is not like a call to eradicate smallpox, but is, in fact, more like a call for the universal establishment of the social and political norms of liberal capitalist societies. And though I will grant that there is much to be said in favour of liberalism (I would not choose to live in an illiberal society), the liberal worldview accepted and reproduced by the new abolitionists is no guarantee against inequality, exploitation, lack of rights, violence and domination. Instead, it is a worldview that presents us with a paradox (Parekh, 1995). No intellectual tradition has been as committed as liberalism 'to thinking through the decisive problem of the limitation of power', and yet liberal ideology can be and has been marshalled in support of the violent subjugation of truly immense numbers of people (Losurdo, 2011: 243).

Liberalism *does* offer an inspiring statement of human equality and freedom, and there is no question but that the legal abolition of chattel slavery is something to be celebrated. The relationship between the two is more complicated than it is widely assumed to be, however, and we forget this at our peril. If the past is to teach us anything that might help to address the inequalities and injustices of our own times, we need something more than the trite story of liberal society reproduced by the new abolitionists, as well as in mainstream liberal popular and political culture. Theirs is a portrait of 'perfect men and noble nations' (Du Bois, 1966), one in which liberal society appears blessed with a 'spontaneous capacity for self-correction' (Losurdo, 2011: 344). To have any hope of developing an analysis that could inform struggles against liberalism's contemporary exclusion clauses, and against contemporary processes of dis-emancipation, we need to attend to histories that acknowledge the powerful associations between modern liberalism and *in*equality and *restraints* on freedom, as well as between it and equality and liberty. More than this, we need to step outside the conceptual binaries that allow us to see *only* the workings of force, and not the workings of agency (or *vice versa*), to picture human beings as either objects or subjects, and to imagine economic and political life as separable, and find ways to acknowledge and engage politically with the ambiguities borne of their simultaneity.

# 2
# Marking the Boundaries of Slavery

What is slavery? And what makes it so uniquely wrong? These two questions may at first appear to be of a different order, the first seemingly a question of fact, the second a matter of moral judgment. Yet in Western post-Enlightenment thought they have in fact been deeply entwined, and in discourse on 'modern slavery' they are entirely indivisible. This chapter introduces some of the theoretical, philosophical and political problems that the definition of slavery and the identification of its singular moral wrongness present. It looks at how the new abolitionism attempts to circumvent them by articulating an essentially legalistic definition of slavery as the reduction of human beings to objects over which powers of ownership are exercised. It then considers this definition against evidence on the historical experience of New World slaves, and against conceptualizations of slavery offered by scholars of slavery from a number of disciplines. It argues that neither history, nor social science, leaves us with a simple, uncontested answer to the question of what slavery is, and what – if anything – makes it peculiarly unjust.

## Slavery, contract and property

Prior to the seventeenth century, in European as well as many other societies, slavery was a social status that could be ascribed only under particular circumstances, or to particular 'kinds' of human being. Those captured in war could be enslaved, for example, or slavery could be imposed as punishment upon convicted criminals (Patterson, 1982). As Tommy Lott (1998) shows in his exegesis of early Enlightenment texts on the rights of slaves, classical social contract theory, which rejected all forms of tradition-based, naturalized authority and emphasized consent as necessary to the legitimate exercise of authority, provided a lens through which the master-slave relationship was simultaneously defined and made morally questionable by its non-consensual nature. This did not immediately rule out the idea of justifiable slavery, however. Indeed, debates about when a person could rightfully be enslaved, as well as about whether some peoples were 'natural slaves', have a long history bridging ancient and modern worlds (Finley, 1964; Haskell, 1998; Nyquist, 2013). Thus, Lott explains, while the key early social contract theorists Thomas Hobbes and John Locke shared a vision of slavery as entailing the non-consensual exercise of authority, they differed on the question of whether, as a result, slavery always represented a violation of natural rights.

Hobbes condemned slavery as 'inherently evil', no matter how slaves were acquired, whereas Locke held that those taken captive in a 'just war' could legitimately be enslaved and 'subjected to "the Absolute Dominion and Arbitrary Power of their Masters"' (Lott, 1998: 109). Yet Hobbes also argued that masters justifiably acquired dominion over servants by means of conquest: the vanquished, to avoid the stroke of death makes a covenant by which 'so long as his life, and the liberty of his body is allowed him, the Victor shall have the use thereof, at his pleasure' (cited in Lott, 1998: 107). As Lott (1998: 114, emphasis original), comments, this looks 'indistinguishable from an act of enslavement', but for Hobbes, the crucial difference was that, unlike the slave, the servant was '*not kept in prison, or bonds*'. In other words, although Hobbes took the absence of consent to be the defining feature of slavery, his model of consent was so expansive that it was only those who actually lost their corporal liberty, being literally imprisoned or held in chains, who were to count as 'slaves'. Those kept in bondage were physically prevented from making the choice between either resisting or entering into a compact with the master. Hobbes could therefore condemn slavery as inherently evil, but still justify the forms of coerced servitude that were widespread in his day.

Locke's vision of consent was more restrictive. For him, 'anyone not free from the "Arbitrary power" of another' would count as a slave (Lott, 1998: 113). Unlike Hobbes, 'Locke considered promises exacted by force to be invalid agreements. Hence, he believed that the subdued parties who have been coerced into a compact have no obligation' (Lott, 1998: 110). But a system of slavery could be transformed into servitude by means of contract: 'For, if once *Compact* enter between them, and make an agreement for a limited Power on the one side, and Obedience on the other, ... *Slavery* ceases, so long as the Compact endures' (Locke, cited in Lott, 1998: 111, original emphasis). In other words, power ceases to be arbitrary once it is consensually exercised, so providing an individual had voluntarily entered into a contract of servitude, she owed obedience to her master come what may.

In these classical social-contract theorists' approach to the questions, 'what is slavery?' and 'what is wrong with slavery?' we see both the centrality of the concept of consent to liberal understandings of slavery, and its flexibility. The meaning of 'consent' is not fixed. It is imagined in relation to wider ideas about free will, volition, and responsibility (among others), ideas which are in turn shaped by conventions that are not only historically variable, but can also be subject to political and social contestation. If you agree to a given form of action when the only alternative is death, is this consent? Or, more pertinent to the new abolitionists' definition of modern slavery, if you remain in a given situation because you are threatened with death if you walk away from it, are you a slave? Thomas Haskell (1998: 315) observes that in classical Christian formalist thought, an individual cannot be driven to do anything against her will; all human action is caused by the will of the individuals involved, and cannot be explained other than as choice:

> Aquinas, the great codifier of Christian doctrine, insisted that even a man at sea, who chooses to throw his possessions overboard rather than risk death in a storm, is acting voluntarily. *'That which is done through fear is voluntary'* said Aquinas *'The will cannot be compelled to act...violence cannot be done to the will'*.

This notion of willing selves is clearly reproduced in Thomas Hobbes' account of the distinction between slavery and servitude, which is one of the reasons why Hobbes provides us with a very straightforward answer to the question, 'what is slavery?' (even if the answer is unsatisfactory through twenty-first-century eyes). His is a hard and fast way to distinguish between slave and non-slave. Those in shackles are slaves; those unshackled can be taken to have consented to their master's dominion and so are not. Locke seemingly offers a way of distinguishing slave from non-slave that is more satisfactory to a contemporary audience, since his acknowledgement that coerced consent is invalid allows us to exclude consent given in fear of death from the realm of the voluntary. But as Lott (1998: 124) points out, for Locke as much as Hobbes:

> the distinction between slavery and servitude is to be understood in wholly legalistic terms – of whether or not the servant has a contract, perhaps combined with a moralistic concern as to whether coercion,

or physical bondage, was involved, but not in terms of ongoing power relations.

This may offer an equally clear basis for delineating the slave from the non-slave (those without contracts are slaves, those with contracts are not) but it compromises the case for treating slavery as morally exceptional, since an individual in contractual servitude could – theoretically and in practice – experience conditions and treatment as harsh at the hands of a cruel and careless master as an individual slave experienced at the hands of 'benign' owner. Once the *ongoing* power relations between masters and their slaves and servants become the focus of attention, as opposed to simply the mode of *initiating* these power relations, the absence of contract does not reveal slavery's unique wrongness, Lott's analysis of the overlap between slavery and servitude reveals.

The raison d'être of the anti-slavery movement is to eradicate slavery, as opposed to any and all constraints on human freedom. Though such an objective need not necessarily imply a privileging of slavery over other forms of oppression, in practice anti-slavery activism has largely framed slavery as a uniquely appalling phenomenon, one that deserves singular moral concern and action. For this reason, slavery's overlaps with other social arrangements and relations of domination and servility represented a chink in the armour of the original anti-slavery campaigners' argument, and one that their pro-slavery contemporaries sought to exploit, pointing, for example, to the appalling conditions under which formally free wage labourers lived and worked in nineteenth-century England (Cunliffe, 1972). Abolitionist campaigners attempted to rebut comparisons between chattel slavery and wage slavery by emphasizing the peculiar injustice of enslavement. One way in which they did so was to rely upon a legalistic definition of slavery.

George Bourne, one of the founders of the American Anti-Slavery Society, wrote that slavery could be indirectly defined as the reduction 'of human beings to the condition of property, the same as other goods, wares, merchandise and chattels' and observed that although there is 'a variety of other ways in which mankind hold control over each other, and sometimes unjustly and oppressively; but if the persons controlled be not held as property, they are not slaves' (1845: 7). The wrong of slavery, he argued, is that it makes 'free agents, chattels – converting *persons* into *things* – sinking immortality into *merchandize*':

We repeat it, 'THE REDUCTION OF PERSONS TO THINGS!' Not robbing a man of privileges, but of *himself*; not loading him with burdens, but making him *a beast of burden*; not restraining liberty, but subverting it; not curtailing rights, but abolishing them; not inflicting personal cruelty, but annihilating *personality*; not exacting involuntary labor, but sinking man into an *implement* of labor; not abridging human comforts, but abrogating *human nature*; not depriving an animal of immunities, but despoiling a rational being of attributes, uncreating A MAN to make room for *a thing!*

(1845: 7–8, original emphasis).

This legalistic approach to the definition of slavery worked perfectly well for anti-slavery campaigners prior to the abolition of chattel slavery. Identifying the object of their concern was simple – a slave was a slave because she was legally defined as property. A servant, no matter how coerced, ill-treated or hard worked, was not. The boundary was clear. So too was the distinctive wrongness of slavery. To legally construct human beings as chattel was to rob them of their free will and personhood.

Matters are not so straightforward for contemporary anti-slavery activists. In a post-abolition world, 'no-one can "be" a slave in the strictest nineteenth-century sense of occupying a legally recognized status category of person as property' (Scott, 2012: 162). There are people who are described as remaining in traditional forms of chattel slavery despite legislation that officially outlaws the practice (although see Bellagamba, 2015), and anti-slavery activists are concerned with their fate. However, this is not the sole, or even the main focus of the new abolitionism. According to organizations like Free the Slaves, Walk Free, and even the more circumspect Anti-Slavery International, the vast majority of the millions of 'slaves' in today's world are victims of modern, not traditional, forms of slavery. But how are we to recognize these modern slaves, and what distinguishes them from non-slaves in the contemporary world?

## Expanding the reach of slavery: the politics of definition

If 'slaves' are defined as those who occupy a legal status category of chattel, then by legislating to abolish the slave trade and chattel slavery, European and North American states transported themselves to a moral high ground. And in fact, from the mid-nineteenth century on, the moral duty to eradicate chattel slavery in 'backward' and 'uncivilized' regions of the world was increasingly presented as part of the justification for colonial expansion in Africa and elsewhere, and a facet of the 'white man's burden' (Kempadoo, 2015; Miers, 1998; Quirk, 2011). But the same states had introduced labour systems that looked virtually identical to the form of slavery they replaced. In the British Caribbean, for example, emancipated slaves were in most cases formally re-designated as 'apprentices' (a very literal expression of their designation as, at best, only nascent persons), who were protected from being bought or sold as chattel, yet also compelled to work without payment for between four and six years, albeit for a maximum of 45 hours a week (Cohen, 2006: 18). Moreover, as the abolition of slavery loomed, a new system of indenture was introduced in British colonies. 'Mauritius and British Guyana were the first of the sugar colonies to recruit Indian workers through agency houses in Calcutta' (Carter and Torabully, 2002: 46), and between 1834 and 1937, more than 30 million people are estimated to have left India as indentured workers, travelling to Mauritius, Guyana, Jamaica, Trinidad, Fiji, Kenya, Uganda, South Africa and other destinations, and at least another five or six million workers from other parts of Asia, in particular China, were 'employed under the coolie system to build infrastructure and to produce goods for the world market either on the plantations or in the mines' (Potts, 1990: 70–1). For critics in the nineteenth and early twentieth centuries, as well as many subsequent commentators (such as Tinker, 1974), what made this 'coolie system' similar to the form of slavery it replaced:

> were the mortality rates on the ships (which, for example, averaged over 17 per cent on ships to the West Indies in 1856), the poor housing and health conditions, the miserable wages, and, above all, the extensive use of penal sanctions...In one year (1892), over 40 per cent of the adult indentured population was convicted under the penal labour laws of Fiji
>
> (Cohen, 2006: 20).

Meanwhile, in other colonies, extraordinarily violent new systems of coerced labour were introduced in the late nineteenth and early twentieth centuries (Nzula et al., 1979). Millions died as a direct result of these systems or trying to resist them (Cohen, 2006). As Aime Cesaire put it, Europe's colonial ventures leave it 'responsible before the human community for the highest heap of corpses in history' (1972: 24). For some (not all) in the anti-slavery movement, the double standards this implied were deeply troubling. Joel Quirk (2011: 103) provides the following quote from a report written by a British anti-slavery activist in 1900:

> We have done much to stop the stealing of blacks in the African interior for sale in the slave markets on the coast,...but we are increasing, instead of lessening, our appliances for bringing under bondage to ourselves, a bondage often more irksome to them than the older slavery, those whom we take credit for having rescued.

The question of whether the term 'slavery' could apply to conditions other than legally and/or socially recognized chattel slavery, and if so, to which conditions and why, was a highly politicized one in the nineteenth and early twentieth centuries. In 1924, the League of Nations established the Temporary Slavery Commission, a body of experts whose thinking shaped the League of Nations' Slavery Convention, 1926. Article 1 of this Convention defined slavery as 'the status of a person over whom all or any of the rights attaching to ownership are exercised', and this continues to be regarded as providing the benchmark legal definition (Allain, 2012). But it is also an extremely vague definition, and its imprecision reflects the political interests of the colonial powers amongst the original signatories to the Slavery Convention. Defining slavery in terms of proprietary powers fitted with what was generally understood as chattel slavery, a legal institution that had by 1926 already been abolished by the 'civilized' European and New World nations.

The Slavery Convention also expanded the reach of the term by requiring states to bring about the complete abolition of slavery 'in all its forms', but the different forms that slavery could take were not listed or explicated. In fact, under pressure from the colonial powers, the extraordinarily brutal regimes of coerced labour that, in the 1920s, were widely imposed by colonial authorities were removed from the Slavery Convention's orbit of concern. Arguing that an attack on forced labour would infringe national sovereignty, they pressed for this issue to be passed to the International Labour Organization (ILO) to be dealt with separately (Drescher, 2012: 99). It was subsequently defined by the ILO's 1930 Forced Labour Convention as 'all work or service which is exacted from any person under the menace of any penalty and for which the said person has not offered himself voluntarily', but the question of what counts as 'forced labour' and whether always amounts to slavery remains contested to this day, as Chapter 6 will show.

The next international legal instrument pertaining to slavery was the United Nations' Supplementary Convention on the Abolition of Slavery, the Slave Trade, and Institutions and Practices Similar to Slavery, 1956.

This 'did not alter the definition of slavery', but it did 'oblige states to abolish related servile conditions of debt bondage, serfdom, servile marriage and child trafficking' (Drescher, 2012: 99). It also added the concept of 'a person of servile status', in order to distinguish between victims of slavery, and victims of 'slave-like' institutions or practices. Again, this was consonant with a view of slavery as a feature of 'backward', 'unenlightened' cultures and an anathema to modern liberal societies (servile aspects of 1950s American and British housewives' condition were not the focus of concern here). However, the alignment of slavery with institutions and practices similar to slavery in the Supplementary Convention did open up possibilities for further expanding what could be addressed under the rubric of 'slavery' in international law, possibilities that were subsequently pursued by actors with very different political interests than those that had held sway in the first half of the twentieth century.

In the context of the 'Cold War divisions and post-colonial politics' of the 1960s, those opposed to apartheid and colonialism were able to press for these to be bundled together with 'institutions and practices similar to slavery' under the heading of 'contemporary forms of slavery' (Quirk, 2011: 263). And as Quirk (2012: 263) argues, this extension of the term 'contemporary slavery' to collective forms of oppression set the precedent 'for the subsequent work of the United Nations Working Group on Slavery'. At its first meeting in 1975, it was agreed that definitions of slavery in existing relevant conventions were inadequate to grasp slavery in all its contemporary forms, and that consideration ought to be given to 'all institutions and practices which, by restricting the freedom of the individual, are susceptible of causing severe hardship and serious deprivation of liberty' (cited in Quirk, 2012: 263). At meetings since then, the Group has taken evidence from NGOs and United Nations bodies on a wide range of phenomena:

It has considered slavery, debt bondage, forced labour, child labour, trafficking in persons, prostitution, pornography, sex slavery, sweated labour, the exploitation of contract and migrant labour, and of illegal aliens, as well as forced marriage, adoption for exploitation, and the use of child soldiers ... other practices brought before the group ... include female circumcision, the honour killing of Muslim women by their relations, marriage practices which discriminate against women, incest and the killing of people in order to sell their organs for transplants.

(Miers, 2004: 11)

The career of the term 'slavery' in international policy circles vividly illustrates the dilemma faced by the new abolitionists. If the term is restricted to the legal construction of persons as chattel or property (as it is in many dictionaries, for example Oxford Dictionaries defines the slave as 'a person who is the legal property of another and is forced to obey them'), then slavery was successfully eliminated with the passage of laws abolishing chattel slavery. But if the term 'slavery' is cut loose from its moorings in the institution of chattel slavery, it starts to billow out uncontrollably, stretching to encompass all manner of human rights violations. Indeed, framed as anything that restricts the freedom of the individual, or causes severe hardship and serious deprivation of liberty, there is nothing solid to stand between the 'slavery' experienced by those who were historically ascribed the legal status 'slave' in the Southern states of the United States, and the experience of today's US Tea Party libertarians who assert their claims against the 'political tyrants' who insist they pay taxes by describing themselves as 'slaves'.

The new abolitionists and other mainstream anti-slavery campaigners take issue with those who would extend the term to cover phenomena such as taxation, abortion, or even female circumcision, honour killing, or sweated labour, arguing that inflating the term in these ways dilutes its potency in terms of marshalling the political will to combat *actual* slavery in the contemporary world. Their concern is with *real* slavery, they say: 'Although its modern forms are different, when we talk about slavery we do not use a metaphor' (ASI, 2013). The new abolitionists therefore need to chart a path between two extremes, extending the boundaries of the meaning of the term 'slavery' beyond chattel slavery, but preventing it from mushrooming out to incorporate any and all restraints on human freedom and well-being. How to do so? Kevin Bales' account of what lies at the heart of slaveries old and new has exerted huge influence on the efforts of contemporary abolitionist organizations in this regard, especially Free the Slaves and Walk Free, and the following section therefore focuses primarily on his writings.

## Heart of slavery: the new abolitionist vision

Bales (2006: 1) acknowledges that the forms of slavery and the details of any particular slave/slaveholder relationship have varied widely historically and continue to be enormously diverse, but contends that it is nonetheless possible 'to parse out the underlying attributes shared by all forms of slavery and to analyze and understand the dynamic and various forms slavery can take in individual cases'. His parsing leads him to define slavery as characterized by three things: 'control based on the potential or actual use of violence; a lack of any remuneration beyond subsistence; and the appropriation of the labor or other qualities of the slave for economic gain' (2006: 2). This, he contends, captures what is at the heart of slavery in all its many and varied forms and regardless of the wider social, political, economic and cultural contexts in which is embedded. It also allows us to maintain a distinction between *real* slavery and other, more ordinary forms of drudgery and oppression that exist in the contemporary world, according to Bales:

> Having just enough money to get by, receiving wages that barely keep you alive, may be called wage slavery, but it is not slavery. Sharecroppers have a hard life, but they are not slaves. Child labour is terrible, but it is not necessarily slavery.
>
> (1999: 5)

It is only when the individual is 'controlled by violence through violence, the threat of violence, or psychological coercion, has lost free will and free movement, is exploited economically, and paid nothing beyond subsistence' that he or she becomes a slave (Bales, 2007b).

Indeed, when attempting to define 'modern slavery', Bales even subdivides the category of bonded labour. 'Debt-bondage' is identified in international law as one of a number of institutions and practices similar to slavery in the United Nations' Supplementary Convention on the Abolition of Slavery, the Slave Trade, and Institutions and Practices Similar to Slavery, 1956.[1] The term has been most commonly applied to situations affecting the rural poor in developing regions, especially South Asia and Latin America, within which individual debtors and/or their families are compelled to labour for the creditor for many years, sometimes even for generations (Brass, 1999). Here, the creditor's claims over the debtor's labour-power are so extensive and so protracted that debt very clearly prevents the debtor from enjoying self-mastery through her/his ownership of labour as a form of property, and is visibly at odds with liberal understandings of freedom.

And yet the ubiquity of indebtedness amongst the rural poor in the developing world means that even these lines are not enough, on their own, to demarcate the boundaries of 'debt slavery' in such a way as to fit with Bales' definition of 'modern slavery'. He thus allows that people can be bound by debt to an employer without being 'enslaved' to that employer. Using the *peshgi* system of bonded labour in brick kiln labour in Pakistan as an illustration, he states that it is 'a terrible way to make a living', one that 'is hard on the children and the adults, but it is only as bad as many other kinds of work in the developing world – and it is better than having no work at all and going hungry' (1999: 167). It only becomes a system of enslavement through 'debt-bondage', according to Bales, when (a) the debt and the piece rate are 'dishonestly' manipulated in such a way as to 'keep the family permanently in debt', and (b) violence is employed 'to enforce the bondage' (1999: 167–8).

In terms of developing a methodological critique of measures such as Walk Free's *Global Slavery Index*, it is important to note that such distinctions evaporate when it comes to quantifying 'modern slavery'. Bales and fellow abolitionists use official and unofficial estimates of the prevalence of 'bonded labour' as if it were data on the prevalence of 'slaves', without regard for such subdivisions. But for the purposes of this chapter, the important point is that Bales draws this distinction through reference to the concept of ownership. Returning to the 1926 Slavery Convention definition, Bales seeks to flesh out the meaning of 'powers attaching to the right of ownership', arguing that it implies the right to possess, and that possession is demonstrated by control, normally exclusive control, and by:

> *The right to use; the right to manage; the right to income...* [and] the *right to capital*, which refers to the right to dispose of the possession, by transfer, by consumption, or by destruction. These 'instances of ownership' – control, use, management, and profit – may be regarded as the central rights of ownership. It is their presence and exercise that can be applied and tested within a situation, such as slavery, where actual legal possession is not permitted.
>
> (2012: 283–4, emphasis original)

The definition of slavery in the 1926 Slavery Convention is thus said to apply not only in *de jure* situations in which a person is legally owned by another, but also in *de facto* situations where legal ownership is prohibited, but the powers attaching to the right of ownership are exercised nonetheless. If one person exercises complete powers of control over another, they in effect make them a chattel. This position informs the 2012 'Bellagio-Harvard Guidelines on the Legal Parameters of Slavery', authored by Jean Allain and Bales among others in the Research Network on the Legal Parameters of Slavery, which states that ownership implies a background relation of control, control is the power attaching to the right of ownership known as possession, and: 'Possession is foundational to an understanding of the legal definition of slavery, even when the State does not support a property right in respect of persons. To determine, in law, a case of slavery, one must look for possession' (Allain, 2012: 376).

In this view, slavery is always defined by possession and its associated elements of control, violence, and exploitation. In the past, this form of possession was legally sanctioned and supported as a status, so that the law drew a vertical line between slaves and free persons, as in Figure 2.1 below. Today, the law does not authorize 'slave' as status, but it can still be used to score a line between slaves and non-slaves, again through reference to possession. This time, however, the line is a horizontal one that cuts through other statuses and identities, as in Figure 2.2.

Legalistic definitions of slavery as ownership have been subject to extensive critique by slavery scholars in anthropology, history, sociology and philosophy, but before turning to these criticisms, I want to draw attention to some problems with the *de facto–de jure* distinction on which the new abolitionism relies by turning it on its head and thinking about the *de facto* freedoms of *de jure* slaves. If Bales had indeed succeeded in parsing out the universal, core elements of slavery, then his definition of slavery ought to allow us to differentiate between all slaves and all non-slaves historically, as well as between slaves and non-slaves today. We would expect to find that every individual legally ascribed the status of 'slave' in the New World, for example, was subject to the close and violent exercise of proprietary powers that the new abolitionists hold to constitute the nucleus of slavery. Is this what historical evidence shows?

| De Jure Enslaved | Free |
|---|---|
|  |  |

*Figure 2.1* The legal line between slave and non-slave historically

|  | Wives | Child labourers | Bonded workers | Migrant workers, etc. |
|---|---|---|---|---|
| Free |  |  |  |  |
| De Facto Enslaved |  |  |  |  |

*Figure 2.2*   The legal line between slave and non-slave today

## Transatlantic slavery and *de facto* freedom

Bales' emphasis on ownership instantiated through control, use, management, and profit, certainly speaks to dominant representations of the experience of slaves forced to live and work on plantations in the Americas. But not every victim of the transatlantic slave trade was involved in plantation work. Consider, for example, Maria Elena Diaz's (2006) research on slaves involved in copper mining in El Cobre, a mountain village in the East of Cuba, between 1670 and 1780. Copper mining in El Cobre, which 'had constituted a large export-based enterprise worked with African derived slave labor', in the first decades of the seventeenth century had declined significantly by the middle of the century. The mines were so neglected that they fell into ruins, and eventually, in 1670, the Spanish crown confiscated them from the private contractor that had, till then, officially operated them and some 270 private slaves became the king's slaves. By 1780:

the small mining settlement had grown into a full-fledged village of some 1,320 inhabitants, of whom 64 percent were royal slaves, 34 percent free people of color (mostly manumitted descendants or relatives of royal slaves) and 2 percent private slaves of these villagers.

(Diaz, 2006: 22)

In the intervening period, the Spanish crown was unable to find another private contractor to reactivate and run the mines as a productive export-oriented enterprise. Copper mining did not entirely cease, however. Instead, the royal slaves 'began to reshape the local mining industry by feminizing it, turning to surface mining, working informally on their own account, and producing mostly, but not exclusively, for a domestic market' (Diaz, 2006: 22). This was an exceptional period, one that fell between two periods of large export-based mining production, and the story of the royal slaves of El Cobre is highly atypical. Nonetheless, the *cobreros* were legally and socially ascribed the status of 'slave' (they were officially recorded as such in the 1670 Inventory of Slaves and the Family Census of 1773 (Diaz, 2006: 37)). But their lived experience was not characterized by what Bales and other new abolitionists identify as the three defining elements of slavery. They were not under the direct, daily supervision of any private contractor or representative of the king. For most of the year, royal slaves were left to support themselves through farming, hunting and mining copper, and with some exceptions in the case of men's contribution to public labour schemes, the *cobreros* were not compelled by violence or its threat to undertake the labour they performed, or controlled and directed by any 'employer'.

The mining activities independently undertaken (mostly by women and children) largely took the form of alluvial and surface mining, and such work is certainly not light or easy. Nor was it especially lucrative. And yet it did give these slave women access to the market and equip them with purchasing power (even if such power was meagre), something that allowed them 'control over their social body and to transcend their fixed place in the established social order' (Diaz, 2006: 31). To the displeasure of some of their contemporaries, women would sometimes use the proceeds of the sale of copper 'to embellish their bodies', acquiring goods and adopting dressing practices that were considered inappropriate and 'arrogant' in slaves (Diaz, 2006: 31).

The *cobreros* were *de jure* slaves who, for a long (albeit finite) period of time, enjoyed *de facto* freedoms in relation to the production, provisioning, and consumption practices of their society (Diaz, 2006: 23). Were we to return to eighteenth century El Cobre and look for people experiencing what Bales defines as the essential ingredients of slavery, we would not find any. This mining settlement was unique in Cuba's history and provides an extremely unusual example, but there is evidence to show that other transatlantic slaves in other settings also sometimes experienced elements of *de facto* freedom. As Geary (2004: 67) notes in relation to Brazil, 'The profile of slave employment ... was considerably more diverse than that implied by a dichotomous plantation model of great plantation owners on the one hand and field slaves on the other'. Slaves were in some cases entrusted with managerial roles in relation to other slaves, or even entire estates.

More generally in the Americas, the small minority of slaves – mostly male – who acquired skills were often leased out and received a wage, intended to cover their subsistence (Beckles, 1987; Camp, 2004; Heuman, 1986). Around this wage were certain customary expectations (sometimes also disputes), and though in law masters had a claim to the wage in its entirety, in practice, some slaves were able to retain a portion of the money they earned. This sometimes equipped them, like the women miners of El Cobre, with access to markets and thus a degree of freedom over consumption practices. Highly skilled slaves could even be, in effect, leased to themselves by their owners. Writing in the United States in 1861, Harriet Jacobs, for example, described her enslaved father as having been such an accomplished carpenter that:

> when buildings out of the common line were to be erected, he was sent for from long distances, to be head workman. On condition of paying his mistress two hundred dollars a year, and supporting himself, he was allowed to work at his trade, and manage his own affairs.
> (2000: 1)

In the French Caribbean, female slaves in particular sometimes managed to secure what Bernard Moitt (2008) describes as 'de facto manumission' for themselves and/or their children through sexual relationships with white men. Known as *libre de savane* or *libre de fait*, these were *de jure* slaves (their manumission was not authorized by the state and so had no legal basis) who were not in fact 'possessed' in the manner taken by Bales to be constitutive of slavery. More generally on Caribbean islands, slaveholders had an interest in allowing some of their slaves the freedom independently to work provision plots and sell their produce at market. In fact, 'By the 1780s the produce of the slave plots in Saint-Domingue and Jamaica furnished the bulk of the food consumed by the whole colony' (Blackburn, 2011: 121–2), and in Barbados too, slave women also played a central role in independent cultivation and the internal market economy (Beckles, 1987).

The *libres de savane* of the French Caribbean in the eighteenth and nineteenth centuries, meanwhile, 'operated ... both in urban and rural areas, as petty traders, selling everything from *pacotille* (scavenged trash) to women's makeup', and sometimes also selling their sexual services

(Moitt, 2008: 164). Still more troubling for the definition of slavery offered by Bales, in some cases, *de jure* slaves could even exercise *de facto* powers of ownership over other *de jure* slaves. Moitt (2008: 164) notes, 'There are cases in slave societies where enslaved women, in particular, occupied positions within the plantation household that allowed them to exploit the labor of other slaves in much the same ways as slave owners did.' He then cites Hilary Beckles' (1987) example of Old Doll, a slave woman in eighteenth-century Barbados who, along with her enslaved daughters and niece, eschewed manual labour and managed and controlled slave attendants of their own.

The eighteenth-century anti-slavery campaigner Olaudah Equiano's (1999) account of his own experience of slavery, first published in 1789, also tells us something about the *de facto* freedoms of the most fortunate amongst the formally enslaved. Towards the end of 1763, Equiano's master in Monserrat agreed to a request from a sea captain to allow Equiano (who had experience and skills as a sailor) to accompany him on his trading voyages around the Caribbean. After a while, Equiano took the opportunity to 'commence merchant' (1999: 85), buying glass tumblers and gin on islands where they were more cheaply available and selling them on at a profit. He continued trading for upwards of four years. Equiano was not closely controlled or under constant surveillance during this time. Indeed, he comments that, 'Had I wished to run away I did not want opportunities, which frequently presented themselves' (1999: 90). Certainly by Hobbes' definition, Equiano would not count as a slave.

None of these examples typify the experience of chattel slavery in the New World. Indeed, Equiano's *Narrative* also testifies to the extraordinarily violent and closely controlled condition under which most of his fellow slaves lived and died at the hands of 'human butchers' (1999: 75). However, even if we turn to the lot of the majority, the fact of being permanently legally constructed as a slave did not necessarily imply lifelong subjection to close and violent control for purposes of economic exploitation. With the passage of time, it could imply something equally terrible, yet different. In his 1845 *Narrative of the Life of Frederick Douglass, an American Slave*, Frederick Douglass describes one his masters' brutally sadistic treatment of a slave girl named Henny, and notes that the secret of his cruelty towards her lay in the fact of a childhood accident in which:

> Her hands were so burnt that she never got the use of them. She could do very little but bear heavy burdens. She was to master a bill

of expense; and as he was a mean man, she was a constant offence to him. He seemed desirous of getting the poor girl out of existence. He gave her away once to his sister; but, being a poor gift, she was not disposed to keep her. Finally, my benevolent master, to use his own words, 'set her adrift to take care of herself'.

(1986: 99)

Similarly, when Douglass' original owner died, his grandmother, 'who was now very old, having outlived my old master and all his children', was left a slave in the hands of strangers, who:

finding she was of but little value, ... complete helplessness fast steal-ing over her once active limbs, they took her to the woods, built her a little hut ... and then made her welcome to the privilege of support-ing herself there in perfect loneliness; thus virtually turning her out to die!

(1986: 92)

In her isolation, Douglass' grandmother was not controlled by force, threat, deception and/or coercion; her new owners did not exploit her through use, management, profit, transfer or disposal. Having cut her adrift, the owners did not exercise any claims or powers of ownership in her.

Were the slaves described above *de facto* free, despite being *de jure* slaves? It is very clear from their writings that Jacobs, Equiano and Douglass' answer to this question would have been a resounding 'no!' I would venture to guess that the *cobreros* were not satisfied either that their *de facto* freedoms amounted to the same thing as the status of 'free'. The fact that many *libre de savane* saved their earnings from market activ-ities to pay the rachat that would allow them to secure formal, legal manumission (Moitt, 2008) suggests that they too perceived a powerful difference between *de facto* and *de jure* freedom. Thinking about the non-commensurability of *de facto* and *de jure* freedom suggests that under transatlantic slavery, being a slave meant something more than simply being treated as an object of property. This in turn raises questions about whether the *de facto* 'unfreedoms' that preoccupy the new abolitionists can be directly equated with *de jure* slavery. Has Bales really managed to identify the universal, transcendental core of slavery?

## Social science and slavery

In a recent discussion of the problem of differing definitions of slavery, Bales notes that where legal definitions seek to locate particular human activities within the rule of law, social science definitions are concerned to describe them as social phenomena (2012: 284). He moves from here to offer 'one social science definition' of slavery. The one he cites is his own. He proceeds to comment favourably on its consistency with the international legal definition of slavery offered by the 1926 Slavery Convention, and thence to generalize and celebrate this 'one social science definition' (his own) as follows:

> What is important is that the fundamental conceptual agreement of both the legal and social scientific definitions means that they point to and can be used to determine the existence of the same human activity – slavery. Furthermore, their coherence points to a general applicability in both the legal realm and the empirical study of slavery in the field.
>
> (Bales, 2012: 284–5)

Bales may be correct to claim there is a fundamental conceptual agreement between his own definition of slavery and that provided in international law, but there is no such agreement between legal and social scientific definitions of slavery more generally. Indeed, there is no consensus amongst the most eminent sociologists and anthropologists in the field of slavery on the defining features of slavery at all.

Some anthropologists have argued that the specificity of slavery lies in the fact that the slave 'is an outcast' (Testart, 2002: 176), others that slavery is best conceived as 'institutionalized marginality' (Kopytoff and Miers, 1977), others still that slavery should be understood as a mode of exploitation, one that differs from other modes of exploitation in respect to how it reproduces itself as a system, such as through acts of political violence, captivity and theft (Meillassoux, 1991). Possibly the most influential sociological treatment of slavery is to be found in Orlando Patterson's (1982) account of slavery as social death. Here, Patterson argues that slavery has three distinguishing features. The first is the slave's powerlessness; the second is the slave's natal alienation. The slave was 'denied all claims on, and obligations to, his parents and living blood relations, [and] by extension, all such claims and obligations on his more remote ancestors and on his descendants' (Patterson, 1982: 5). Slaves were socially dead, isolated from their social heritage and their social relations with the living, alienated from all rights or claims of birth and not belonging, in their own right, 'to any legitimate social order' (1982: 5). The third constituent element of the slave relation, according to Patterson, concerns the 'chronic, inalienable, dishonour' of the slave (1982: 12). A slave is a human being degraded and without means to achieve the power that is necessary to defend a sense of honour. Patterson thus offers the following 'definition of slavery on the level of personal relations: *slavery is the permanent, violent domination of natally alienated and generally dishonored persons'* (1982: 13, original emphasis).

Patterson's emphasis on dishonour, natal alienation and powerless takes us beyond slavery as merely the 'ownership' or 'possession' (control, use, management and profit) of one individual by another, to a view of slavery as a social relation and location, and this is one of the great virtues of his analysis. His definition allows us to see slavery as 'about individuals' relations to each other, their imagined communities and their sense of personhood' (Brace, 2004: 164–5). Note, however, that this is not a definition that is easily translated into an instrument that would help 'measure-kind-of-guys' to count 'slaves' in a world where nobody is legally ascribed that status. In fact, even Patterson's claims about the essential, distinctive features of slavery have been contested. Some hold that it is a mistake to imagine slavery as 'a monolithic, one-size-fits-all phenomenon, characterized by features such as natal alienation, persons-as-property, coercion, or "social death"', as Richard Eaton (2006: 1) puts it. Moreover, when taken as a literal description of the experience of the enslaved, the concept of 'social death' can work to conceal the ways in which the enslaved managed to turn slavery 'into collective forms of belonging and striving, making connections when confronted with alienation and finding dignity in the face of dishonor' (Brown, 2009: 1236).

Though the distinguishing characteristics of slavery are the subject of (often heated) dispute within anthropology and sociology, the one point on which most slavery scholars (including classicists, philosophers and political theorists as well as anthropologists and sociologists) appear to agree is that modern legalistic definitions of slavery fail to grasp the complexity, diversity and distinctiveness of the systems of slavery that have historically existed (e.g., Finley, 1964; Patterson, 1982; Kopytoff, 1982; Blackburn, 1988; Meillassoux, 1991; Lott, 1998; Turley, 2000; Testart, 2002; Miers, 2004; Brace, 2004; Quirk, 2011).

## The limits of legalistic definitions: slavery, persons and things

Semantic and legal definitions (as well as the new abolitionist definition) of slavery emphasize the legal, cultural and conceptual marking of human beings as 'things' that can be owned and controlled as property as its core feature. In contemporary liberal societies, as for George Bourne, this also provides the answer to the question of what is wrong with slavery. In a civilized society, only things, never persons, can properly be bought, sold and possessed, we are told. Hence, 'To determine, in law, a case of slavery', the Bellagio-Harvard Guidelines state, 'one must look for possession', and in essence, possession 'supposes control over a *person* by another such as a person might control a *thing*' (Allain, 2012: 376, emphasis added).

Such seemingly straightforward and widely accepted ideas about human non-commodifiability mask a more troublesome and complicated relationship between the realm of the human and that of the market, as well as between the forms of control exercised over persons and things, and the background relations and structures that support these forms of control. Slavery cannot, in practice, be distinguished from all other social relations through reference to the exercise of proprietary powers over slaves, slavery scholars argue. This is partly because 'property' is a concept that stands in for 'a miscellaneous collection of equities, rights, interests, claims, privileges, and preferences' (Bunzel, cited in Kopytoff, 1982: 219). As Orlando Patterson puts it, to define slavery *only* as the treatment of human beings as property is inadequate, since 'proprietary claims and powers are made with respect to many persons who are clearly not slaves' (1982: 21). Married people, he observes, have 'in actual and sociological terms... all sorts of claims, privileges and powers in the person, labour power and earnings' of their spouses, while parents have proprietary claims and powers in their children. Such examples:

> reveal the speciousness of the ownership concept in definitions of slavery... ownership is simply another name for property; it can only mean claims and powers *vis a vis* other persons with respect to a given thing, person or action. This is what a master possesses with respect to his slave, it is also exactly what a person possesses with respect to his or her spouse, child, employee or land.
>
> (1982: 22)

Or, in Claude Meillassoux's words (1991: 10), other categories of dependants, such as cadets, wives and pawned people 'are, like the slave, subject to the absolute power of the head of the family'.

For Patterson, it is merely a matter of convention that 'we tend not to regard "free" human beings as objects of property' (1982: 22). To distinguish the slave from the non-slave, we should focus not on the fact that a slave was legally and socially imagined as the *object* of property, but rather on the fact 'he could not be the *subject* of property' (Patterson, 1982: 28). This is what rendered the slave a person without power. Certainly, this is one of the things that makes *de facto* freedom and/or even kindly treatment a poor substitute for *de jure* freedom. As has been seen, Olaudah Equiano was not always subject to the direct or violent control of his master, and he employed his freedoms to engage in profitable trading activities. However, because he was a slave *de jure*, his property rights in goods and money were not protected in law. His narrative is littered with examples in which white people cheated or robbed him of the stock he had managed to accumulate, as well as instances of brutal assault by white strangers, acts against which he, as a slave (and even, later, as a freed black man), had no redress in law.

The right to be the subject of property is critical to political subjectivity in liberal thought, and the fact that in law, slaves were both treated as property *and* excluded from property rights was, for some nineteenth-century anti-slavery campaigners, a crucial part of the wrongness of slavery. As Frederick Douglass noted in a speech in 1850, the corollary to the master who 'claims and exercises a right of property in the person of a fellow-man' is the slave, who is:

> a human being divested of all rights – reduced to the level of a brute – a mere 'chattel' in the eye of the law ... In law, the slave has no wife, no children, no country, and no home. He can own nothing, possess nothing, acquire nothing.
>
> (cited in DeLombard, 2012: 6)

Or as George Bourne (1845: 7) put it, the slave's exclusion from property meant 'His right to himself is abrogated ... To *use himself* for his own good is a *crime*. To keep what he *earns* is stealing. To take his body into his own keeping is insurrection'. For anti-slavery campaigners like Bourne, all of this amounted to the legal eradication of the slave as a person, *ergo* the legal constitution of the slave as an object or thing.

However, Patterson (1982: 22) also takes issue with the 'common definition of a slave as someone without a legal personality'. 'No legal code I know has ever attempted to treat slaves as anything other than persons in law', he remarks (1982: 23). For whilst the law in slave societies did erase many aspects of their humanity, slaves were nonetheless deemed legally and morally responsible for any criminal act they committed. They were tried, sentenced and punished as human agents. The revised 1856 edition of what was then America's leading reference on the subject, Bouvier's *Law Dictionary*, notes that 'slaves are sometimes ranked not with persons but things', then proceeds: 'But sometimes they are considered as persons; for example, a negro is in contemplation of law a person, so as to be capable of committing a riot in conjunction with white men' (cited in DeLombard, 2012: 8–9).

Unlike the livestock to which they were routinely compared, transatlantic slaves were arrested, tried, and punished for committing outlawed acts, 'precisely because whites recognized...blacks' capacity for reason (with *mens rea* swiftly becoming the main legal ingredient of criminal culpability)' (DeLombard, 2012: 8). And as Jeannine DeLombard also points out, the fact that white Americans sometimes preached to and prayed for those they held in slavery further indicates a recognition that slaves were human, not merely animal. Slaveholders, she argues, 'purchased, mortgaged, willed, and speculated on women and men, girls and boys, cooks and carpenters, field hands and fancy girls, not an assortment of dehumanized "its"' (2012: 8). We may wish to qualify this statement with the observation that some slaveholders did treat some slaves as 'its' for the purpose of trading them. Equiano (1999: 79), for instance, reported that 'I have often seen slaves, particularly those who were meager, in different islands, put into scales and weighed; and then sold from three-pence to six-pence or nine-pence a pound'. But even slaves bought and sold in this manner were acknowledged as human in the sense of being deemed criminally culpable. As Joan Dayan (1999: 411) puts it:

> Legal thought relied on a set of fictions to sustain such precepts as the absolute concept of property and the alternating distinction of slaves as things or persons, depending on whether the context was civil action (as article of property, utterly deprived of civil capacity) or criminal action (as capable of crime, recognized as a rational being). In both cases, what is legally possible or impossible demands the give-and-take between categories such as contract or tort, public or private, thing or self, physical or incorporeal.

And though masters might sometimes have weighed and bought slaves like so many pounds of horse meat, the fact that they bought human beings, not mere flesh, made it impossible for owners to possess and manage slaves in the same way that they possessed and managed the property they held in inanimate objects or non-human animals. For while in 'legal terms, the slave is described as an object, a possession...given the nature or his or exploitation, the assimilation of a human being to an object, or even an animal, is an untenable and contradictory fiction' (Meillassoux, 1991: 9). Bales speaks of the 'involuntariness' of slavery, but as Turton (2003: 11) has pointed out, strictly speaking, 'An act is involuntary when it is done without thinking, without deliberation, as when I let out a cry of pain after dropping something on my foot'. One person can command another to perform a certain action, but he or she cannot literally appropriate the self and will of another and *cause* them to perform it. Classical Christian formalism was onto something in this respect.

When slaves were given orders by owners or their representatives, they had no simple reflex action to obey, they did not act automatically. Bales says that the control of the slave by the slaveholder 'transfers agency, freedom of movement, access to the body, and labor and its products and benefits to the slaveholder', but *agency* cannot be transferred. Slaves were not directly controlled by the will of their owner. This fact was recognized in relation to the insurance of slaves as commodities when transported across the Atlantic by British ships, which came to exclude losses attributable to insurrection on the part of the commodities themselves (Rupprecht, 2007). It was also recognized in the practice of paying compensation to the owners of slaves (things) who were found guilty of crimes and sentenced (as persons) to life imprisonment, transportation or death, instituted in Jamaica in 1717 (Paton, 2001). If ownership of a slave implied possession of the slave's will, and so becoming the motive force of the slave's action in the same way that possession of a gun implies becoming its motive force, the idea of compensating a slaveholder for the loss of a slave who had committed murder would have looked as odd as the idea of compensating a gun murderer for the confiscation of his gun.

As willing selves, slaves had to actively decide whether or not to comply with orders given by their legal owners. They had to make choices, as attested by the tragedy of Margaret Garner, an enslaved woman who, when her attempt to escape with her family failed, elected to kill her beloved three-year-old daughter with a butcher's knife 'and attempted to kill the other children rather than let them be taken back into slavery by their master' (Gilroy, 1993: 65), as well as in several slave narratives that include memories of, and thought-provoking reflections on, moments during the author's enslavement when he or she either refused, or contemplated refusing, to obey the command of a master or overseer (e.g., Ball, 2014; Bibb, 2008; Douglass, 1986; Henson, 2008; Jacobs, 2000; Northup, 2012; Roper, 2003), and in the fact of slave revolts and revolution (Brown, 2009; James, 2001; Williams, 1970). It follows that the control exercised by slaveholders over slaves was *not* control over them 'such as a person might control a thing' (Allain, 2012: 376). Rather, the slaveholder's control rested on forms of subjugation that made compliance the most likely outcome of slaves' mindful deliberations about how to respond to commands. Considered in this light, more or less every aspect of the system of domination upon which transatlantic slavery relied for its everyday operation reflected a recognition of the enslaved as humans, not 'things'.

## Not possession but subjugation

Except in the case of murder and execution, which did actually transform the slave into a mere body and nothing but a body, the wide array of coercive practices with which transatlantic slavery was associated were designed to produce compliance, not literally to transform the slave into an object (and even the murder and execution of some was designed to terrorize others into submission). As Saidiya Hartman (1997) points out, the slave had a 'bifurcated existence' as both property and person, object and subject and the tension between these two aspects of the slave's existence is graphically expressed in the extraordinarily sadistic punishments often meted out by owners. Had the Jamaican planter, Thomas Thistlewood, actually regarded the slaves he owned as equivalent to the property he held in material objects, or even non-human animals, for example, he would hardly have felt it worthwhile to devise and impose upon them the sickening penalties that he so assiduously recorded in his diaries (Burnard, 2004). These punishments horrify precisely because of their peculiar and cruel engagement with specifically human emotions, such as disgust and humiliation.

Likewise, slave owners were aware of the fact that, as human beings, slaves had powerful affective ties to family and community, and they 'manipulated these human relationships so as to maximize slaves' tractability and profitability' (DeLombard, 2012: 8; see also Wong, 2009). Equiano (1999: 77) remarks on the fact that when slaveholders wished to punish female slaves, they would sometimes make husbands flog their own wives, a practice which again speaks to a form of identification with the humanity of slaves that must have preceded its violent repudiation. Such practices are often described as dehumanizing, but nothing can actually transform a human into some other category of being. What we label 'dehumanizing' are practices that constitute an active refusal to acknowledge a fellow human's humanity, and in this sense a disavowal of something known to be true. Even the decision to cut 'useless' slaves adrift expressed an awareness of slaves' humanity. Henny and Douglass' grandmother had to be exiled from the community of slaves in which they lived because, had they remained, their fellow slaves, being human, would have offered them care and support, using time and resources that the owners imagined as not theirs to give.

By the same token, slaveholders could have particular interests in particular slaves because of the human relationship they had forged with them. Again in the slave South, the law had to grapple with the twofold character of the slave, as Dayan (1999: 408) illustrates with a case that came before the Court of Errors in Columbia, South Carolina in 1841 on appeal from the judgment of the circuit court:

> The question before the court was whether Joyce, a young female slave, had to be returned bodily to the plaintiff or whether the defendant could replace her by paying money damages as remedy for her loss. The decision turned on whether slaves are to be regarded as chattels – things personal and movable, mere merchandise, perishables in the market – or real estate, affixed to or growing upon the land. In this case, Joyce is argued to be no 'mere toy' or 'snuff box' but a valuable entity.

The fact that it would be impossible to go to market on any day and buy 'an able, honest, and faithful slave' in the same way that one might buy 'a bale of goods, or a flock of sheep' revealed that Joyce was not a fully fungible commodity. She was property, but of a special species (Dayan, 1999: 408, see also Josiah Henson's, 2008, account of the trust vested in him by his first owner).

## Revisiting the questions: what is slavery and what is wrong with slavery?

In pursuit of a universal, transhistorical definition of slavery, Bales treats certain identifiable elements of the historical experience of certain slaves as if these elements can be abstracted both from each other, and from any specific historical context. 'It is a simple yet potent truth that slavery is a relationship between (at least) two people' he states (2006: 1). But an equal, if not more potent, truth is that slavery has historically been a legally and/or socially recognized and sanctioned status. This made slavery relational not merely in the sense it implied a particular kind of relationship between the individual slave and the individual slaveholder, but also in the sense that it placed the slave in a particular position in relation to the society or community as a whole. Herein lies an important difference between contemporary cases in which women and girls have been held in captivity and abused for many years (Josef Fritzl's daughter in Austria; three women held for ten years by three brothers in Cleveland, Ohio, for example), and slavery. In the former cases, the women were victims of what is socially and legally recognized as a crime. Their social status did not license their captors to deprive them of their liberty and exploit them for their own purposes. As pertinently, Charles Ball's (2014) slave narrative contains an account of case in which a white woman was kidnapped by two male slaves and held captive by them for a few days. It would be nonsensical to describe her as having become a *de facto* slave, despite the violence to which she was subjected, and equally nonsensical to describe her abductors as *de facto* slaveholders, given the even more barbarous violence to which they were subject when caught.

If we focus on slavery as a status, the obstacles to Bales' ambition to 'parse out' its universal, underlying features becomes very obvious. This ambition overlooks the fact that, as Finley (1964: 247) put it, all human beings, unless they somehow manage to live alone on an island, 'are bundles of claims, privileges, immunities, liabilities and obligations with respect to others. A man's status is defined by the total of these elements which he possesses or which he has (or has not) the potential of acquiring'. Attempts to unpick the bundles that made up the status of slave in a series of radically different historical and cultural settings and identify their shared elements will tell us very little about the nature or meaning of that status, because it is the particular ways in which claims, privileges, immunities, liabilities and obligations are bundled up *relative to each other* that matters.

Unravel and decontextualize the elements, and, as will be seen in Chapter 7, the white wife and daughter of the transatlantic slaveholder look to stand in the same relation to him as his slaves. (Mary Prince (2004) describes once having had to intervene to prevent her violent and alcoholic master from beating his own white daughter to death.) And yet the parallels between the condition of wives and children on the one hand and chattel slaves on the other hardly rendered their experience equivalent. Viewed as entire bundles, we see that the white wife had certain obligations with respect to her husband that he did not have to her, but at the same time shared with her husband certain privileges and immunities with respect to slaves. It is only by attending to the totality of these elements, and how they intersected and contrasted with other bundles or statuses in a given society, that we can hope to produce reliable descriptions of slaveries (not slavery) as a social phenomenon. And even transatlantic or New World slavery was not one single, unitary system. The bundle of elements that made up the status of 'slave' varied over time and between different slave and colonial states. This is one reason why slaveries challenge even the best efforts to identify the universal, transcendent features of slavery *per se*. Attention to 'slave' as one of a number of social statuses that differentially distributed claims, privileges, immunities, liabilities and obligations in a given society also reveals why it is so difficult to identify slavery's unique moral wrongness.

For the new abolitionists, as in dominant liberal discourse, the immorality of slavery lies in its treatment of persons as things: commodities to be bought, sold and used for profit. This leads to a legalistic definition of slavery that assumes slaves are first and foremost differentiated, controlled and subordinated by their construction (either *de jure* or *de facto*) as objects of property. As Bales said on the release of Walk Free's 2013 *Global Slavery Index* : 'We're not talking about bad choices, we're not talking about crummy jobs in a sweatshop. We're talking about real life slavery – you can't walk away, you're controlled through violence, you're treated like property' (Hume, 2013). Yet under transatlantic slavery, the techniques and social and legal machinery that suborned slaves to the will of slaveholders appear to have been as much, if not more, concerned with slaves as human beings and willing selves (persons), than with slaves as objects (things).

This leaves us with the problem of slavery's overlaps with other systems of domination, in particular, as the following chapters show, class, caste, race, nationality and gender, overlaps that together constitute an overwhelming obstacle to differentiating between 'slave' and 'non-slave' in the contemporary world. The new abolitionist analysis of slavery does not provide a satisfactory answer to the question 'what is slavery?' or allow us to identify what is uniquely morally wrong with it.

# 3
# Slavery and Wage Labour: Freedom and Its Doubles

In a 2012 TEDx talk titled 'Photos that bear witness to modern slavery', a photographer talks us through what the publicity blurb describes as her 'hauntingly beautiful images...illuminating the plight of the 27 million souls enslaved worldwide'. Lisa Kristine, a slim, young white American woman, with neat blonde hair and a startlingly white shirt, stands spotlit on a stage. Behind her, images of impoverished developing world black and brown men, women and children are projected onto a huge screen. As the photographs appear, Lisa recounts the story of her work with Free the Slaves. It was, she tells us in a voice husky with suppressed emotion, a journey into 'Dante's inferno', a hidden world where 'modern slaves' are forced to labour with 'primitive tools' in unbearable heat (Kristine, 2012). On her journey, she met people engaged in brick production and stone quarrying in India and Nepal, brothel prostitution in Nepal, silk dyeing in India and informal gold mining in Ghana.

In the Himalayas, Kristine tells us, she found and photographed 'children carrying stone for miles down mountainous terrain to trucks waiting below. The sheets of stone weighed more than the children' (Kristine, 2012). They, like other workers she met, were not paid for their backbreaking work, but many did not even realize they were slaves 'because they've been slaves all their lives' and knew no different. But, she continues, one group of villagers did attempt to resist their exploitation. In response, the 'slavers' burned down their homes, and the villagers 'were so petrified they wanted to give up'. Yet one woman:

> rallied for them to persevere and abolitionists on the ground helped them get a quarry lease of their own. So that now they do the same backbreaking work, but they do it for themselves, and they get paid for it, and they do it in freedom.
>
> (Kristine, 2012)

It seems likely that she is referring to a case that is presented by Free the Slaves as a success story, in which 'hereditary slaves in a stone quarry' in northern India were helped 'to stand up to their masters and renounce slavery' and subsequently 'embarked on new lives, many of them now running their own quarry. The children went to school and some ex-slaves even ran for elected office' (Bales, 2007a; FTS, 2014b).

I do not doubt that these villagers were in an extremely oppressive situation, or that they managed to improve that situation in certain respects through their collective action. But I do wonder what it is that leads organizations like Free the Slaves and Walk Free to describe such workers as 'modern slaves', and what *kind* of freedom they wish to bestow upon them. Take artisanal gold mining and stone quarrying work, for example, both generally classified under the broad heading of 'Artisanal and Small Mining' or ASM. The term refers to 'informal mining activities carried out using low technology or with minimal machinery' (Fraser Institute, 2012). Definitional problems, the absence of reliable and cross-nationally comparable official statistics, and the fact that workers are often involved on a seasonal and occasional basis mean that all statistics on it should be treated with caution. However, it is estimated that, in the developing world, there are 'at least 25 million artisanal miners, with 150–170 million people indirectly reliant on ASM' (Fraser Institute, 2012).

The employment relations associated with ASM vary widely, not merely between different countries and regions, but also within them, and even within a single mine. In Ghana, for instance, labourers in artisanal gold mining may be working on a seasonal or more permanent basis, with seasonal workers often having migrated from poorer rural regions in the north; they may be hired by the day or working on a self-employed, entrepreneurial basis (Okyere, 2012). In South Asia, ASM includes workers on permanent and casual employment contracts (though not usually written contracts), self-employed producers, dependent producers, unpaid family members and bonded labourers. Many workers are indebted, in some cases leading to forms of bondage transferrable between family members, or generationally, and the vast majority are migrants from other regions of the same country (ILO, 2005; Lahiri-Dutt, 2006). As 'internal migrants', they are often unable to access basic entitlements to housing, health facilities, education and banking services, or to secure 'social security and legal protection' (UNICEF, 2014) and, in addition, such workers are in the main drawn from extremely poor and marginalized communities, *Dalit* (or Scheduled Caste) or *Adivasi* (or Scheduled Tribes) (almost half of India's *Adivasi* population of 84.3 million live below the official poverty line, Nilsen, 2012: 1).

Whatever the nature of the employment relation, ASM workers in the developing world typically labour without proper equipment or safety gear and the conditions they face are notoriously harsh (Hilson et al., 2013; Okyere, 2012, 2013). Occupational hazards affecting *all* workers in ASM in South Asia (in other words, the 'free' as well as the bonded) include:

> respiratory problems, silicosis, tuberculosis, leukemia, arthritis, poor vision and deafness to reproductive tract problems. They occur due to constant exposure to dust and noise, poor water supply and sanitation. Whereas major accidents claim mostly the lives of men due to their preponderance in the underground jobs, minor accidents due to blasting or falls are also common for both women and men. Snake bites in conditions of inundation can also claim lives.
>
> (Lahiri-Dutt, 2006: 25)

Workers generally earn either only enough for daily survival or too little to avoid becoming mired in debt. In many places, 'Living and working conditions are deplorable; small and low temporary huts with plastic sheets for roofing, no clean and safe accessible drinking water supply, no electricity, no health services and no educational facilities for the children' (Lahiri-Dutt, 2006: 30). Samuel Okyere's ethnography of an artisanal gold mine in Ghana reveals similar living and working conditions (2012, 2013).

The new abolitionists are not, of course, in favour of such hazardous and miserable conditions, or of inequality, poverty or caste/tribal discrimination. But they imagine these problems as separable from what they call 'slavery'. More than this, the new abolitionists believe that ending 'slavery' and enabling workers like those Lisa Kristine photographed to 'work in freedom' is part of the solution to the problem of poverty and global inequality. What they dub 'modern slavery' is presented as an anachronism that can and will disappear when economic development and modernization is combined with proper anti-slavery law and law enforcement. As Kevin Bales (2010) puts it:

> Slavery has been pushed to the criminal edges of our global society and to the very edge of its own extinction...freed slaves given opportunities today generate economic growth through a 'freedom dividend'.

Though workers liberated from bondage may not immediately enjoy a standard of living, working conditions or social protections comparable to that enjoyed by people like Kevin and Lisa themselves, they have been gifted the basic building blocks of 'freedom'. Now they can participate in capitalism proper. Their freedom, carefully managed and mixed with good, honest toil, will ultimately pay dividends that will allow them to lift themselves and their descendants from poverty and deprivation, and help their countries to develop economically.

Again, there are strong echoes of nineteenth century European thought. Gyan Prakash (1993: 134) describes a letter to the civil court authorities in Calcutta written in 1808 by a minor official of the East India Company, which denounced British tolerance of slavery in India, arguing that its abolition 'would inspire progress and prosperity in the region', and that 'free labor would bring the benefits of a market economy and promote population growth and industriousness'. The new abolitionists, it seems, rely on the same 'transition narrative' that has historically been deployed in liberal defences of various European colonial ventures (Chakrabarty, 1992), 'a heavily ideological narrative' in which history unfolds as progress from the 'primitive' to 'civilised' and from feudalism into capitalism, culminating with 'the modern individual' at the story's end (Brace, 2004: 210).

This chapter critically explores that narrative against the history of wage labour in liberal capitalist societies, then returns to consider what is masked, forgotten or glossed over in depictions of workers like those photographed by Lisa Kristine as 'slaves'.

## 'Freeing up' wage labour

In feudal European societies, material production and human reproduction were visibly united. A person's position at birth determined their role in the process of material production, and material production was arranged with a view to sustaining and reproducing the human relations that characterized the society, as well as human life itself: 'all of what we might now call "society" was understood in terms of kinship or kin-like bonds of loyalty or fealty on the model of the patriarchal household' (Slater, 1998: 138). There was profound political inequality, but those at the top of the hierarchy had certain obligations to their dependants lower down the hierarchy, as well as rights in relation to them. According to the standard liberal account of the history of liberal societies, and also to orthodox sociological theory, the two cycles – production and reproduction – were wrenched apart in the transition to capitalism. Productive activity was no longer suborned to the imperative to preserve a society organized around kin-like bonds, and status hierarchies were gradually eliminated and replaced by contractual relations between free and formally equal buyers and sellers of labour. The transition to capitalism was a linear process of incremental liberation from the hierarchically arranged constraints of the old regime.

For Marx too, Derek Sayer (1991: 56) observes, capitalism appears as 'a distinctively modern form of sociation', one that 'entailed – or was – a revolution in what might... be called the elementary forms of social life: individuality, relationship and community'. However, in contrast to the orthodox liberal version of history, in which the movement that 'changes the producers into wage-labourers appears... as their emancipation from serfdom and from the fetters of the guilds' (Marx, 1954: 875), Marx's story begins with the politically orchestrated, and extremely violent process of 'primitive accumulation' that was an essential precondition for the emergence of the economic structure of capitalist society (Nichols, 1980).

In Europe from the fifteenth century on, private landlords, lords and rich farmers, employed a variety of strategies to 'eliminate communal land property and expand their holdings', 'engrossing' or 'enclosing' land such that they amassed wealth, while independent proprietors and peasants increasingly lost their traditional rights of access to the common resources upon which they depended for food, fuel, bedding and shelter (Federici, 2004: 69). Land privatization was supported by an emerging discourse of 'improvement' which asserted that 'land held in common fields was often spoiled through lack of good husbandry' and so 'constituted the sin of wasting God's workmanship' (Brace, 2004: 17). At this stage, prior to the industrial revolution, there was not enough paid work to absorb all those thrown off the land and denied access to customary ways of subsisting. 'Masterless' men, women and children therefore frequently wandered the country, relying upon begging, tinkering, peddling, pilfering, horse-thievery, prostitution, fortune-telling and any other means by which they could subsist.

'Vagabondage' (or people roaming freely and without obligations to any master to fix them geographically and socially) was identified as a serious threat to the established status quo of sixteenth-century England. Before 1530, there was 'almost no legislation on this subject... From that year, however, until the end of the century the rogues and beggars received constant attention from Parliament' (Aydelotte, 1913: 56). This legislation drew a distinction between 'sturdy' and 'impotent' vagabonds, allowing that the latter deserved some relief, but insisting that the former must be set to work. The most brutal physical punishments were also reserved for the 'sturdy' (such as whipping, stocking, branding, ear cropping and execution). In 1547, a statute (repealed two years later on grounds that it was too severe) even decreed that able-bodied persons not working could be seized by their former masters, branded with a V on the breast, and made slaves for two years. They could then 'legally be chained, given only the coarsest food, driven to work with whips or subjected to any other cruelty . . . . If they ran away and were caught, they were to be branded S on the chest and made slaves for life' (Aydelotte, 1913: 63).

State controls over mobility introduced in the sixteenth century as a response to the perceived menace of the masterless poor cast long shadows into the future. The Vagrancy Act of 1597 provided that 'persistent rogues could be banished to "parts beyond the seas" at the behest of members of the Privy Council' and in this way prefigured the practice of transportation (Jordan and Walsh, 2007: 39). Meanwhile, measures to contain vagabondage by forcing the uprooted back to their social and geographic 'place' were consolidated in the Poor Laws of the seventeenth century, especially the 1662 Poor Relief Act, which not only 'ordered that poor relief or work could only be given to those who were "settled" in a parish or who were in their parish of birth', but also sanctioned the expulsion of the 'unsettled' poor 'to their last parish of settlement or their parish of birth' (Anderson, 2013: 22–3). The right claimed by the state to determine who may settle where, as well as to forcibly move people across geopolitical boundaries, anticipated contemporary immigration controls.

The system of settlement, or 'parish serfdom', represented a means of coercing the poor into labour, but as it was also a means of preventing their mobility, it did not create a labour market (Polanyi, 2001). The labouring poor were not free to take their labour-power and sell it where they pleased; they still 'belonged' to the parish. Throughout the eighteenth century, even as the Settlement Acts were being less rigorously enforced, vagrancy legislation continued to be used to fix people in their geographic and social 'place' (Rogers, 1994). However, while these measures were working to prevent the mobility of the masterless, a second wave of enclosures, which took place between 1760 and 1870, operated to dispossess and displace yet more people. This time, land privatization was orchestrated through some 4,000 acts of parliament, by means of which 'about 7 million acres (about one sixth the area of England) were changed . . . from common land to enclosed land' (Fairlie, 2009). Now, 'arguments of property and improvement [were] joined to arguments of class discipline' (Thompson, 1991: 163). As one proponent of enclosure put it in 1810:

> The appropriation of the forests . . . would . . . be the means of produc-
> ing a number of additional useful hands for agricultural employment,
> by gradually cutting up and annihilating that nest and conservatory
> of sloth, idleness and misery, which is uniformly to be witnessed in
> the vicinity of all commons, waste lands and forests.
>
> (cited in Thompson, 1991: 163)

To prevent people from subsisting through their own endeavours rather than through paid employment, avenues for independent survival were further closed down by a series of increasingly restrictive Game Laws. The Waltham Black Acts of 1722, for instance, made it a capital offence to hunt deer, hares and rabbits, for example (McLynn, 1989), and even after their reform in 1831, convictions for poaching increased. During the 1840s 'in some rural counties, 30 to 40 percent of all male convictions were still for infractions of the Game Laws', and some hold that the 'majority of convicts that Britain exiled to Australia' had either been convicted of poaching or crimes associated with it, such as resisting arrest (Perelman, 2000: 44). The Black Acts reveal the system of property that was being established as very much what G. A. Cohen (1995) has described as a distribution of freedom and unfreedom, with one individual's freedom to own land as private property being directly predicated on denying many other people the freedom to live from the land, and the process of enclosure was both accompanied and propelled by swathes of equally brutal legislation extending the range of activities that were defined as crimes against property to similar effect. Christopher Hill (1967: 181) observes that between 1688 and 1780, the number of offences that carried the death sentence increased from 50 to 5 times that number, most of which were offences against property, and the main 'offenders' (in London at least) were people under 20 years of age.[1]

Commenting on this history, Marx (1954: 669) noted that the English wage labourers who arrived at market to sell their labour-power, free from bonds to any lord, master or slaveholder, had become 'sellers of themselves only after they had been robbed of all their own means of production, and of all the guarantees of existence afforded by the old feudal arrangements'. They were stripped of all protection, and 'hurled as free and "unattached" proletarians on the labour-market' (Marx, 1954: 669). Without an alternative means of subsistence, and without anyone with an obligation to provide for them, dull economic compulsion forced the dispossessed to treat their bodily capacity to labour as a commodity on sale to the highest bidder. The form of primitive accumulation that robbed 'various categories of agricultural producers [of] access to land' can thus be 'conceived as a process of *proletarianization*', Robert Miles comments (1987: 36, emphasis original), since it is a process that 'creates a worker with only labour power for sale, i.e., a proletarian. It is therefore synonymous with the creation of a labour market and the commodification of labour power'.

## Wage labour and the location of freedom

The double freedom of Marx's ideal–typical proletarian (free of both an owner and of any means of subsistence other that wage labour) seemingly stands in very sharp contrast to the double dependency of the ideal–typical chattel slave. Proletarian workers take their own commodified labour-power to market to sell where they choose; slaves are dependent upon the will of their owners as to whether, and to whom, they are sold, leased, exchanged, gifted or bequeathed. Proletarian workers are free independently to arrange their own sustenance, clothing, accommodation, medical attention and so on (and also to die independently for want of these supports), whilst slaves depend on their owners to make these provisions (or not, as they choose). Wage workers are driven to sell their labour-power as commodity by impersonal forces such as hunger and other wants; chattel slaves are forced directly to surrender their labour-power by the person who legally owns them. Slavery depends upon theft – slaves must be stolen or born of parents or ancestors who were stolen – and so seemingly produces *objects*. Wage labour is based upon consent – the wage labourer voluntarily enters the employment contract – and so seemingly produces *subjects* (Marx, 1973: 464–5).

Nevertheless, for all these sharp contrasts with slavery, wage labour remained, for Marx, a system of domination. He not only showed that it required a powerful legal apparatus to coerce one portion of society to produce for another through the system of wage labour, but also that the contractual exchange of labour-power for wages is the mechanism by which relations of inequality and domination are reproduced. By purchasing the commodified labour-power of workers who have no alternative but to sell it, and harnessing that labour-power to existing capital, capitalists are able to set in motion a labour process that generates surplus value, which they then appropriate as profit and invest in more capital (Nichols, 1980). The social and economic power of the capitalist class is sustained by and dependent upon the labour of wage workers, just as the social and economic power of feudal lords was sustained by the labour of their serfs, and that of the slave-owning class by the labour of their slaves. In *appearance*, however, relations of domination had been transformed. Power now appeared to be mediated by 'things', rather than God-given to one class or group of persons to exercise directly over another.

The newness of capitalism as a social formation was a central preoccupation for Marx, just as the novelty of modernity was more generally the core concern of nineteenth- and early twentieth-century social and political theorists (Sayer, 1991), and his work draws attention to the enormous social and political import of this altered appearance of power, its commodity fetishization. Whether or not Marx believed capitalism had wrought changes of a type that ruled out the continued use of slave and other forms of unfree labour is a matter of dispute amongst Marxists, however (e.g., Miles, 1987; Davis, 1975; Brass, 2010). Rather than entering these vexed debates, I want to focus on the distinction Marx drew between relations in the labour market, and relations in the actual process of production. This distinction was and remains of great significance for questions about the kind of freedoms that wage labourers enjoy in capitalist societies.

In the orthodox transition narrative, once people were released from the traditional, political ties that fixed them to a lord or parish, and were in a position to take the property they held in their persons (their labour-power) to market and voluntarily enter into a contract to sell it, they were free. But as Marx showed, the wage labour exchange is not like (most) other market exchanges. What employers buy, and what workers sell, is not a fully alienable 'thing'. The human capacity to labour cannot be detached from the *person* of the labourer. A price can be set upon an individual's ability to pick apples, but farmers cannot go to market, purchase a certain quantity of that ability, and take it back to use in their orchards without also taking the human being in whom that ability inheres – 'the worker must be present when the commodity she has parted with is consumed by its purchaser' (Lebowitz, 2003: 4).

This makes human labour-power a 'peculiar commodity', for what 'the worker sells, and the capitalist buys, is *not an agreed amount of labor, but the power to labor over an agreed period of time*', as Harry Braverman (1974: 54, original emphasis) put it. The contract between buyer and seller is therefore very unlike the contracts that facilitate most other market exchanges. To begin with, the wage labour exchange involves a transfer of powers over persons, not the exchange of one 'thing' (money) for another (labour), for when employers purchase workers' power to labour, what they wish to obtain is the right to direct workers to do their bidding for the period of the contract. Thus, though the wage labour contract is ostensibly a contract between equals, it is also, as David Graeber (2011: 120) observes, 'an agreement between equals in which both agree that once one of them punches the time clock, they won't be equals any more'. Having voluntarily entered the contract, the two parties leave the marketplace, the employer striding ahead, 'smirking, intent on business', the worker 'timid and holding back, like one who is bringing his own hide to market and has nothing to expect but – a hiding', and move to the private arena of the workplace, the 'hidden abode of production' (Marx, 1954: 172). In this location, wage labour – which was free whilst circulating in the market – becomes unfree: 'Once labour-power becomes the property of capitalists, the labourers are subject to discipline and supervision' (Nichols, 1980: 75; Weeks, 2011).

The paradox is strengthened by the 'over a period of time' element of the agreement. Because employers want to buy a human capacity or potential, not a thing, the wage labour exchange cannot be executed instantaneously, as when a shopper pays cash and immediately takes receipt of, say, a kilo of apples. The 'commodity' that employers buy has to be delivered over a certain period of time. During this period of time (no matter how long or brief), the exchange is incomplete. The worker stands as a debtor to the employer, having promised to deliver up her capacity to labour for a set period in exchange for some benefit, but not having yet done so. Again, though debt is a promise made between equals – 'or at least potential equals', people who will be made equal again once the debt is repaid – so long as 'the debt remains unpaid, the logic of hierarchy takes hold' (Graeber, 2011: 121).

For the term of the contract, the employer has a claim in the *person* of the worker, and the worker has a duty to follow the orders of the employer. The labour contract may begin with equality – the exchange of equivalents in the marketplace – but it is followed by hierarchy in the sphere of production (Lebowitz, 2003: 5), and contract does not automatically replace or rule out the exercise of personalistic power in this latter sphere. In principle, it licenses employers to exercise the right of command in relation to the worker that the slaveholder enjoys in relation to the slave – 'In the factory code, the capitalist formulates his autocratic power over his workers like a private legislator, and purely as an emanation of his own will' (Marx, 1977: 549–50; cited in Hairong, 2008: 14). A new abolitionist might object that the slaveholder's power

of command differs because it is unlimited both temporally and physically – the slave cannot walk away. It is certainly true that contracts
*can* impose strong limits on employers' freedom to treat workers as they
please. But as will be seen below, it is equally true that labour contracts
*can* bestow almost unlimited powers on employers, and for extremely
protracted periods of time.

If we combine Marx's insights about the nature of the relationship
initiated by the wage labour contract with attention to features of
modernity that were longstanding and timeworn, as opposed to novel,
it becomes clear that the creation of a market in commodified labour-
power cannot be the end of the story for anyone concerned with
questions about workers' exposure to forms of coercion, violence and
exploitation from which they cannot walk away. Under certain circumstances and in particular conditions, these experiences can be initiated
by contract.

## Contract and dependence

Reflecting on the demand for chattel slaves in eighteenth-century
America, Benjamin Franklin stated that the attraction of slaves was that
they 'may be kept as long as a Man pleases, or has Occasion for their
Labour; while hired Men are continually leaving their Master (often
in the midst of his Business) and setting up for themselves' (cited in
Perelman, 2000: 265). This observation about hired men certainly spoke
to the problems faced by some would-be capitalist colonists (see Nichols,
1980: 73), but it was hardly an accurate description of relations between
most masters and labourers in eighteenth-century America or Europe.
As Paul Craven and Douglas Hay (1994: 71) note:

> slavery was just one of many legal statuses defining employment rela-
> tions in the common law world. Apprentices, journeymen, labourers,
> indentured servants, 'industrial' immigrants, slaves and masters were
> the main categories, but within each there was a plethora of legal
> definitions at common law and in legislation, setting the limits of
> freedom that 'free' servants (and masters) enjoyed.

The liberty to 'walk away' from an employment relationship was
one of the key aspects of freedom that was differentially limited by
such laws, and in so doing, the law produced – in varying degrees –
labourers' dependency upon the masters to whom they were bound.
In seventeenth-century England, some groups of workers were actually

tied to their masters for life. There were iron founders in South Wales and some salters and miners in Scotland whose resemblance to chattel slaves extended to 'having to wear collars engraved with their master's name' (Perelman, 2000: 249). Such lifelong servitude was far from the norm (though it is worth noting that these arrangements lasted into the eighteenth century), but seventeenth-century English law nonetheless locked most workers into lengthy relationships with their masters. Apprentices were tied to their masters and expected to reside with them for at least seven years; resident servants typically served by the year and those who left before their term had expired were treated as 'runaways'; even labourers and artificers could not depart from an agreed term of service for a master (Steinfeld, 1991: 23–35). The immobility of these non-slave workers was enforced by the threat of imprisonment.

The 'early law of the American colonies followed the basic pattern of this English law', though terms of service for colonial indentured servants were longer – often three to seven, sometimes even 11 years – and penalties for departing prior to the end of the term were generally harsher (Steinfeld, 1991: 4; see also Hadden, 2001). Amongst the servants in seventeenth- and eighteenth-century America were children who had either been dispatched by the state as vagrants or sent by their parents in the hope of a better future and British convicts sentenced to transportation and servitude. Indeed, the approximately 50,000 British convicts transported to America between 1718 and 1775 represented 'roughly a quarter of all British arrivals and half of all English arrivals in this period', according to Grubb (2000: 94). But many servants (roughly two-thirds according Coldham, 1992) were people who had been free to go to market and sell their labour-power. They were, in other words, free in the Lockean sense of having entered voluntarily into a contract to exchange the property they held in their person for a specified sum or benefit. They were even sometimes referred to as 'free-willers' (Jordan and Walsh, 2007: 14).

However, the contract they voluntary entered initiated and licensed power relations that had much in common with those between slaveholder and slave, and that were in fact virtually identical to those between masters and convicts forcibly transported into servitude:

> While under contract in America indentured and convict servants were largely indistinguishable with regard to fulfilment of their contracts, the legal and customary rights and restrictions placed on their and their masters' behavior, the range of work performed, and the restoration of freedom upon contract completion.
>
> (Grubb, 2000: 95)

For the term of the contract, 'free' indentured servants could not quit and their independent mobility was criminalized. And in fact, Benjamin Franklin had good cause to know that non-slave workers could not always simply up and leave their Master. Franklin himself started out as an apprentice to a printer in Boston – his own brother, James Franklin – to whom he was legally bound by a contract of indenture until the age of 21. 'Tho' a Brother, he considered himself as my Master, & me as his Apprentice; and accordingly expected the same Services from me as he would from Another', Franklin reminisced (cited in Waldstreicher, 2004: 4). James' treatment of his younger brother was 'harsh and tyrannical', including corporal punishment, and Benjamin Franklin 'did what unfree people did as last resort... He ran away' (Waldstreicher, 2004: 4).

Employment relations in the North American colonies of the eighteenth century still included both slavery and servitude, then, and during the early part of the century 'both slave and servant imports increased rapidly... in response to a very real and widely perceived labor shortage' (Waldstreicher, 2004: 19). The trade in supplying servants (whether indentured or convict) was, like the transatlantic slave trade, a profitable business. Private shipping firms arranged the movement of indentured servants and convicts, often on the same voyage. The servants were then sold to the highest bidder in America, 'with the monies received going to defray the shippers' transportation expenses' (Grubb, 2000: 195). In addition to this, 'a remarkably fluid internal market for bound workers' developed in America (Waldstreicher, 2004: 19–21). Servants, as well as slaves, were rented out and sold on to new masters and mistresses. When the runaway Benjamin Franklin later did manage to establish his own printing shop, he ran advertisements offering 'soap, goose feathers, sugar, coffee, servants, and slaves, sometimes in the same ad':

> 'TO BE SOLD, A Dutch Servant Man and his Wife, for Two Years and Eight Months, a genteel riding Chair, almost new, a Ten Cord Flat with new Sails and Rigging, a Fishing Boat, and sundry sorts of Household Goods'.
>
> (Waldstreicher, 2004: 24)

'No labourer escaped dependency during the colonial period', Laura Edwards (1998: 320) remarks. For the duration of the contract, all hired workers legally surrendered not just claims over their labour-power, but also control over other aspects of their lives. The master's authority extended to 'what they wore, what they ate, where they lived, what they did in their leisure time, and with whom they associated' (Edwards, 1998: 320). In America, it was not until the nineteenth century that indentured servitude came to be viewed as an illegitimate restriction on individual freedom, and only after the 1830s that penal sanctions ceased to play a 'role in the lives of adult white wage or contract workers in the United States' (Steinfeld, 2001: 254). Adult black wage workers in Southern states were often legally forced into relations of dependency for more than another century (Davis, A. 2003), and employers across the United States (and in Canada) also began to make use of migrant labour involving employment relations that 'comprised a spectrum of consensual and coercive elements' (Peck, 2000: 8; Steinfeld, 2001). As will be seen in Chapter 6, some groups of migrant workers continue to be locked into relations of dependency upon their employers by immigration law.

In the standard liberal tale of the rise of free market capitalist society (and even in some Marxist accounts), it is assumed that in England, *laissez-faire* thinking led to the incremental repeal of the provisions of the sixteenth-century Tudor legislation that embedded labour relations in the old social order, such that by the nineteenth century, state regulation of the labour market had been largely eliminated. But as Robert Steinfeld (2001: 41) shows, in reality, some of the provisions of the Tudor legislation, in particular those providing criminal sanctions for contract breaches, were actually *revitalized* in the eighteenth and nineteenth centuries. Indeed, it was precisely as the old order that tied wives, children, apprentices, servants and labourers together as the dependents of a head of household began to loosen in the eighteenth century (causing propertied white men to bemoan the insolence and insubordination of the plebians), that William Blackstone in his 1765–69 '*Commentaries on the Laws of England* established "master and servant" as the legal categorization of all employment relations' (Hairong, 2008: 16).

In England, Masters and Servants' legislation – which was not repealed until 1875 – came to cover factory workers as well as agricultural and domestic workers, and made worker absence and desertion, as well as insubordination, unsatisfactory work and damaging property punishable by imprisonment 'usually for three months, with perpetual re-imprisonment possible if the servant refused to go back to work' (Craven and Hay, 1994: 88). The meaning of *modern* employment relations in England was thus centrally defined by a very *traditional* understanding of the master and servant relationship. The 'coding of employment relations as master and servant stressed that the employer-master has legally sanctioned property in the service of the servant-employee...the contract has built-in legal relations of subjection', notes Yan Hairong (2008: 16). This model also shaped the development of modern employment relations in the American North as well as the South. In the early nineteenth century, courts in Northern states 'affirmed the centrality of dependency in the labor relationship. Legally, the workplace became the capitalist's private domain, beyond the reach of public debate and exempt from community standards' (Edwards, 1998: 321). The master–servant relation thus lay at the heart of the forms of contract labour that were represented in nineteenth-century 'free labour ideology' as the opposite of slavery.

The new abolitionists hold that where workers are unable to 'walk away' from an employment relation characterized by severe exploitation and violence or its threat, they are *de facto* slaves. But English and American labourers of the seventeenth through to the latter half of the nineteenth century could also be subject to violence or its threat as a means of labour discipline, their wages frequently covered only subsistence, or were clawed back by mechanisms such as the Truck System and the Tommy Shop (Hilton, 1960), and most lived under threat of imprisonment and/or elongated bondage should they attempt to escape their master. Applied retrospectively, the new abolitionist definition of slavery makes these workers 'slaves', a point that, if conceded, would lead to the sociologically surprising conclusion that the development of capitalism ushered in not free wage labour, but 'modern slavery' on a momentous scale.

Some contemporary anti-slavery activists (not necessarily those driving the new abolitionism) might say that the servants and labourers described above *should* be recognized as victims of a form of slavery, albeit not one identical to chattel slavery. But against this, I would argue that the historical evidence outlined above underlines the dangers of de-contextualizing elements of human experience or relationships from entire bundles of rights, obligations, immunities and privileges that go with particular social statuses at particular moments in time and treating them as definitive of 'slavery'. One of the dangers is that it deflects attention from the means by which (some) workers managed to change the nature and degree of restraints on their freedom. This allows us to forget that, in Ben Rogaly's (2008: 1444) words, 'The state at different levels – local, national and international – is a potential enabler and, at the same time, discipliner of capital', and which of these roles it most enthusiastically fulfils at any given moment is an outcome of political struggle (see also Lebowitz, 2003).

## Freedom in the balance

The heavy restraints on the freedoms of free white adult male citizen workers that were tolerated in mid-nineteenth century North America and Europe were gradually lifted. Though change was uneven, by the post-World War Two years, the experience of this group was, in the main, radically different from that of their nineteenth-century forebears, as well as from the experience of chattel slaves. But change was not secured through campaigns against slavery, nor was it willingly granted by enlightened capitalists on the basis that freer workers would make more productive workers. One of Marx's fundamental insights was that the process of creating labour markets is simultaneously a process of class formation (Brass, 2010), and 'the degree of organization and fighting strength of the working class enters in to affect the degree to which free wage-labour can be said to be "free"' (Nichols, 1980: 76). If we ask why free white adult male citizen workers looked so much more free in, say, the 1960s than they did in the 1860s in North America and Europe, the answer, in broad brush strokes, has to do with workers' political struggles and the manner in which their demands were accommodated (Papadopoulos, 2012).

As Steinfeld (2001: 234) argues, 'the regime of contract rules we refer to as modern free labor ... must be seen as a product of labor's struggle to improve its position in a market society'. And struggles over the kind of power relations that contracts can legitimately initiate were connected to wider political struggles over the background structures of the social order that lead people to enter into labour contracts in the first place. Class struggle was not merely an effort to ensure that workers got paid for their backbreaking work, were protected from employer violence and enjoyed the formal right to freely retract from labour contracts. It was also a struggle for social and economic rights, for freedom from dependency on the market as well as from dependence on individual employers.

Indeed, the very idea of a market in labour, and the fiction of the human capacity to labour as a fully alienable commodity, such that an employer could have property rights in a worker's labour-power without any obligations towards the worker beyond paying an agreed wage, had been resisted from the very start. In England, the old, customary relations of dependency were not quickly or entirely replaced by those based on a view of labour as a commodity that could be subject to narrowly defined, explicitly contractual, market relations. Instead, the emerging market in labour co-existed with reciprocities, obligations and

a complex web of long established, traditional cultural and social relationships (Price, 1986: 21). Indeed, class struggles in early industrial
England centred precisely on struggles to defend such customary bundles of reciprocities (Thompson, 1963). In America too, labour reformers
and workers insisted on the immorality of a market in which employers
could treat workers in the same way they might treat any other piece of
merchandise. They fiercely protested the construction of employment
as the purely market relation exemplified in the US lawyer H. G. Wood's
1877 formulation of the 'employment at will' rule, whereby 'employment of an indefinite duration can be terminated at any time, for any
reason, with or without cause' (Hairong, 2008: 16). Such arguments
formed part of a debate on 'the labour question' that ultimately 'gave
rise to legislation on issues ranging from tenement sweatshops to the
right to join unions and the hours of work', and 'contributed directly to
the reshaping of liberalism' (Stanley, 1998: 97).

This reshaping of liberalism represented an accommodation of worker
resistance, though not the victory of labour over capital. In fact, it simultaneously tempered and enforced the double 'freedom' of free wage
labourers, for it entailed state interventions that, on the one hand,
placed certain restrictions on employers' freedom to fully commercialize
their relations with workers, but on the other, disciplined and punished
those who refused to accept dependency on wage labour (e.g., beggars
and vagrants) (Stanley, 1998). A model of 'worker citizenship', by which
certain social rights and protections would accrue to citizens who performed wage labour was internationalized by the International Labour
Organization in the twentieth century (Standing, 2008: 356), and lay at
the heart of the political accommodation between capital and labour in
post-war welfare capitalist states. Such states intervened in the market
exchange processes of a capitalist economy by providing social security payments and public services that, to a greater or lesser degree,
provided individuals and families with 'a level of insulation from total
dependence on the labour market for survival' (O'Connor, 1998: 188).
They in effect 'decommodified' certain aspects of social reproduction
(Esping-Andersen, 1990; Offe, 1984).

Post-war welfare regimes and Keynesian economics reflected a commitment to guarantee propertyless proletarians not merely economic
security but also the right to 'a share in the full social heritage and
to live the life of a civilized being according to the standards prevail-
ing in the society' through their 'social citizenship' (Marshall, 1964:
78). But more than this, states penetrated the 'hidden abode' of production, intervening to moderate and monitor workplace relations and

practices, adopting policies that afforded (some) workers certain forms of protection *in* employment as well as *from* the market and that eroded the employment-at-will rule (Hairong, 2007: 17; Papadopoulos, 2005). The aim was to ensure the capitalist no longer enjoyed the liberty to formulate his autocratic power over his workers purely as an emanation of his own will, but was constrained by legislation that afforded workers minimum labour rights and standards.

Worker citizenship was not only a paradoxical political accommodation from a class perspective, but also, since it foundered on and reproduced divisions and inequalities in terms of gender, age, race and nationality, a profoundly problematic one in other respects (Sharma, 2006). But it nonetheless implied significant political and material gains for many working class people. Unlike their nineteenth-century counterparts, (most) adult male worker citizens of capitalist welfare states in the 1960s could depend on the state to ensure they and their families were nurtured in infancy and provided for in old age, and that they did not face a choice between either remaining with a violent, abusive, or otherwise unsatisfactory employer – or destitution. Yet their dependency did not erase their political subjectivity: worker citizens were formally constructed as equals. Thus, in the heyday of welfare capitalism, (some) markets in human labour-power were embedded in a system of rights such that they bore very little likeness to chattel slavery or even to servitude (Harvey, 2007). This was a model that sought to balance liberty and equality.

Those gains were not won once and for all, however. Since the 1970s, what Marxists term 'the balance of class forces' has changed, as has the geography of production. Those pressing to extend market forces, both globally and within nations, have reclaimed political ground, a trend that was both allowed by, and has allowed for, processes of deindustrialization in the global North and the expansion of manufacturing sectors in the global South. In the neoliberal economic restructuring that has gathered pace globally since the 1990s (and that has been reinforced by the 2008 global economic crisis), the social protections and labour rights of worker citizens in affluent, economically developed nations have been eroded (see, for example, TUC, 2008). The consequences for the mass of the people in less economically developed countries, where the model of industrial citizenship was already more weakly established and social rights necessarily more limited, have been even more brutal. Where 'the Keynesian period brought with it an active expansion of the population systematically valued as workers and consumers', the global expansion and 'deepening of capitalist relations of production over the past 20 years' has led to 'a sharp growth in the numbers of people that have been "expulsed"', as Saskia Sassen (2010: 24) puts it. This returns us to the subjects of Lisa Kristine's photographs.

## Tradition or neoliberal capitalism?

Lisa Kristine's photographs are a close fit with a trope widely employed in new abolitionist representations of 'slavery' in the global South, and one that has been very effectively critiqued by Kamala Kempadoo (2015), namely that of colonized peoples as helplessly trapped by their 'traditional' cultures, hopeless drudges endlessly repeating Sisyphean tasks, objects not subjects, eternal victims who can only be liberated by a White Saviour. Yet most serious analysis of the settings in which workers dubbed 'modern slaves' are found suggests that their condition is very much a product of the contemporary moment. In particular, it is an outcome of the twinning of neoliberal structural adjustment policies with export-oriented industrialization strategies in developing countries, a policy 'combo' which, Alessandra Mezzadri (2015) notes, has 'ensured the availability of a cheap labour force that, even when not fully divorced from the land, became a reserve army of labour' for export-led industries such as garments, mining, sugar and many more. Indeed, it is this combination that has made it so profitable to shift production from the global North to the South over the past 30 or 40 years.

In India, for instance, the business and political elite has, since 1975, pursued economic development and growth through what is known as the 'low route', and this has entailed concerted efforts:

> to discipline the labourers and restructure production to achieve the maximum of flexibility and a docile and cheap workforce. Government support for the private sector, anti-union policies and activities by companies weakened organized labour, and the more overt liberalization government policies from the early 1990s onwards have strengthened the anti-labour hand further.
>
> (Lerche, 2007: 443)

One effect of this has been to encourage the expansion of the informal sector (Breman, 2013). Jan Breman (2009: 35) notes that over the last 20 years, this has meant, amongst other things, the end of the large-scale textile industry in South Asia:

> In Ahmedabad... more than 150,000 mill workers were laid off at a stroke. This did not mean the end of textile production in the city.

Cloth is now produced in power-loom workshops by operators who work twelve-hour days, instead of eight, and at less than half the wages they received in the mill; garment manufacture has become home-based work, in which the whole family is engaged day and night. The textile workers' union has all but disappeared. Sliding down the labour hierarchy has plunged these households into a permanent social and economic crisis.

Liberalization has also been associated with increased internal, often seasonal, migration, for as Svati Shah observes:

neoliberal economic reforms have reduced or eliminated agricultural subsidies and forced farmers to compete in global markets amid unstable prices for commodities like cotton and sugar. Deepening poverty in rural areas has meant that survival for landless workers there is decreasingly viable, prompting greater numbers of people to migrate for work and contributing to an expanding pool of labor in urban informal economies.

(2014: 9)

For marginalized Adivasi communities, it is structural adjustment's links to continuing processes of dispossession that deprive them 'of access to the land and forests that have traditionally undergirded their subsistence-oriented agrarian livelihoods' which lies behind rural–urban migration (Nilsen, 2012: 2).

Though traditional aspects of the social fabric in the form of caste, gender and age hierarchies shape the experience of such workers in informal economies (just as traditional hierarchies of race, ethnicity, gender and age shape the experience of workers in Europe, North America and Australia), 'tradition' does not explain why they have moved to work, why they are undertaking the work they are under-taking or the conditions under which they labour. The ASM workers photographed by Lisa Kristine in the Himalayas, for example, are not quarrying stone to build their own 'traditional' dwellings or places of worship – they are producing for a modern, capitalist market, under con-ditions that are very much a creation of the informalization process in India set in motion by 'the new international labour-unfriendly regime, or neo-liberal globalization' (Lerche, 2007: 446). The same goes for tex-tiles workers in South Asia (Mezzandri, 2015), and for brick kiln workers, and for sugar workers in Tamil Nadu. The latter are also often recruited by intermediary labour contractors who offer advance, lump-sum loans:

that can be used to cover immediate expenditures – say a marriage ceremony or medical fees – and offer a modicum of job security. However, the pittance wages leave the workers with very little at the end of the season, making it difficult to pay off their debt. Many are thus trapped into returning to the highly crowded and unhygienic makeshift camps of cane cutters year after year.

(Richardson, 2015)

Likewise, the miners Kristine photographed in Ghana are not continuing a centuries-old tradition. Here, as in a number of other African countries, informal economic activity and seasonal migration is very much a legacy of the IMF/World Bank sourced structural adjustment programmes implemented in the 1980s, when 'Stringent fiscal reform measures saw a virtual collapse of already very poor delivery of public sector services to the rural population', and the focus on recovering export earnings from cocoa encouraged highly uneven forms of economic development (Medhekar-Smith, 2003: 153). Involvement in artisanal gold mining also links to contemporary processes of dispossession. The Ghanaian site studied by Okyere (2013: 82), for example, came into existence only after farmers and other locals lost their subsistence land to a subsidiary of Newmont Mining Corporation that wished to set up an industrial mine – 'In the resulting destitution and hardships suffered by residents of the area who had mostly lived off their land...some, joined by others from across the country, began small-scale mining activities at the location'.

Rather than shining a light on 'modern slavery', then, it could be argued that Kristine's photos of workers in ASM and other informal sector work in India and Ghana reveal one of contemporary capitalism's many faces. This, I want to conclude by arguing, highlights not only problems with the new abolitionist vision of contract as the harbinger of both liberty and equality, but also difficulties faced by those seeking to reframe the experience of such workers within critiques of contemporary capitalism.

## Double troubles: agency and force

In one sense, new abolitionist discourse emphasizes the power of social structures. 'Slaves' as well as 'slavers' appear to be people blindly driven by cultural forces they can neither see nor name (the 'slaves' in Lisa Kristine's TEDx talk 'did not even know they were slaves', for example). But at the same time, the new abolitionists are centrally concerned with agency, for it is through reference to the voluntariness of contract and the ability freely to walk away that they mark the boundaries of 'modern slavery'. Two individuals working and living alongside each other in the same appalling conditions in ASM, for example, can be distinguished according to whether or not they consented to take on the work, and whether or not they are directly prevented from 'walking away' by another individual. Bonded brick kiln workers can be sorted into two groups according to whether the creditor-employer is dishonest and/or violent (in which case, they are 'slaves'), or sticks to the terms of the contract and refrains from using physical force (in which case they are 'free') (Bales, 1999: 167–8). And so on. Such distinctions reflect a preoccupation with the form of compulsion produced by the exercise of direct, personalistic power, and so a very narrow and distinct understanding of 'force'. Certainly, it is an understanding of 'force' that misses:

the way in which social structures force fates on people while appearing to leave their fates up to them. When Marx wrote that the wage-worker 'is compelled to sell himself of his own free will' (C, I, p. 766), he was not being arch or paradoxical. He was telling us both how force works in capitalism and why it is unseen.

(Reiman, 1987: 23)

To draw a line between bonded and non-bonded labourers in ASM in India, or to subdivide bonded brick kiln workers in Pakistan, is to discount the fact that precisely the same unseen forces can be at work on both sides of this line, and so to privilege a very particular kind of 'freedom' – namely, 'the bare bourgeois freedom which distinguishes the most abject proletarian from the slave' (Cohen, 1995: 101).

Take Lisa Kristine's description of the stone quarry workers she photographed as now working 'in freedom'. I think it safe to assume that Kristine would not consider herself liberated if she woke to discover the only way in which she could now secure even basic subsistence was by carrying huge slabs of stone down mountainous paths. When she describes the workers as 'free', she means that in the absence of an individual 'slaver' exercising powers of ownership over them, they are at liberty to access the market directly, and to secure recompense – however paltry – for their backbreaking labour. More fundamental questions about why undertaking quarry work to produce stone for sale across a market (whether sold by a third party or by themselves) is the only way in which they can subsist, about the global and national economic and political order in which their work is set, and the legal and social exclusions that produce them as the kind of persons who must perform such labour, are all bracketed off. Once these questions are sidelined, contract can perform its equalizing magic. Lisa and the villagers now appear to enjoy a common freedom. She and they alike enjoy self-sovereignty. She and they are equally at liberty to make voluntarily contracts to sell their labour-power and skills, or its products, whether in the form of stone slabs, or photographs of people carrying stone slabs. Contract renders the villagers' experience equivalent to Lisa Kristine's.

In this respect, her TEDx talk, like new abolitionist campaign literature more generally, implicitly connects us back to a tradition of liberal thought in which contract is the solution to the problem of both tyranny and slavery. The histories briefly highlighted in this chapter tell a different story. They not only show that contract can uphold systems of domination, but further reveal that the line between what is understood as 'freedom' and what is taken as its opposite is, itself, a site of political struggle. That boundary does not stand still but shifts over time and according to the balance of forces pressing for different models of 'freedom'. Her talk, and the new abolitionism more generally, also reflects and revitalizes a liberal vision of a world in which people are *either* abject, passive objects and slaves *or* freely contracting subjects. It thus functions to conceal the social structures that force fates on people while appearing to leave their fates up to them, and here, Marxist inspired critiques of neoliberal capitalism are enormously helpful as tools with which to dismantle the blinds and uncover how force works. Once this is visible, the idea that it is possible to draw a sharp line between 'slaves' and 'non-slaves' in the kind of informal sector work discussed above through reference to whether or not they can choose to 'walk away' is revealed as a nonsense.

However, the new abolitionists' portrait of people as *either* objects *or* subjects also operates to obscure the agency that people (children as well as adults) exercise in choosing between the narrow range of fates available and working them as best they can to meet their own interests and goals. In this regard, Marxist critiques do not always provide a clear counterpoint. In fact, there is sometimes an alarming congruity between the representations of 'modern slaves' produced by new abolitionists and depictions of exploited workers of the Global South found in some Marxist writings on informalization, labour migration and oppression under neoliberal capitalism. Alpa Shah (2006) has remarked on this tendency in relation to representations of seasonal casual labour migrants in India, which often place such heavy analytic emphasis on economic structures as to make the migrants concerned appear as non-agential objects, swept along like flotsam and jetsam by structural forces. The same tendency is particularly apparent in some research and activism on child labour, and even more so on women and girl's involvement in prostitution (of which more will be said in Chapter 8), where some strands of feminist thought, as well as some Marxian inspired analyses, lead to representations of those who sell sex as abject victims of structural compulsion (e.g., Barry, 1995; Jeffreys, 1997). In reaction against this, other commentators strongly emphasize the agency of such workers and/or construct their action as a form of resistance against patriarchal norms or the exclusionary forces of neoliberal capitalism (e.g., Agustin, 2007; Jeffrey and MacDonald, 2006).

Vincent Brown's (2009: 1235) comments on how studies of transatlantic slavery 'often divide between works that emphasize the overwhelming power of the institution and scholarship that focuses on the resistant efforts of the enslaved' also speak to a dilemma faced by scholars and activists in relation to contemporary groups of workers like those photographed by Kristine. When writing against contemporary processes of neoliberal economic reform, those at the sharp end of these processes can easily (if unwittingly) be worked as figures that stand in for capitalism's ideally subjugated, precarious workers. Their story is told in such a way as to reveal the workings of force under capitalism, and so to emphasize the overwhelming power of the structures that oppress them. A very obvious, and very serious, problem that arises from their reduction to mere personifications of economic categories, as much as from their depiction as 'modern slaves', is that it encourages policies designed to prevent internal migration, eliminate child labour, suppress prostitution and so on, thereby further limiting the possible livelihood strategies open to those whose choices are already heavily restricted (Okyere, 2012; Rogaly, 2008; Shah, 2014). However, simply to invert the discourse and celebrate the self-activity of such workers as either a form of resistance or an expression of their resilience and creativity, runs the danger of reinscribing the liberal association between consent and freedom.

It is, however, possible to tread a course between these opposing narratives, and there are a number of examples of ethnographies that do just this. Svati Shah's (2014) ethnography of migrant women in Mumbai whose livelihood strategies included both sex work and other forms of paid labour makes visible the workings of agency as well as of force. Alpa Shah's study of migrant brick kiln workers in Tapu village in Bero Block of Ranchi District is another case in point. Though brick kiln labour is harsh and can be associated with violently coercive employment relations (as illustrated by a recently reported case in which bonded labourers who ran away from a brick kiln were horribly mutilated in punishment, Hawksley, 2014), Shah shows that it can also provide a space for individuals actively to pursue ends they would not otherwise be able to attain. These ends are not always primarily economic. She found that those who migrate into such work from Jharkhand neither saw:

> brick kiln migration just in terms of money; nor as the irredeemable torture and drudgery that much of the literature portrays. Rather, they view their migration as a temporary escape from a problem at home and an opportunity to explore a new country, gain independence from parents, and live out prohibited amorous relationships... For many migrants, life at the kilns is seen as 'free'.
>
> (2006: 93)

Shah does not argue that brick kiln labour gives freedom to Tapu migrants, but rather that it is significant that Tapu migrants themselves 'often describe the kilns as a place where they can live "freely"' (2006: 93).

Okyere's research also allows us to see the agency of those described as 'slaves' or as 'the expulsed', at the same time as revealing all too clearly the structurally generated limits on the choices open to them. The people who were displaced from their subsistence land in Kenyasi by the Newmont Mining Corporation strongly resisted their exclusion from employment and other earning opportunities associated with mining development, and fought for the right to mine independently. As importantly, his research challenges dominant discourse on 'child slavery' in ASM in Ghana. In this discourse, any person below the age of 18 is a 'child', and as such, incapable of entering into valid contracts. In addition, ASM is a 'worst form of child labour'. All children working in ASM are therefore 'modern slaves' (FTS, 2013a). But Okyere's ethnography reveals that teenagers can be found working in artisanal gold mining in Ghana not because they have been driven and forced into it by wicked individual 'slavers', but because, in the absence of a well-funded and effective system of welfare upon which to depend, such work represents the only or best means through which to secure their needs and pursue their life-goals, often including education.

Moreover, where abolitionist commentary, including Lisa Kristine's TEDx talk, leaves us with the impression that artisanal gold mines in Ghana are lawless 'infernos' where the strong prey viciously upon the weak, Okyere's (2012, 2013) ethnography shows that, in Kenyasi at least, those engaged in mining have organized themselves into a community run along democratic lines, that protects younger workers (under 16) from the most hazardous forms of mine labour (underground work, working with mercury). This does not mean that working and living conditions for either children or adults are safe or desirable. But many of the risks and dangers children face – such as from snake bites and poor sanitation – are identical to those they face when performing what are described as tolerable forms of 'child work' by new abolitionist and other commentators, that is to say, unpaid labour performed for their own families in rural settings (see also Hashim and Thorsen, 2011; Howard and Morganti, 2015). These are all studies that neither reduce their research subjects to abject victims and suffering bodies, nor romanticize them as 'heroic subalterns' (Brown, 2009: 1235), but instead work with a model of agency, or will, as inalienable; a model of 'agency as the capacity to act – differential, context specific, and always, in some fashion extant', as Svati Shah (2014: 199) puts it. It is only by using this model that we can escape the pull of the transition narrative which represents the modern individual as free, and contract as an alternative to domination.

As will be seen in future chapters, the tensions between force and agency discussed here are of equal relevance for debates on 'trafficking' and 'forced labour' involving international migrants. Before considering these debates, however, it is necessary to think about another system of domination – its links to transatlantic slavery, its post-emancipation career, its contemporary expressions and its place in new abolitionist discourse – namely race, to which the following chapter now turns.

# 4
# Mastery, Race and Nation: Prisons and Borders, Afterlives and Legacies of Transatlantic Slavery

In speaking of transatlantic slavery, contemporary anti-slavery activists are always at pains to avow and condemn the role of race and racism. But race vanishes from their analysis of 'modern slavery'. Indeed, they tend to open any discussion of 'modern slavery' by simultaneously dissociating it from transatlantic slavery (the focus of the original anti-slavery movement's successful campaign for the legal abolition of chattel slavery), and attempting to decouple it from race. Offering a definition of modern slavery on its website, Anti-Slavery International (2015) tells the reader that 'Contemporary slavery takes various forms and affects people of all ages, gender and races', while Kevin Bales (1999) insists that one of the key differences between 'new' and 'old' slavery is that where race was significant to the latter, ethnic and racial difference are unimportant in contemporary slavery. 'Modern slavers are color-blind', he tells us, and the common denominator in vulnerability to slavery today 'is poverty, not color' (Bales, 2004: 11–12).

It is true that the phenomena described by the new abolitionists as 'modern slavery' could be said to involve exploitation and violence that, in racialized terms, is sometimes white-on-white, as well as brown-on-brown, black-on-black or any combination thereof. But one very obvious objection to talk of 'colour-blind slavery' is that according to the global slavery 'indexes' produced by new abolitionists, including Bales himself, the overwhelming majority of those dubbed slaves are found in the places once colonized by Europe and America (Woods, 2013). To suggest that their poverty has nothing to do with 'colour' is to forget both that they are predominantly drawn from populations historically subject to the exclusion clause of the racial contract (Mills, 1998), and the centrality of that exclusion clause to patterns of economic development and underdevelopment in the contemporary world (Rodney,

1989; Williams, 1964). The language of 'colour-blindness' also seems disingenuous in view of the fact that, with the exception of materials referring to what is termed 'sex trafficking', the visual representations of 'modern slaves' in new abolitionist campaigning materials are overwhelmingly images of children, women and men who are not racialized as 'white'.

Where the previous chapter was very much concerned with overlaps between the historical experience of chattel slaves and that of servants and labourers in the modern world, this chapter is concerned with what was distinctive about transatlantic slavery, namely, its association with the idea of race as constitutive of borders between flesh and blood human beings in terms of their capacities, moral worth and rights. It examines how the freedom/slavery binary of liberal thought came to map onto an imagined racial binary between white and black (and non-white more generally), such that citizenship, which implied enjoyment of the 'rights of man' including mastery over self and others, was coded as white, and therefore impossible for those racialized as black, whether or not they were enslaved.

Neither the freedom/slavery nor the white/black binary arise from nature; both are ideational, political constructs. Keeping them fastened together was no simple task, indeed, their contiguity was constantly under threat (the enslaved resisted the freedom/slavery binary by running away, while slaveholders and others racialized as white undermined the white/black binary by raping or forming sexual alliances with the enslaved, for example). Constant attention to the legal, social and physical boundaries by which freedom was reserved for those racialized as white was required to maintain this status quo even while chattel slavery existed as a legal institution. In the American South, Stephanie Camp (2004: 12) observes, slavery 'entailed the strictest control of the physical and social mobility of enslaved people, as some of the institution's most resonant accouterments – shackles, chains, passes, slave patrols, and hounds – suggest'. Its abolition potentially threatened to undo what she describes as the 'geographies of containment' that produced race (and so white privilege), as well as slavery.

'One of the values invented by the bourgeoisie in former times and launched throughout the world was that of *man*', remarked Aimé Césaire (1972: 57); the other 'was the nation'. Both were understood to be white when invented, and for those who believed in the fiction of race and white superiority (which included many white abolitionists), the legal abolition of slavery therefore represented a political dilemma. If those racialized as black were unfit to bear 'the rights of man' and to 'belong' to these invented nations, what was to be done with them? Without slavery, what would contain the millions of black former slaves whose minds were, in William Wilberforce's words, so 'uninformed' and 'debased' as to be 'almost incapacitated for the reception of civil rights' (Festa, 2010: 14)? The second half of the chapter is concerned with responses to this quandary. It considers first the 'prison industrial complex' (PIC) in the United States, locating it in what Saidiya Hartman (2007: 6) terms 'the afterlife of slavery', and then explores the history of immigration controls as a living legacy of transatlantic slavery. Though the afterlife of slavery in the form of the devaluation and imperilment of black lives 'by a racial calculus and a political arithmetic that were entrenched centuries ago' (Hartman, 2007: 6; Black Lives Matter, 2015), and the legacy of transatlantic slavery in the form of borders are not identical, and should not be conflated, the PIC and immigration controls are both closely connected to dilemmas about how to fix racial boundaries in the absence of chattel slavery. Both also today imply extensive, harsh restrictions on human freedom. And yet the new abolitionists do not campaign against either of them. Why not?

## Liberty, equality and dependency

Classical liberal theorists' vision of the 'man' who enjoyed political freedom and held rights was deeply embedded in religiously inspired ideas about improvement: of the earth, of society and of the individual (Brace, 2004). The natural liberty given to man by God had to be 'perfected' to meet God's designs for mankind, something achieved when man learned to use 'his moral judgement to restrain his exercise of personal freedom' (in other words, when his reason led him to the social contract) (Marden, 2009: 93). As not every human being had learned this, some lacked the moral worthiness that was a necessary qualification for rights-holding. Such exclusions may sound illiberal, though they are not actually out of line with Kant's formulation of the meaning of Enlightenment. 'Immaturity', Kant (2009: 2) said, 'is the inability to use one's own understanding without direction from another'. Enlightenment only promised release from *self-incurred* immaturity, which is to say, it promised release only to those who did possess the capacity to use their understanding (those who were rational) but who had hitherto lacked the will and fortitude to use it independently. Those who were seen to be *actually* immature were unqualified for the exercise of freedom, and so needed to be protected both from others and themselves.

This case was most explicitly elaborated by classical liberal theorists in relation to children, who were excluded from the terms of the social contract on grounds that, since they had not developed the capacity for reason, they were not qualified for the exercise of freedom and needed to be protected from their own irrational actions, as well as from others (Archard, 1993; O'Connell Davidson, 2005). However, the same basic model was also transposed onto colonized peoples through a narrative of social development through time that mirrored individual human development from birth, and through this to African slaves and their descendants (Hall, 2002; Nyquist, 2013; Parekh, 1995). Women's nature, meanwhile, left them perpetual minors, 'lacking the capacities for public participation', and so forever fixed in the private, domestic realm under the governance of men (Pateman, 1998: 245).

The human beings who were excluded from the rights and freedoms that self-evidently belonged to 'all men' had in common that they were constructed as dependants. Dependency, as Roland Marden (2009: 94) points out in a discussion of 'rights talk' in late-eighteenth century North America, disqualified individuals for full civil status because it was taken to signify the absence of 'free will' or 'moral mastery' that was required to play a part in political society. To be dependent was to be subject to the will of another person, a condition that was seen to enfeeble, degrade, infantalize and 'unman'. Thomas Paine held that freedom 'is destroyed by dependence', while his associate Candidus described freedom and dependency as 'opposite and irreconcilable terms' (Marden, 2009: 95). Thus, Marden (2009: 95–6) continues:

The new state constitutions that proudly proclaimed their commit-ment to equal rights explicitly denied the right to vote to a range of categories of persons considered de facto dependent on the will of others: wives dependent upon their husbands, minors and sons still living at home upon their fathers, servants and slaves upon their masters, tenants and renters upon their landlords, aliens upon their native countries, Catholics upon their church, debtors upon their creditors, and the poor and insane upon their community. For those that lay outside of these categories, a further indication of independence was required in the form of property ownership.

The opposition between freedom and dependency made it possible to reconcile the apparent contradiction between a belief in the liberty and equality of *all* men, and the persistent exercise of hierarchical, tradition-based forms of authority over *some* men, as well as over women and children. Indeed, liberalism licensed highly illiberal relations within the private, domestic realm. As master of all those included in his private household as dependants, the free, modern, liberal subject who emerged from the seventeenth century had a right to control, direct and discipline his wife, children, servants, apprentices and slaves, should he hold them.

The source and nature of the authority masters exercised is well illustrated by the division in English law first drawn in 1352 between murder, and petty or petit treason (Dolan, 1992). If a man killed his wife or servant, he would be charged with murder, but where a subordinate (a wife, child, servant or apprentice) killed 'the person who had legitimate authority over him or her (husband, father, or master) [it] was considered treasonous within the household, a crime analogous to treason against the state' (Paton, 2001: 931). Until 1790 in England:

> punishments for petty treason were different than those for murder and drew attention to the crime as a particularly egregious assault on social and political order... Women convicted of petty treason ... were sentenced to the same punishment as those convicted of high treason: they were burned at the stake.
>
> (Dolan, 1992: 318)

When introduced, this legal category of petty treason reflected the commonplace early modern 'analogy between the household and the commonwealth, and the fluid boundaries between domestic and political life' (Dolan, 1992: 317), and it is revealing that it was not repealed in England until 1858.

Historically, then, the liberal state subcontracted certain of its powers over various categories of person to the white, adult, propertied male citizens whose amalgamated will constituted its own legitimate authority (and the 'masterless' poor who did not 'belong' to any citizen were frequently reclaimed and directly controlled by the state in prisons or workhouses, or transported into servitude in the colonies). Relations between masters and their dependants were legally 'private', and this legal and social privacy was increasingly given physical expression in the walls and fences used to enclose land. Camp (2004: 5) comments on the Fence Law of South Carolina, amended in 1827 in such a way as to erode 'common access to land, waterways and roads', and guarantee 'property holders "exclusive use" of their land. Inside fenced boundaries, property rights were sacrosanct', including those exercised over household dependants.

As Laura Edwards (1999: 758) notes, this 'kind of privacy did not mean that domestic relations were wholly free from legal oversight'. Husbands were authorized to discipline but not kill their wives. Likewise, in seventeenth-century England, the master's right to physically chastize his servants did not extend to a right to mutilate or murder them at whim (although it is worth noting that in Adam Smith's view, should a servant 'die under his correction it is not murther, unless it was done with an offensive weapon or with forethought and without provocation', 1982: 456, cited in Losurdo, 2011: 68). Nor were slaveholders always and everywhere given legal sanction to dispose of their slaves by killing them. In 1839, Thomas Ruffin, Chief Justice of the North Carolina Supreme Court, stated that though 'the law generally left the degree of punishment to the master's "judgment and humanity"... "the master's authority is not altogether unlimited. He must not kill"' (Tushnet, 1981: 103).

Nonetheless, the white male head of household was licensed to exercise powers over his subordinates that amounted to what are generally taken to be powers of possession, and dependants were explicitly denied rights to resist violent control, whether by fleeing the households in which they were held, or by physical retaliation. Ruling on the legal limits of self-defence in the case of slaves in 1847, for example, Chief Justice Ruffin argued that just as a child who killed a parent during punishment 'was guilty of murder because the act could be seen only as "a malignant and diabolical spirit of vengeance"' so only a slave 'with "a bad heart"... "intent upon the assertion of an equality, social and personal, with the white, and bent on mortal mischief in support of the assertion"' would kill a white man who battered him or her (Edwards, 1999: 765–6).

Did the fact that slaves, servants, wives, and children (among others) were judged incompetent to exercise liberty mean that they all stood in the same relation to their masters and the state? This is where race takes on particular significance.

## Transatlantic slavery and the invention of race

The idea that certain 'kinds' of human being were natural slaves, or could rightfully be enslaved, has a very long lineage, bridging ancient and modern worlds (Finley, 1964; Haskell, 1998; Nyquist, 2013). Likewise, the idea of certain 'kinds' of human being as Other, and Otherness being signified by deviation from certain phenotypical and cultural norms, has a history that predates the transatlantic slave trade (Miles, 1989: 17). However, these two sets of ideas were only imbricated as the trade in slaves from Africa to the New World grew in economic significance through the seventeenth century. As it developed, slavery was more explicitly legally codified, and ideas about Africans as Others both informed, and became more pronounced as a result of, this process of codification. So, for example, the *legal* status of the first shipments of Africans to Virginia was not clearly distinguished from that of white indentured servants (except in the sense that many servants arrived with legal contracts of indenture), so that both groups could be and were alternately described as servants or slaves. But their *social* status was perceived to be different. Hence, the servitude of Europeans was regarded as time-limited, whereas that of Africans was customarily taken to be lifelong (albeit in the absence of a legal framework to prevent Africans from making the transition to free status, there were initially a small number of exceptions (Vaughan, 1989)). Legal and social status were brought into line in 1661, when 'the Virginia State Assembly became one of the first legislative bodies to equate enslavement with racial standing' by legally coding 'Slave' as 'synonymous with African/Black' (James, 2005: xxv).

Likewise, the legal status of Africans (also 'Indians' brought from Suriname) transported to and sold in Barbados was initially unclear. The first Africans arrived in 1627, but it was not until 1636 that Governor Henry Hawley issued a proclamation stating that '*Negroes* and *Indians* that come here to be sold, should serve for Life, unless a Contract was before made to the contrary' (Beckles, 1987: 11; Vaughan, 1989: 341). But once again, this proclamation 'merely gave legality to custom', for non-Europeans had already been singled out for hereditary life slavery (Beckles, 1987: 12). As the colonial powers established statutory slavery, they at the same time produced race as the category that marked the distinction between those who could and should be slaves, and those who could and should not. The 1661 Barbadian 'Act for the better ordering and governing of Negroes', for instance, provided the colony's first comprehensive slave code, and in its preamble, 'the slaves were described as "heathenish", "brutish" and "a dangerous kind of people", whose naturally wicked instincts should at all times be suppressed' (Beckles, 1987: 21). The law provided that masters should feed, clothe and accommodate the slave within the 'customs of the country' and specified the various punishments to which slaves should be subject when found guilty of given crimes. Subsequent amendments extended and consolidated the framework that fixed people racialized as black as slaves, excluded them 'from the socio-economic property accumulation and social mobility, and ensured that they were policed constantly, both within the production process and within civil society' (Beckles, 1987: 22).

'It is notable', David Bryon Davis (2003: 17) remarks, 'that the Hebrew, Greek, and Latin words for slave carried no ethnic connotations (*ebed, doulos, servus*)'. The word 'slave' derives from the ethnic designation in Latin *sclavus* (Slav) given to the inhabitants of the Dalmatian coast, who were victimized by Italian slave traders between the 1200s and 1400s. This trade, Davis (2003: 18) argues, 'foreshadowed almost every aspect of the soon-to-appear African slave trade' and when the African trade did appear, it linked the term 'slave', and the stigma that attached to it, to people 'with supposedly visible African ancestry'. Gradually, 'somatic or physical characteristics came to signify a new kind of social and psychological boundary' (Davis, D., 2003: 30). The racial encoding of this boundary was fortified by the emergence and growth of the pseudoscience of race (Gould, 1996; Lott, 1999). This pseudoscience taught that 'race' referred to distinct categories or types of human being and:

> purported to demonstrate not only the number and characteristics of each 'race', but also a hierarchical relationship between them...Moreover, science purported to demonstrate that the biological characteristics of each 'race' determined a range of psychological and social capacities of each group, by which they could be ranked.
>
> (Miles, 1989: 32)

The rise of scientific racism during the period of transatlantic slavery meant that 'slavery became indelibly linked throughout the Western Hemisphere with people of African descent...the dishonor, humiliation and bestialization that had universally been associated with chattel slavery now became fused with Negritude' (Davis, D., 2003: 29). Race came to structure and legitimate the refusal to grant to certain human beings 'the moral status to which their presumptive personhood should have entitled them' (Mills, 2011). This is important to the analysis of transatlantic slavery's overlaps with other systems of domination operating at the same historical moment.

## Racing mastery and dependency

The condition of chattel slaves was in some respects analogous to that of white servants, labourers, apprentices, wives and children who also lived and laboured 'within a legally "private" relationship in which they were subject to the rule of their household heads' (Edwards, 1998: 312). However, the fiction of race also worked to separate slaves from other categories of dependant. Slavery not only implied inescapable and life-long dependency, but also a caste-like condition inherited by the children of the enslaved. As Liam Hogan (2014) points out in a critique of the mythology that represents Irish indentured servants in the West Indies as 'slaves', neither of these devastating restrictions applied to white servants. Crime and punishment were also racialized, as Diane Paton shows in her study of how the principle of 'petit treason' was incorporated into slave law in seventeenth-century Jamaica: 'A violent act by a slave against a white person could never be just that; it always carried with it the implicit threat of slave rebellion and the overthrow of white power' (2001: 931). Similarly in early nineteenth-century Maryland, Josiah Henson (2008: 3) observed in his autobiography, 'A blow at one white man is a blow at all; is the muttering and upheaving of volcanic fires, which underlie and threaten to burst forth and utterly consume the whole social fabric.' The punishment was therefore extreme. William Dickson, who lived in Barbados in the 1770s and '80s, commented that 'the punishments of capital crimes of negroes against whites in Barbados [were] dreadful and excruciating, to a degree far beyond any idea [he] could have formed of the duration and poignancy of human suffering' (Beckles, 1987: 69).

Though in one sense mirroring the way in which servants' crimes against masters and wives' crimes against husbands were conceived, the notion of slaves as racially alien added another dimension to the powers that were subcontracted to slaveholders. Male masters had a right to chastize wives, children and servants in their households as they saw fit, but the slaveholder's power to punish slaves was far more overtly constructed as the deputation of state authority. The 1664 Jamaican slave code:

> explicitly delegated state sovereign claims to the slaveholder, requiring that 'all small... misdemeanours shall be heard and determined by the master of the Slave or Slaves.'... As well as legitimating the slaveholder's direct right to punish, the state provided resources for the punishment of slaves on the private authority of their masters. Slaveholders could hire state employees to flog their slaves.
>
> (Paton, 2001: 927)

Moreover, while not necessarily legally authorized to kill their slaves, in most of the New World at most times, slaveholders did, in effect, hold the power of life or death over their slaves and murdered with impunity when they chose to do so (Losurdo, 2011).

The racialization of the line between freedom and slavery also had implications for the relationship between state, master and slave that did not pertain with regard to other categories of dependant. In addition to licensing propertied white men to exercise certain powers of sovereignty over the dependants in their household, powers that were especially wide-ranging in relation to slaves, New World slave states made white society (non-slaveholders as well as slaveholders) *collectively* responsible 'for the control and regulation of blacks. It was the civil duty of all whites to enforce the slave laws' (Beckles, 1987: 23; Hadden, 2001). Certainly, the civil duty to enforce and respect private property also applied in relation to men's property rights in their wives, servants and children, but what is distinctive in the case of slaves is that this duty was simultaneously a private matter and a public, political one. White people could be, and were, brought before the courts for failing to discharge their duties with respect to controlling and regulating slaves (Beckles, 1987: 23), and slaveholders were often under a legal obligation to treat their slaves in the manner deemed appropriate by the state, as opposed to the manner they saw fit as private individuals.

In Alabama in the 1850s, for example, various criminal statutes prevented a slaveholder from simply deciding to let a slave live as though she or he were free. The origin and purpose of this 'wise and conservative' legislative policy, as explained in a Supreme Court ruling on one manumission case, was 'to prevent the demoralization and corruption of slaves, resulting from a withdrawal of discipline and restraint from them, and to prevent the pernicious effect upon the slave community of the anomalous condition of servitude without a master's control' (cited in Tushnet, 1981: 199). Men had no equivalent legal responsibility with regard to wives, or as time went on, to servants (though it is worth noting that to this day in liberal societies, parents continue to be legally required to exercise certain forms of control over children).

More generally, laws governing manumission speak to the fact that whilst the right of property may be foundational to the 'rights of man' (Sichel, 1972), that right is subordinate to man's obligations to the central political power that acknowledges him as a rights-holder. Slave states restrained slaveholders' freedom to do as they pleased with their slave property when it came to manumission because masterless slaves were as anomaly: who would govern them, and who would provide for them if destitute? Thus, the Spanish slave code of 1789 prohibited the manumission of slaves as a means by which slaveholders could rid themselves of the burden of supporting aged and infirm slaves (though the prohibition was not always observed (Titus, 2009: 84)). Elsewhere, a surety to the parish or a rachat to the state had to be paid before manumission was authorized; and in Southern slave states, manumission was often permitted only with the proviso that the freed slave must leave the territory of the state. Indeed, the notion that ownership implies 'the right to dispose of the possession' – which Bales (2012: 283) takes as one of the central rights of ownership – rarely held in its entirety in New World slave societies, as strict legal limits were set on slaveholders' right to dispose of their slave possessions by transferring ownership to slaves themselves (Blackburn, 2011; Moitt, 2008; Patterson, 1982; Tushnet, 1981). Such laws remind us of the 'double character' of the slave (Hartman, 1997). The slave could be owned as a 'thing' but not freely *dis*owned precisely because she was a 'person', not a material object, and crucially, because she was a person racialized as black.

Again, there are overlaps between slaves and white indentured servants as well as wives and children in the sense that measures to prevent masters from simply turfing out dependants they had wearied of were not uniquely applied to slaves. And they are still at play in certain elements of divorce law, in laws making biological fathers responsible for child support payments, and in immigration controls that require citizens who sponsor family members' or spouses' entry onto the territory to pay bonds or demonstrate that they can maintain and accommodate their 'dependant' 'without recourse to public funds' (Anderson, 2013: 65). Those to whom the state delegates 'petty sovereignty' cannot just renounce the obligations it implies as it suits them. Race was, nonetheless, a differentiating factor. White indentured servants could complete their contract and make the transition to free status, and a white wife could be widowed or even abandoned or divorced and still have a place in her society. However, state controls over manumission seared the freedom/slavery binary onto the imagined racial binary of white/black in such a way as to make freedom white only.

In Georgia in 1853, for example, ruling on a case in which the right of free black people to own slaves was at issue, Judge Joseph Lumpkin stated that a freed black person was 'in a state of perpetual pupilage or wardship', and:

> The act of manumission confers no other right but that of freedom from the dominion of the master, and the limited liberty of

locomotion; it does not and cannot confer *citizenship*, nor any of the powers, civil or political, incident to *citizenship*.
(quoted in Tushnet, 1981: 150)

He continued to explain the impossibility of citizenship for freed slaves in explicitly racial terms – 'the taint of blood, adheres to the descendants of Ham in this county, like the poisoned tunic of Nessus' (Tushnet, 1981: 150). The racial character of rights and freedom was also made explicit in the notorious 1857 *Dred Scott* decision of the US Supreme Court, which 'judged that blacks were "beings of an inferior order" with "no rights which the white man was bound to respect"'(Mills, 2011).

The idea of race and racial hierarchy as biological realities (i.e., racism) generated a system of domination and subordination that cut across the assumed oppositional binary of slavery and freedom. In the United States, what James Stewart (1998: 182) terms 'racial modernity' – a white supremacist 'polity premised on the uniform assumption that nature had always divided black and white as superior and inferior and always must' – had been established in the 'free' North by 1840, undermining the Slave South/Free North distinction that remains so important to popular representations of the pre-Civil War United States (including in Steve McQueen's recent film *12 Years a Slave*). In Spanish colonies too, the whiteness of freedom and citizenship was enshrined in a series of restrictions on the freedoms of 'free coloured populations' (restraints on movement, legal disabilities, prohibitions against holding public office, practising professions, being buried in a cathedral compound, making use of educational facilities and even prohibitions against women wearing jewels) (Titus, 2009: 84).

The system transatlantic slavery and the ideology of race had together produced large numbers of people racialized as black living on specific political territories in the New World. So long as slavery persisted as a legal institution, these people were socially fixed in these geopolitical spaces as perpetual outsiders. Manumission was possible, but it was regulated and limited by the state, and arranged in such a way as to be an exception that in no way undermined the general rules governing the associations between race and slave or free status (Wolfe, 2004). Whether born to free status, or freed from slavery, 'people of colour' were not citizens. The institution of slavery provided the moorings for race as much as race provided the ideological justification for slavery. What, then, would be the status and position of those racialized as black in its absence? This question was politically divisive even amongst abolitionists.

## Anti-slavery politics and race politics

In an account of her flight from slavery in the early 1840s, abolitionist campaigner Harriet Jacobs explains that she managed to get to Philadelphia by boat. Here, a friend bought her a ticket to continue to New York by train, apologizing that it had to be second-class since, 'They don't allow colored people to go in the first class cars'. Jacobs reflected, 'This was the first chill to my enthusiasm about the Free States. Colored people were allowed to ride in a filthy box, behind white people, at the South, but there they were not required to pay for the privilege' (2000: 163).

Like Frederick Douglass and many others who struggled for the abolition of slavery (including some white as well as black activists), Jacobs simultaneously articulated demands for an end to bondage *and* for racial equality. But this was by no means true of all those who campaigned for slavery's abolition. Indeed, Du Bois' (1966) comment on the demand that we forget what is discomforting 'and simply remember the things we regard as creditable and inspiring' also rings true in relation to the history of the anti-slavery movement. Some of the white figures that are today held up as icons of that movement did not regard the black brethren they sought to release from the bonds of slavery as fit for inclusion as equals in white political society (Davis, 1975).

William Wilberforce's reservations about the capacity of the enslaved to exercise freedom, for example, were so great that his primary concern was to end the transatlantic slave *trade* and not slavery *per se*. His hope was that by abolishing the slave trade, 'a disposition to breed instead of buying' would be produced amongst the planter class, he wrote in a diary entry in 1818, elsewhere explaining that 'our object was by ameliorating regulations, and by stopping the influx of uninstructed savages, to advance slowly towards the period when these unhappy things might exchange their degraded state of slavery for that of free and industrious peasantry' (quoted in Jordan, 2005: 180–1). Such comments, along with his efforts to suppress 'the nascent working class, the trade union movement, and their demands for political and labour rights' through his Society for the Suppression of Vice and Encouragement of Religion led radical writer William Hazlitt to describe Wilberforce in 1825 as 'as fine a specimen of moral equivocation as can be conceived' (Pupavac, 2015).

But alliances between class radicals and radicals in the abolitionist movement could also be undermined by racism. Chattel slavery and wage slavery were regarded by many in the Chartist and other working class movements as twin evils to be simultaneously opposed, but they were also sometimes framed as 'negro' and 'white' slavery respectively, and some prioritized struggle against the latter because it reduced those who ought 'naturally' be free to the condition of 'slaves' (Cunliffe, 1979). Gender politics further divided the anti-slavery movement, prompting coalitions between those calling for racial equality and those calling for women's rights (coalitions that quickly broke down following slave emancipation in the United States).

Nineteenth-century abolitionist institutions were rooted in a 'grammar of difference', Catherine Hall (2003) argues, and the imagined division between public and private, along with the trope of the family, made it possible for white middle-class male abolitionists to accommodate the idea of gifting 'freedom' without also acknowledging equality (see also Wood, 2010). Indeed, the family provided 'a way of managing inequality, for children must be guided by their parents, wives by their husbands, the young by the old' (2003: 481). The race, class and gender tensions running through the abolitionist movement are vividly brought to life in Benjamin Robert Haydon's famous painting of the 1840 World Anti-Slavery Convention in London, organized by the British and Foreign Anti-Slavery Society, Hall notes. The painting captures a moment when powerful anti-slavery sentiment sat alongside acceptance of the 'rule of difference' to produce a picture in which 'middle-class white men carried power both for themselves and on behalf of others, black men were there on sufferance, women could not speak, and the Irish were at the margins' (2003: 485).

For all these reasons, the 'old' abolitionism leaves behind a complex, fractured and fracturing legacy, and certainly not one that can today be straightforwardly picked up and celebrated by all alike. But while Kevin Bales (1999, 2005) flags up racism as a feature of transatlantic slavery and accepts that it remained a powerful, damaging force in US society following abolition, he does not address its presence in the anti-slavery movement. Nor does he dig very deep into the historical relation between slavery and race. In the past 'ethnic and racial differences were used to explain and excuse slavery', he says, and:

> Maintaining these differences required tremendous investment in some very irrational ideas...The 'Founding Fathers' of the United States of America had to go through moral, linguistic, and political contortions to explain why the 'land of the free' only applied to white people...Most of them knew they were lying, that they were betraying their most cherished ideals. They were driven to it because slavery was worth a lot of money to a lot of people in Colonial

America...at that time, they felt they had to make moral excuses for their economic decisions.

(1999: 10)

Why then did white racism continue to structure economic, political and social life after abolition? Bales' answer appears to be that racism and racial inequality in the United States is a 'vestige' of the system of racial slavery that once operated (1999: 7). Racism is wrong, but it has nothing to do with the new system of slavery operating in the contemporary world, which is 'color blind' (Bales, 2004: 11). Patricia Williams' (1997: 2) comments on the discourse of colour-blindness as power-averse come to mind. To characterize racism as but a 'very irrational idea' that unfortunately happened to continue to haunt liberal societies post-abolition is to evade thought about how racism is incorporated into the living tissue of contemporary liberal societies. It is to forget that 'the same developments of modernity that brought liberalism into existence as a supposedly general set of political norms also brought race into existence as a set of restrictions and entitlements governing the application of those norms' (Mills, 2008: 1394). And forgetting about race as a system of domination allows the new abolitionists to sidestep questions about a form of unfreedom found in the contemporary United States that does continue to produce racialized patterns of exclusion from citizenship, and that *is* regarded as modern or neo-slavery by some black radical thinkers (see James, 2005), namely, the Prison Industrial Complex.

## From slave emancipation to mass incarceration

Immediately after the American Civil War and Lincoln's Emancipation Proclamation, the Slave Codes of former slave states were reformulated as Black Codes, which, as Angela Davis (2003: 28) explains, allowed 'the behaviour of free blacks' to be regulated in much the same way that slaves' behaviour had been controlled during slavery. Some of these codes laid the foundations for the Southern system of peonage through which significant numbers of persons racialized as black were locked into a set of social and labour relations closely resembling chattel slavery well into the second half of the twentieth century. In Mississippi in 1865, for example:

> 'An Act to confer Civil Rights on Freedmen' barred the freedman from renting land outside city limits, thus ensuring that blacks could not begin farming on their own. Further, by the following January, and

annually thereafter, each freedman had to hold written proof of lawful employment (i.e., a labor contract). The absence of such evidence was prima facie proof of vagrancy. Should a freedman breach his contract 'without good cause,' he was subject to arrest by the police or other civil officer. The arresting officer was entitled to a reward of five dollars (plus ten cents per mile travelled), to be paid out of the laborer's wages.

(Novak, 1978: 2–3)

Other black codes 'foreshadowed Jim Crow laws by prohibiting, among other things, interracial seating in the first class sections of railroad cars and by segregating schools' (Alexander, 2010: 28). The enactment of black codes 'was accompanied by violent attacks on the freedmen and women by white vigilante groups' (Blackburn, 2011: 424).

Then followed 'the relatively brief but extraordinary period of black advancement known as the Reconstruction Era', during which the black codes were 'overturned, and a slew of federal civil rights legislating protecting the newly freed slaves was passed' (Alexander, 2010: 29). In this short moment, the *Dred Scott* decision was swept aside, and it appeared possible that not just chattel slavery, but also the racial caste system it had spawned, could be abolished. But this was not to be. An extraordinarily violent backlash by white conservatives wishing to 'redeem' the South, and the withdrawal of federal troops after the 1877 Hayes-Tilden Compromise (said to be a 'gentlemen's agreement' struck to resolve dispute over the 1876 presidential election) paved the way for 'the re-subordination of blacks under the new regime of Jim Crow', the system of racial segregation or apartheid 'given formal federal sanction in the 1896 *Plessy vs. Ferguson* decision' (Mills, 2011).

Alongside this, from the 1880s to the 1920s, the practice of lynching operated as a form of 'racial–sexual terror' (James, 2005: xxx), one that served as spectacular proof that, in the words of Richard Wright, 'the law is white' (1947: 44, cited in Marriott, 2000: 6). Race became, if anything, a more significant marker of social and political inclusion and exclusion in the aftermath of abolition (Wolfe, 2004). Amongst the post-emancipation measures that stripped those racialized as black of any rights to which their presumptive 'freedom' entitled them was the southern convict lease system. This system allowed people convicted of offences such as vagrancy (also 'mischief' and 'insulting gestures') to be contracted out as labourers, and subject to brutal regimes of coerced and unpaid labour in lumber camps, brickyards, railroads, farms, plantations and other privately owned businesses (Alexander, 2010: 31; Blackmon,

2008). It 'transferred symbolically significant numbers of black people from the prison of slavery to the slavery of prison' (Davis, A., 2003). In essence, what vagrancy laws criminalize is not merely poverty, but masterlessness, as seen in the context of the 'freeing up' of wage labour in England, and in the Mississipi Act to confer Civil Rights on Freedmen mentioned above. Its extensive use to coerce freed black men and women into a condition of that implied both rightlessness and severe labour exploitation in the post-emancipation US South speaks to the strength of the political resistance on the part of the ruling white elite to accept people racialized as black as morally worthy of inclusion in civil society, and to the perspicacity of the abolitionist Wendell Phillips' comment on the ratification of the Thirteenth Amendment: 'We have abolished the slave but the master remains' (Stewart, 2015: 132).

In contemplating this history, Kevin Bales can see racism and its connection to what he considers to be slavery. He describes systems and practices such as share cropping and convict labour schemes as techniques of 're-enslavement' (Bales, 1999, 2005; Bales and Soodalter, 2009). Fast forward to the 1970s, and Bales can still see racism in US society, but its links to what he considers to be the 'obscenity' of slavery (i.e., that it 'is not just stealing someone's labor; it is the theft of an entire life', 1999: 7) have now become opaque. And yet it was at precisely at this point that a new carceral turn was being taken in the United States. This took off in earnest in the 1980s as a result of the 'War on Drugs', which Michelle Alexander describes as 'the engine of mass incarceration, as well as the primary cause of gross racial disparities in the criminal justice system and in the ex-offender population' (2010: 184).

The Reagan administration was determined to get 'tough on crime' through more extensive use of prison sentences and longer sentences. It initiated a 'massive project of prison construction', and as 'the U.S. prison system expanded, so did corporate involvement in construction, provision of goods and services, and use of prison labor', inspiring the use of the term Prison Industrial Complex (Davis, A., 2003: 12). The federal 'three strikes and you're out' law endorsed by Bill Clinton in 1994 was one of a number of 'reforms' that helped to ensure a growing supply of inmates for the industry. For instance, California's three strikes law 'mandates a sentence of 25 years to life for recidivists convicted of a third felony, no matter how minor', leading to 'sentences of 25 years without parole for a man who stole three golf clubs from a pro shop, and 50 years without parole for another man for stealing children's videotapes from a Kmart store' (Alexander, 2010: 89). The prison population soared, and by 1995, one study suggested that almost one in three black men between the ages of 20 and 29 were imprisoned, on parole or on probation (Davis, A., 2003: 19). By the millennium, the prison population had reached 2 million, and by 2009, some 2.3 million people were imprisoned, the vast majority of whom (two-thirds) were 'people of colour' (Loyd et al., 2012: 7). Approximately half a million of these people are serving time for drug offences, mostly involving minor infractions of drug laws, such as possession of small quantities of marijuana (Alexander, 2010: 59). Almost 5 million people more 'are under direct state supervision through the parole and probation systems' (Loyd et al., 2012: 7).

Inmates constitute the raw materials processed by for-profit private corporations involved in the PIC, but they are also often exploited directly as a source of labour-power. Writing in 2008, Noel Zatz observes that 'well over 600,000, and probably close to a million, inmates are working full time in jails and prisons throughout the United States' and 'prison industries generate $2 billion in revenue annually' (2008: 868–9). Prison industries take a number of different organizational forms. The 'contract' system that was widespread in the nineteenth century, then largely disappeared in the twentieth century, and that 'places these functions within a private firm that operates the program pursuant to a contract with the prison' is reemerging as one of them, but the most widespread yet least visible, form of prison labor Zatz (2008: 870) terms 'prison housework', in which the prison both:

> manages production and also consumes its output, as inmates contribute directly to prison operations by cooking meals, doing laundry, or cleaning the facilities. Inmates also may be used directly by other units of the jurisdiction incarcerating them, such as the Iowa prisoners who bake cookies for the Governor's holiday parties and other events. Placing a value on this work is difficult, but one Kentucky county estimated that inmate labor saved it $3 million during 2006.

The scale of the savings is explained by the fact that inmates provide extraordinarily cheap labour, well below the federal minimum wage – 'Wage rates vary widely by program and jurisdiction, but in 2002, the average statewide rates ranged from $0.17 to $5.35 per hour' (2008: 870–1). Kevin Bales remarks that:

> Prison labor is a particularly thorny question, because the accusation that it constitutes enslavement depends primarily on the legitimacy of the government in control and the fairness of its justice

system. When people are held against their will and without due process, threatened or coerced with violence, and robbed of their labor power – all features of the current situation in Burma ... then it is reasonable to assess this as a form of state-sponsored slavery. When an inmate of a British prison is voluntarily enrolled in a work project for which he or she is remunerated, this can hardly be described as slavery.

(2005: 58)

If Bales picked British prisons because he imagines they offer a less controversial example than US prisons, he should note that privatization and prison expansion have also been features of British experience since the 1990s (Sudbury, 2005a); that Britain has also witnessed growing political preoccupation with crime and crime control over the past two decades, and increasing criminalization of behaviours deemed 'antisocial' (in 2006, 'a Manchester school girl was £75 for leaving a wooden lolly stick on a walk, a woman in Luton was fined £75 for throwing a Cheesy Wotsit from a car' (Rodger, 2008: xiv)); and that 'There is now greater disproportionality in the number of black people in prisons in the UK than in the United States' (Prison Reform Trust, 2013: 5).

Indeed in Britain, as in the United States, processes of criminalization have been raced – as Stuart Hall et al.'s (1978) seminal work, *Policing the Crisis*, showed, and this places an extremely large question mark against 'the fairness of the justice system'. In the United States, moreover, to serve a prison sentence is to be cut adrift from the political community not merely for the duration of the period of incarceration, but also on release. Most former prisoners emerge from prison deeply in debt, to face legally authorized discrimination in employment, housing, education, and public benefits. In addition, the right to vote, which is denied to felony prisoners, continues to be withheld in most states when prisoners are released on parole, and 'Even after the term of punishment expires, some states deny the right to vote for a period ranging from a number of years to the rest of one's life' (Alexander, 2010: 153). In 2010, 5.85 million people in the United States were disenfranchised due to a felony conviction, and:

1 of every 13 African Americans of voting age is disenfranchised, a rate more than four times greater than non-African Americans. Nearly 7.7 percent of the adult African American population is disenfranchised compared to 1.8 percent of the non-African American population.

(Uggen et al., 2012: 1–2)

In some states, the percentage of African Americans disenfranchised rises to 23 percent (Florida), 22 percent (Kentucky) and 20 percent (Virginia) (Uggen et al., 2012: 2). These high levels of disenfranchisement place a question mark against the legitimacy of government.

Angela Davis (2014) describes the recent police killings of black youth in the United States as part of 'an unbroken stream of racist violence, both official and extra-legal, from slave patrols and the Ku Klux Klan, to contemporary profiling practices and present-day vigilantes', and these measures constitute a similarly direct and uninterrupted line back to slavery. Release from prison today, like manumission in the past, leaves human beings standing between captivity and freedom, denied the powers, civil or political, incident to citizenship, clothed in 'the poisoned tunic of Nessus'. That such policies are so much more likely to affect people of colour lends weight to Loic Wacquant's (2002) contention that the PIC is the fourth of America's 'peculiar institutions', the first three being slavery, Jim Crow, and the ghetto, all of which had in common that they were 'instruments for the conjoint *extraction of labour* and *social ostracization* of an outcast group deemed unassimilable by virtue of the indelible ... stigma it carries'.

It is not my contention that those held captive in the PIC are the *real* 'modern slaves', for I believe 'modern slavery' names a set of moral and political arguments, not any specific phenomenon. But I do believe that the US penal system grossly violates what US state actors elsewhere describe as fundamental human rights; that as James Stewart (2015: 132) puts it, it involves forcible detention 'for the raw monetary value' of the victims' bodies, and often represents the theft of entire lives; and that it constitutes an important element of anti-blackness (Woods, 2013), which is to say, 'the afterlife of slavery – skewed life chances, limited access to health and education, premature death, incarceration, and impoverishment' (Hartman, 2007: 6). That the new abolitionists do not wish to include the PIC in their discourse on contemporary practices that debase, brutalize, and exploit human beings reveals much about the nature and cause of their 'colour blindness'. Their failure to attend to the history that connects contemporary immigration controls back to racial slavery is similarly worrisome.

## Race, citizenship and the threat of abolition

Because slavery and race had grown into interlocking categories under transatlantic slavery, in the early nineteenth century, a free, black citizen was almost as inconceivable as the idea that white Britons ever, ever could be slaves. Projects seeking to settle freed slaves in African colonies spoke to this perceived problem. The British established 'the colony of Sierra Leone in 1787 as a refuge for blacks freed during the American War of Independence' (Davis, D., 2003: 65), and it, along with a British colonial outpost, McCarthy Island, the Gambia, was subsequently used as a 'resettlement site for slaves intercepted' in illegal slave ships in the Atlantic 'and repatriated to Africa's shore' (Webb, 1994: 136). In the United States, the American Colonization Society (ACS), formed in Philadelphia in 1816, founded the colony of Liberia in 1822 (Jordan, 2005) and dedicated itself 'to promoting the manumission of slaves, with an undertaking that, once free, they would agree to be shipped to Liberia or some other African destination' (Blackburn, 2011: 245).

The idea of 'repatriation' did actually find favour amongst some slaves in the 1700s, who, having been kidnapped and transported to America, wished to return (Davis, D., 2003). This included Quobna Ottobah Cugoano, although writing in 1787, he was already aware that the absence of 'a treaty of agreement... with the inhabitants of Africa' seriously compromised plans for Sierra Leone as a free colony, and expressed doubt that freed slaves would ever 'be settled, as intended, in any permanent and peaceable way' there (1999: 104–5). However, the impulse to resettle slaves in Africa (and remember that many enslaved people in the Americas had been born there, including as the children of their white owners) did not necessarily spring from any regard for the wishes or humanity of the enslaved. It was also inspired by anti-black sentiment. Sierra Leone's designation as a resettlement site strongly reflected the fact that 'The large numbers of emancipated slaves taken to Britain after the American Revolution were not welcome in a white nation that had tried to deport all blacks in the late sixteenth century' (Davis, D., 2003: 65). Even Granville Sharp, hero of the British antislavery movement, expressed concerns about 'swarms of negroes' arriving in England (Blackburn, 2011: 151). Likewise, the ACS appealed to white Philadelphians who objected to the state's growing black population. Indeed, policies to promote the emigration to Africa of people racialized as black speak forcefully to the fact that whilst the human body has long served as 'the pervasive metaphor of the body politic' (Grosz, 1994: 106), the body politic of liberal thought is 'a masculine domain of whiteness' (Puwar, 2004: 13).

Abolition was a problem for the many white Americans who – whether or not they found chattel slavery a morally acceptable institution – shared Judge Lumpkin's reservations about the possibilities of incorporating black bodies into citizenship. So long as the legal machinery of slavery existed, race was constituted as a hereditary, caste-like, social marker. There was no possibility of 'swarms of negroes' agitating for equal rights, and no means by which those racialized as black could alter their position in the social hierarchy by dint of their own efforts. To dismantle the institution of chattel slavery would potentially also be to dismantle the legal, social and political mechanisms through which racial difference and hierarchy were produced, policed and perpetuated, thereby eviscerating whiteness of its privilege.

Such fears help to explain why, following the Civil War, interracial marriage and 'miscegenation' became important to debate on 'what freedom would for former slaves was to mean, what sort of citizenship African Americans would possess, what power they would hold relative to other free people' (Rosen, 2005: 291). The absence of slavery and its associated controls over sexuality was perceived to imply 'the specter of black economic mobility and its consolidation, through racial integration, of a world in which race had no visible significance' (Rosen, 2005: 299). The same anxieties also help to explain measures taken in Southern slave states to exclude people from their territories even before the Civil War in response to perceived threats to the institution of slavery, in particular the enactment of The Negro Seaman Act (1822). This Act was designed to control and prevent the entry of free black seamen on their soil. It provided that as soon as their vessel docked, black sailors were to be seized and imprisoned, and, if their jail fees went unpaid, they were to be sold into slavery. It was initially introduced as one of several 'quarantine laws' guarding entrance into South Carolina following the discovery of the 1822 Denmark Vesey plot in Charleston,[1] Edlie Wong (2009: 184) explains, but it was strengthened and more vigorously enforced following the abolition of slavery in the British West Indies.

Similar legislation was soon also enacted in North Carolina, Georgia, Florida, Alabama, Louisiana, and Texas. Defending such laws, a South Carolina lawyer, Benjamin Faneuil Hunt, argued as follows:

the civilized man can secure his family against the contagion of the dissolute or depraved, by closing his doors, or selecting his visitors; – So, every sovereign state, has the perfect right of interdicting all intercourse with strangers, or of selecting those whose influence or example she may fear, and confining the exclusion to them. A master of a family receives or excludes his visitors, according to the peculiar situation and feelings of his own household. A State must be the sole judge to decide what strangers may or may not enter. The power to exclude or to admit strangers, implies the right to direct the terms upon which those who are admitted shall remain. As an individual may direct what apartment his guest shall occupy, a state may confine strangers to such limits, as its own policy may dictate.

(quoted in Wong, 2009: 197)

The introduction of more stringent means of controlling admittance onto the territory of the state at a time when the transatlantic system of racial slavery was beginning to break down (and with it, the containment of black bodies within the private households of petty sovereigns), and the use of the analogy between home and state by those supporting such measures, were also features of the history of the post-abolition British Empire (Sharma, 2006). Indeed, some argue that the origins of contemporary immigration controls lie in this history.

## From slaves to coolies to immigration controls: race, state sovereignty and the power to exclude

In Europe, state control of human mobility originally centred on immobilizing the poor and expelling the seditious from the sovereign's territory, and systematic regulation and control of the entrance of 'aliens' only began to be implemented from the end of the eighteenth century (Anderson, 2013: 21; Cohen, 2006). From the late nineteenth century, powers of exclusion and controls over the terms on which 'aliens' could enter became the primary focus of state efforts to control human mobility in Europe, Australia and North America, a preoccupation that gradually extended around the world through the twentieth century. Today, 'The global monopoly of a system of states over the international movement of people seems an unremarkable fact' (Mongia, 1999: 527). The state's right to control its borders is regarded as virtually unquestionable, and is defended by a range of thinkers. The communitarian political philosopher Michael Walzer (1983: 61–2), for instance, describes the state's right to choose an admissions policy as a fundamental one:

for it is not merely a matter of acting in the world, exercising sovereignty, and pursuing national interests. At stake here is the shape of the community that acts in the world, exercises sovereignty, and so on. Admission and exclusion are at the core of communal independence. They suggest the deepest meaning of self-determination.

This makes it sound as if there is something natural and timeless about a community's need to exercise powers of admittance and exclusion, an idea that is today widely accepted as a fundamental truth of political existence. And yet communities have historically existed without exercising such powers, and the distinction between citizens and migrants is a relatively recent invention (Anderson, 2013: 21). British colonial states, for example, 'did not exercise a monopoly of control over the mobility of people' in the nineteenth century and this only began to change in the aftermath of slavery's abolition (Mongia, 1999: 533). In the British Empire of the nineteenth century, those racialized as black, brown and yellow were, in theory, included alongside those racialized as white as subjects of Queen Victoria's munificent rule (even if in practice, forms of dominion over them and clear racial hierarchies were licensed by colonial states). Thus, in her Proclamation to the Princes, Chiefs and People of India in 1858, Queen Victoria stated that 'we hold ourselves bound to the natives of our Indian territories by the same obligations of duty which bind us to all our other subjects' (Anderson, 2013: 33).

This early version of 'colour blindness' meant that on abolition, emancipated slaves in distant lands could more readily be reimagined (at least by those in Britain) as belonging to her Empire than the more proximate emancipated slaves in the United States could be reconceived as citizens, albeit (or precisely because) they would belong on highly unequal terms. But the abolition of slavery nonetheless presented colonial rulers with the problem of a potential shortage of labour, and it was, Radhika Mongia (1999) argues, the solution to this problem – namely the system of indentured labour, or the 'coolie system' – that ultimately brought into being the controls over mobility that today are read as rights that states must 'naturally' hold. As noted in Chapter 2, the conditions under which coolies lived and laboured resembled those endured by the chattel slaves they replaced, and their spatial and social mobility was heavily restrained. They could not leave the plantations or other work settings without passes, they could not change their employer, and so their alienage from citizenship and belonging in the territory on which they laboured was assured (Cohen, 2006; Potts, 1990; Tinker, 1974). It is also instructive to note that the large scale movement of Indian coolie labour from the mid-nineteenth century had been preceded by forced movement of Indian convicts to serve as a labour force in 'the enclaves of the rising British Empire in Southeast Asia' (Yang, 2003: 185).

The coolie system was controlled by states under emigration legislation. However, these controls 'covered *only* the large-scale movement of indentured labor to specific countries' – those who migrated without having entered into contracts of indenture before leaving home, as well as those who were not engaged in 'manual labour', were still 'free to travel unhindered, especially between parts of the British empire' (Mongia, 1999: 532–3, original emphasis). And it was when Chinese and Indian migrants began to take advantage of opportunities to travel independently within the British Empire, moving to what were deemed to be 'white' settler colonies that their freedom of mobility came to be regarded as a problem in need of a solution. In Australia from the late 1870s, Chinese migration was increasingly represented as a threat to a 'white man's country' (Lake, 2014). Around the same time, the free migration of Indians to Natal provoked similar anxieties (Anderson, 2013: 33), as did Indian migration to Canada in the first decade of the twentieth century (Mongia, 1999).

In Australia in 1881, 'the Victoria government moved...to introduce new immigration restrictions, including a poll tax on Chinese, and to disenfranchise those who enjoyed the vote under the local provision for manhood suffrage' (Lake, 2014: 98). Such measures were deemed necessary to prevent Chinese from arriving 'in hordes' and 'swamping' the white population, but were difficult to enact in relation to migrants from Hong Kong, who were in theory also subjects of the British empire. The same difficulty beset the Canadian Government, which devised various measures intended to act as a barrier to the entry of Indians, and called for the introduction of passports to further control and restrict their movement, only to meet with strong objections from the Indian Government. Indeed, the latter refused 'to participate in a passport system to restrict emigration to Canada, grounding its refusal in the principle of "complete freedom for all British subjects to transfer themselves from one part of His Majesty's dominions to another"' (Mongia, 1999: 548).

The problem, as Bridget Anderson puts it, 'was that to limit mobility of "Europeans" was unthinkable, yet any mention of "race" could threaten to undermine assertions of equality and benevolent rule' (2013: 33). The solution, as the Victoria government discovered in 1888, was to formulate 'the issue of immigration restriction as one of national sovereignty, the right of a self-governing, "free and independent state" to self-preservation' (Lake, 2014: 101). Likewise in Canada, restrictive immigration laws and an end to the special status accorded to British subjects across the empire were defended in terms of national sovereignty, and in language similar to that employed by Benjamin Faneuil Hunt. An opposition party MP told the Canadian House:

Canada is mistress of her own house and takes the authority and responsibility of deciding who shall be admitted to citizenship and the privileges and rights of citizenship within her borders...This is not a labor question; it is not a racial question; it is a question of national dominance and national existence.

(cited in Mongia, 1999: 550)

In the same debate, a former prime minister, Wilfrid Laurier, made explicit the fact that questions of national dominance and existence were in fact racial questions when he said, 'The people of Canada want to have a white country' (Mongia, 1999: 550). The pressure for the introduction of passports became irresistible, and the Indian Government yielded to it. In 1914, the Viceroy of India accepted the notion that countries 'have an inherent right to decide whom they will or will not admit within their borders', and determined that the solution was 'to furnish passports to emigrants entitling them to admission into the Colonies and India respectively. The number of these permits or passports would be limited by agreement' (Mongia, 1999: 553). This allowed:

a principle of pseudo-reciprocity and thus pseudo-universality to be inscribed within the passport system. The passport emerges here as a state document that purports to assign a national identity rather than a racial identity...Simultaneously and crucially, however, this formation of the passport generates 'nationality' as the intersection between the nation and the state. Inscribed on the body of the migrant are the traces of both the state and the nation-race. This produces...the 'nationalized' migrant.

(Mongia, 1999: 553–4)

Such analyses suggest that, whether the state's right to exclude is likened to the patriarch's 'natural' powers over his household (as in Hunt's defence of this right), or imagined as licensed by and democratically exercised on behalf of 'the community' (as in Walzer's account), such explanations are back-to-front. The practices of admission and exclusion are what *create* a political community (or a patriarchal household), not simply the expression of the will of a pre-existing 'community' or 'family' whose boundaries somehow sprung from 'nature' (Chow, 1999). Far from existing in some natural, timeless or ahistoric form, the 'creation of a geopolitical space dominated by the nation-state' took place in the context of 'raced-migration', that is, the movement of peoples deemed to be racial Others (Mongia, 1999: 528; McKeown, 2008). It was this that prompted states to claim the right to admit or exclude, to produce 'race' as a 'national attribute' and codify it 'in the state document of the passport' (Mongia, 1999: 528–9). As Nandita Sharma (2006: 7) has shown, modernist ideas of 'home' remain crucial to this interlacing of the state, the nation, and race, helping 'to organize and legitimate the differential treatment of those living within the same space'. The nation as home metaphor discursively constructs nationality as biological connection, as a 'natural' form of belonging, and:

> as ideologies of highly racialized nations as natural homelands became hegemonic, people's understanding of geographical movements profoundly shifted. Indeed, as borders became more fixed, migrants increasingly were portrayed as trespassers. In other words, as the nation became more homey to those seen as its members, migrants were made even more homeless.
>
> (Sharma, 2006: 11)

Or, we might say, in the presence of racism but the absence of the system of racial slavery that had once both allowed and required petty sovereigns to contain racial Others in their private households, it became increasingly important for states to directly police and control the social and physical boundaries of racial power. Like freed slaves in the United States, migrants racialized as black, brown and yellow were Outsiders unrestrained by a master. As I hope to show in the next two chapters, the immigration regimes that today govern who is, and is not, allowed lawful entry to states, and that impose heavy restraints on the freedoms of many of those who are admitted, reflect a similar concern with unmoored or masterless 'aliens'.

The dynamics that produced race as a national attribute were not identical to those at play in the production of racial slavery. Borders are a living legacy of transatlantic slavery and are associated with forms of exclusion and domination, but their construction did not ineradicably mark the category 'migrant' with the stigma of slavery in the way that racial slavery fused blackness and slavery, thereby permanently destabilizing 'the position of any nominally free black population' (Sexton, 2010: 36). It is important to remember the specificity of the anti-black racism spawned by transatlantic slavery and the particularities of its continuing aftermath (Fannon, 1970; Sexton, 2010). This is one strong reason to reject new abolitionist talk of a new, colour-blind slavery, one that affects more people 'today than at any time during the trans-Atlantic Slave Trade' (IJM, 2015), but that excludes the millions of African-Americans incarcerated and disenfranchised by the US government. Another, separate and distinct, reason to reject it is that the same discourse also fails to challenge the 'right' claimed by states to restrict human mobility, even though state-imposed restrictions on freedom of movement are closely associated with many of the phenomena dubbed 'modern slavery' (as well as other forms of harm that new abolitionists do not consider to be 'slavery').

# 5
# 'Trafficking' as a Modern Slave Trade? Mobility, Slavery and Escape

'Human trafficking' is described as a process that reduces its victims to objects of trade – mere things or commodities to be bought, used and discarded – and it is routinely compared to the transatlantic slave trade by politicians and by the new abolitionists (Bravo, 2011). 'Human trafficking is the modern day slave trade – the process of enslaving a person', Free the Slaves (FTS, 2014b) tells us, and according to Ambassador John Miller, the man George W. Bush appointed to lead the US State Department's Office to Monitor and Combat Trafficking in Persons from 2002: 'We need to bring the same passion and commitment to this struggle that the abolitionists of this country brought to the struggle against slavery based upon color 160 years ago' (2006: 4). Such is the US Government's commitment to this struggle that it has donned the mantle of the world's moral police officer, establishing a Trafficking in Persons (TIP) Office that collects and publishes in its annual TIP Report information 'about other nation states' efforts to combat trafficking', ranking them in tiers according to their degree of compliance with the standards set by the US' Trafficking Victims Protection Act (2000), and threatening 'under-performing' nations with sanctions (O'Brien and Wilson, 2015: 124). But how can states combat this 'modern day slave trade'?

'Say the words "slave trade" and most people picture wooden ships leaving Africa for the New World', Kevin Bales (1999: 250) remarks, but, he continues, it has evolved and transmuted – the 'modern version uses false passports and airline tickets. It packs slaves into trucks and bribes border guards. It covers its tracks with false work contracts and fraudulent visas'. The solution, Bales says, is tighter border controls and more intensive policing which will allow 'slaves' to be identified and rescued, and work to drive the 'slavers' out of business. If there really were a contemporary version of the transatlantic slave trade through which millions of people were being kidnapped, forcibly moved and then sold into slavery, this might sound a reasonable plan of action. But there is no such contemporary trade.

As defined in the UN trafficking protocol (2000), 'trafficking' does not refer to a single, unitary act leading to one specific outcome, but is rather an umbrella term to cover a *process* (recruitment, transportation and control) that can be organized in a variety of ways and involve a range of different actions and outcomes (Anderson and O'Connell Davidson, 2003). Of itself, this makes 'trafficking' a vague and elastic concept. But the fact that it seeks to describe a process, not an event, introduces a temporal element that further complicates it. Indeed, herein lies an important difference between what is described as 'trafficking' and the transatlantic slave trade. Though there are some documented cases in which people have been kidnapped and moved against their will, then brutally exploited; in the vast majority of cases described as 'trafficking', the individuals concerned actively wanted to migrate and invariably had excellent reasons for wishing to do so. The same cannot be said of the Africans transported to the New World as chattel slaves between the fifteenth and nineteenth centuries. It required overwhelming physical force to move them there.

In fact, at the point of departure, the story of 'trafficking' and that of transatlantic slavery could not be more different. There are no modern equivalents of the many fortresses and castles that dotted the Western coast of African slave trading regions, in which people destined for New World slavery were held in dungeons, sometimes for periods of weeks, before being loaded and shackled on slave ships. Those described as Victims of Trafficking (VoTs) very rarely set off on their journey as Olaudah Equiano did, hoping 'that death would soon put an end to my miseries' (1999: 34). Today, whether people are queuing outside recruitment offices in the hope of an opportunity to work abroad, gladly accompanying recruitment brokers on journeys to cities or farms or mines where they have been offered jobs, setting off to the airport armed with their fake travel documents, climbing atop freight trains or waiting for word from a boat owner who has agreed to take them across the Mediterranean, we are not talking about human beings snatched, manacled and transported as *objects*. We are talking about people moving as *subjects*, albeit subjects whose choices are framed by the limited alternative options open to them.

Very often, those described as VoTs are depicted as naïve and gullible dupes. Yet evidence on the forms of migration that carry the greatest risks of exploitation and abuse suggests that migrants are frequently well aware of the dangers, but choose to proceed nonetheless. Consider the many people from Sub-Saharan African countries, Syria and Palestine currently waiting at the North African coast to make extraordinarily dangerous journeys to get to Europe (Andersson, 2014a; Stock, 2013). Journalists and politicians often describe those who die as 'trafficked' (those who survive the journey are more likely to be named 'smuggled' persons or 'illegal immigrants'). They generally know the risks, which have recently increased exponentially as a consequence of policies adopted by the EU border agency, Frontex, to make entry to Europe more difficult, coupled, since November 2014, with the scaling back of search and rescue efforts funded by the European Commission (Crawley, 2015). Despite the many tragic and widely publicized shipwrecks, and immense loss of life, migrants continue to be willing pay large sums to people who promise to facilitate their movement. As a young Albanian man who had made the almost equally dangerous sea crossing to Italy a decade earlier told Maurizio Albahari (2006: 27), 'I had finished my studies, what should I have done stuck in Vlorë? My life, sitting all day in a café doing nothing, was not worth living, so I crossed, even if I knew people had died in the attempt'. For the many migrants currently stuck in Libya, the alternatives are even bleaker (HRW, 2014).

People's willingness to take such risks connects to two other significant differences between the transatlantic slave trade and the forms of movement today discussed under the banner 'trafficking'. First, where being carried to the New World as a slave inevitably led to an utterly appalling outcome, migration (whether through irregular channels with fake documents or through state sanctioned channels with legitimate contracts and visas) does not. Instead, it is very often associated with highly positive outcomes, which is precisely why people actively choose to migrate. Second, where victims of the transatlantic slave trade were generally doomed to lifelong exile and enslavement, even amongst those contemporary migrants for whom things go most badly wrong, it is rare to find instances of their being permanently locked into a slavery-like relationship with a 'trafficker', creditor or employer.

The fact that the experience of harsh labour, heavy restraints on freedoms and sometimes also violence is usually time-limited rather than perpetual does not make it any the less morally or politically wrong, but it does make a difference to those weighing up their alternatives. Some, like the 'free-willers' who entered into seven-year-long contracts of indenture in the colonies in the seventeenth and eighteenth centuries, will proceed even knowing the costs and dangers. Paying third parties to assist with unauthorized migration, and/or to arrange travel and employment in another country or region may be taking a risk, but for many people, there are also risks associated with *not* moving (sometimes even absolute certainties about the extremely negative consequences that will attend on immobility), and risks are always balanced against the potential gain if the gamble pays off.

Dominant discourse on 'trafficking as modern slavery' glosses over the start of the story, skipping quickly to the point at which the victim finds herself trapped and abused at the point of destination. But if we look more closely at the scene of departure, and think about the fact we are almost always talking about people who *want* to move, it should lead us to question the simple, neat narrative that unfolds again and again in anti-trafficking campaign materials and political rhetoric (Molland, 2012). Admitting the desire for movement shifts the backdrop to the tale. Instead of continuing the history of chattel slavery (which everyone now agrees was wrong), it moves us onto much more difficult and contested political territory: that of state control over human mobility. In fact, as this chapter sets out to show, if we want to find a historical parallel between the experience of many of today's international migrants and that of transatlantic chattel slaves, we would do better to focus our attention on the attempted and actual movement of people seeking to escape *from* chattel slavery, than on their transportation *into* it. Here, the continuities are much more evident and they arise from the correspondence between structures and mechanisms set in place by slave and colonial states historically, and those employed by states today, to control and manage the mobility of groups deemed to be outsiders and subpersons.

## Freedom of movement and state control of mobility

Mobility is fundamental to human life. The basic human need and desire to move is one of the reasons why, when injury, impairment, illness or old age restrict our mobility, we consider ourselves disabled; why imprisonment, and even house arrest, implies such a profound and terrifying punishment; and why 'false imprisonment' is considered such a serious crime. The right to freedom of movement is enshrined in Article 13 of the Universal Declaration of Human Rights, while Article 12 of the International Covenant on Civil and Political Rights provides that 'Everyone lawfully within the territory of a State shall, within that territory, have the right to liberty of movement and freedom to choose his residence', and that 'Everyone shall be free to leave any country, including his own'. In this and other international covenants and treaties dealing with freedom of movement, we see a recognition that, while the range of different individuals' movement may vary, mobility is everywhere, and has always been, an integral and essential part of people's economic, social, cultural and political lives (Anderson, 2013).

However, human mobility has long been perceived as having another face, in particular one that threatens state sovereignty. It is not just the mobilization of foreign armies and violent seizure of political power that is regarded as a potential threat, but also the mobility of subordinate groups within a given territory that could potentially allow them to evade the control of a sovereign power, or subvert the social order it seeks to impose. Thus, states have historically had an interest in preventing exodus and fixing those under their rule to a given geographical and social place, and/or forcibly exiling those who refuse to remain immobilized, hence the deployment of measures such as the laws on vagabondage, vagrancy and transportation mentioned in Chapter 3. Hence, too, the restrictions on women's freedom of movement that will be discussed in Chapter 7, measures that help to prevent women from breaking out of patriarchal family structures endorsed by the state. Indeed, Papadopoulos et al. (2008: 43) argue that it is precisely the human agency expressed in the capacity to move, to escape, take flight, desert (also in acts of subversion, refusal and sabotage, or simply to act 'beyond or independently of existing political structures of power') that prompts the sovereign power to devise such mechanisms of control.

In the context of the historical movement towards a market, capitalist society in England, what Bridget Anderson describes as the coalescence of 'authority, bureaucracy, and violence' that embodies state control of human mobility was focused on the movement of the poor, the sovereign's own subjects (2013: 21). These are the restrictions on free movement that are addressed in the international human rights declarations and covenants mentioned above. By contrast, the state's right to regulate and control the entrance of aliens, discussed in the previous chapter, continues to be vigorously asserted by state actors, and defended by a range of thinkers. However, in claiming the right to authorize or deny people entrance onto its territory, the state *produces* 'illegal' immigration (De Genova, 2002; Düvell, 2011; Samers, 2003). Human mobility is an existent phenomenon – people can and do move – but 'illegal immigration' and 'legal immigration' have no prior ontological existence. Nor do the many categories that are used to subdivide them ('asylum seeking', 'smuggling', 'trafficking', 'temporary labour migration', 'migration for family reunion' and so on). These are social, political and legal constructs that reflect states' systems for classifying human movement rather than ethnographically or experientially meaningful differences between different forms of mobility.

For this, amongst other reasons, it would be as facile to equate any one 'type' of contemporary migration with the movement of slaves who sought to escape slave states as it is to equate any one 'type' with the transatlantic slave trade. Though some migrants today are fleeing to escape threats that were also faced by slaves (including torture, execution, starvation or indefinite detention in labour camps), migration – whether legally sanctioned by states or not – is rarely simply driven by 'push' factors. Instead, migration scholars argue it is the outcome of an extremely complex interplay between macro-level structures, micro-level institutions and individual agency. Broader social, economic and political structures provide the context in which individuals and groups decide whether or not to migrate, but their decisions are strongly influenced by their own personal histories, identities and resources; their connections with social networks in a destination country (family, friends or community that will assist with finding accommodation, employment and so on); and by the extent to which out-migration from their country or region is institutionalized (Anderson, 2013; Kofman et al., 2000; Massey et al., 1993).

However, so far as those who contemporary immigration laws and regulations are primarily designed to control are concerned (which is to say, those who are not wealthy, who are not nationals of affluent countries and/or who belong to racial groups deemed incompatible with 'national attributes'), it is possible to identify one commonality with fugitive transatlantic slaves. Slaves who sought to escape to 'free' states, or territory where they could not be held in slavery, were willing to face the enormous risks implied by running away because they knew, or thought they knew, that their status and life-chances would be radically improved by the move. Likewise, many people who today aspire to migrate to more affluent and economically developed nations (or regions within their own country) regard migration as a strategy to pursue goals and advance plans that would be very difficult or impossible to realize without moving. Today, these goals may include travel itself and for its own sake, since the desire for adventure, diversion, and to see something of the world are factors that contribute not just to affluent Western gap-year students' eagerness to travel, but also to that of less privileged young people in developing countries (Alpes, 2011; Andersson, 2014a; Esson, 2015).

Yet there are massive asymmetries between the opportunities for legally authorized migration open to those from poorer countries and those from more affluent nations (Neumayer, 2006), and:

> Across the world, national states, especially in what the *Economist* likes to call the 'rich world,' are imposing ever more restrictive immigration policies. Such state efforts are being enacted at precisely the time when migration has become an increasingly important part of people's strategies for gaining access to much-needed life resources.
>
> (Anderson et al., 2011: 5)

Many of those wishing to move therefore seek ways to evade these restrictions, and there are some very obvious points of comparison between the techniques designed by slave states to thwart slaves' ambitions in regard to unauthorized movement, and those employed by states (including liberal democratic states) to prevent 'illegal' migration today.

## Controlling slave mobility

Though slaves were constructed as 'things' in the sense of being treated as property, they nonetheless remained human beings. The 'double character' of the slave as property *and* person, object *and* subject, presented slaveholders with problems that they did not face with regard to their property in inanimate objects and non-human animals. One of these problems concerned mobility. While slaves could not 'walk free', escape – or *marronage* – was a 'surprisingly frequent reaction to slavery in the Americas' (Price, 1979: 1; Heuman, 1986). The ever-present risk that their property would take flight meant slaveholders had strong interests in controlling slave mobility. Yet it was not in their interests literally to imprison slaves. A slave held permanently captive in a dungeon would not be a productive asset. Nor was it always in slaveholders' interests physically to constrain slaves' mobility by means of balls and chains and other such instruments. It was instead, to varying degrees, expedient for owners to permit slaves certain forms of movement.

Slaveholders in the New World often relied on their slaves to run errands and transport produce; they sometimes wanted to set them to work on farmland at a distance from home; they also often hired their slaves out, or required slaves to hire themselves out, even to seek new masters when the owner wished to sell them; sometimes they required slaves to accompany and serve them on their own travels. At many times and in many places, Sunday was customarily a day when slaves did not have to labour at their normal duties, but were expected instead to perform tasks necessary to the reproduction of their own labour-power: to wash and mend clothes, to go hunting wild game, to tend their provision plots, to make their own cooking and eating utensils, to perform paid work elsewhere furnishing them with the money to buy small necessities of life, and so on (Ball, 2014; Beckles, 1987; Bibb, 2008; Blackburn, 2011; Camp, 2004; Douglass, 1986; Henson, 2008; Mason, 1893).

For all these reasons, it was to owners' advantage to allow (some) slaves a certain level of mobility. But this ran alongside an equally strong interest in repressing other forms of movement. As individuals, slaveholders were seldom in a position to manage their contradictory interests in slave mobility. Indeed, though slaves were legally con-structed as private property, slaveholding was far from a private matter. Most slaveholders in most places and at most times were utterly reliant upon the political community to legally enshrine and daily repro-duce their effective property rights in slaves – 'Lawmakers created the state-backed principles of restraint that criminalized and enclosed slave movement' (Camp, 2004: 16). For example, the Barbados Slave Code of 1661 was revised in 1688 to introduce a pass system, making it manda-tory for slaves to carry a pass or ticket when leaving their plantation. It also placed the burden of policing this system on *all* white men, requiring them 'to give wandering slaves with no ticket a sound whip-ping, and detain them til the owner could retrieve them' (Beckles, 1987; Hadden, 2001: 11).

South Carolina mimicked the Barbados Code, introducing a curfew for all slaves and a pass system for all travel and trading in 1687, laws which remained in place until 1865. From 1690, it became a white man's legal duty to capture and return runaways. Over time, colony-sanctioned patrols to 'monitor slave movement and behavior' emerged and again, whiteness implied an obligation on men to take part in patrols, whether or not they owned slaves (Hadden, 2001: 38). Harbouring runaway slaves was criminalized (Camp, 2004). Even white people who were not residents of the colony were under legal compulsion to support the effort to control slaves' mobility. From 1642 in Virginia, ship cap-tains were prohibited from setting sail with passengers who had no pass, for example (Hadden, 2001). Here and elsewhere, a series of extremely punitive sanctions were introduced against captains and owners of ves-sels found carrying fugitive slaves to freedom (Ogden, 1858), as well as against anyone offering succour and assistance to fugitive slaves as they made long, difficult and extremely dangerous journeys by foot, laws that remained in place until abolition (Camp, 2004).

In the American context, the duty of third parties to return runaway slaves to their owners extended beyond the boundaries of individual slave states and was formalized in the original US Constitution. Though slavery was a divisive issue amongst delegates to the Constitutional Convention of 1787, with some recognizing the contradiction between the fact of slavery, and the representation of the American Revolution as a movement based on the 'self-evident' truth that 'all men are created equal', ultimately, none were 'inclined to jeopardize the "species of property" that accounted for nearly 60 percent of the entire wealth of the southern states' (Lubet, 2010: 9). A number of provisions that protected slaveholding were therefore approved by the Convention, including the Fugitive Slave Clause, which stated that:

> No Person held to Service or Labour in one State, under the Laws thereof, escaping into another, shall, in Consequence of any Law or Regulation therein, be discharged from such Service or Labour, but shall be delivered up on Claim of the Party to whom such Service or Labour may be due.
>
> (cited in Best, 2004: 80)

Though the clause vividly illuminated the contradiction at the heart of chattel slavery (can property steal itself? And if not, what, precisely, was criminal in slaves' fugitivity? Best, 2004), it was subsequently reinforced through further statutes passed by the US Congress, and by the Fugitive Slave Act of 1850. The latter reinforced a view of the federal state as having no right to meddle with individual states' decisions as to the morality or wisdom of slavery, but at the same time having a crucial role to play in ensuring that the property rights of slaveholders were upheld across the entire union (Lubet, 2010). For the fugitive slave subject to such law, rendition implied not merely being returned to slavery as property, but potentially also to face criminal sanctions as a person. Punishments provided in law for captured runaways included whipping, stocking, ear cropping and other mutilations.

The meaning of this legal edifice for those who sought to escape chattel slavery is chillingly described in many fugitive slave narratives. Consider, for instance, Frederick Douglass' account of his reflections when contemplating (an ultimately unsuccessful) plan to escape with a number of his fellow slaves:

Our path was beset with the greatest obstacles... At every gate through which we were to pass, we saw a watchman – at every ferry a guard – on every bridge a sentinel – and in every wood a patrol. We were hemmed in upon every side (1986: 123).

Solomon Northup described his situation having run away from his owner as follows:

Not provided with a pass, any white man would be at liberty to arrest me, and place me in prison until such time as my master should 'prove property, pay charges, and take me away'. I was astray, and if so unfortunate as to meet a law abiding citizen of Louisiana, he would deem it his duty to his neighbour, perhaps, to put me forthwith in the pound. Really, it was difficult to determine which I had most reason to fear – dogs, alligators, or men! (2012: 87).

The journey to freedom was often across harsh physical terrain, and usually without benefit of map or geographical knowledge. For example, following the 1848 Treaty of Guadalupe Hidalgo many slaves from Texas sought to cross the border into Mexico, where slavery had been abolished in 1829, but:

the route to Mexico was difficult and hazardous... Some [slaves] fought against armed slave-hunting parties... Others had to combat loyal slaves who tried to prevent their fellow blacks from running away. If the [slaves] did escape into the semi-desert regions, further hardships awaited. Few slaves knew the route to Mexico. They often got lost and had to risk their freedom to ask directions... Even if the former slaves knew the direction to Mexico, they might be captured by the nomadic Comanches or Apaches, who roamed the semi-desert regions of the state.

(Tyler, 1972: 3)

One conclusion to which all of this points is that the new abolitionists' focus on slavery as a relationship between *individuals* is of limited utility in understanding the nature and meaning of slavery in the New World. Slaveholders were only able to hold vast numbers of people in slavery because they enjoyed the backing of a legal system that sanctioned their violent domination, enforced slaves' dependence upon their owners and savagely suppressed resistance to their owners' control. It took states to construct a framework that simultaneously penned (most) slaves in *and* allowed them to circulate as both commodities and workers. And the basic structure of this framework was not unique to slavery, nor did the abolition of slavery spell an end to any such framework.

## Blocking escape: rewind

New World slave societies were not the first to find it necessary to simultaneously and differentially allow, but control, human movement in order to preserve a hierarchically structured social and political order. In feudal European societies, the ambition to fix the lowly in their social and geographic place as serfs and servants did not imply an absolute prohibition on all forms of movement. Pilgrimages (including military pilgrimages or crusades) were tolerated, and this legitimated certain forms of nomadism: 'Nomads referred to themselves – in order to legitimise their mobility – as pilgrims from Egypt, which in English then became "gypsies". These were often joined by others who were then referred to as "counterfayte Egyptians", as bogus or disguised "gypsies"' (Papadopoulos et al., 2008: 44). Such 'bogus' pilgrims were seen to belong to the ranks of paupers and 'vagabonds' whose movement was to be suppressed.

In Elizabethan England, recognition that it was both necessary and desirable to allow some of the 'deserving' poor to move and to beg, albeit in certain prescribed ways, ran alongside the strong desire to fix the 'able-bodied' to the parish where they 'belonged' and set them to labour there. Thus, from 1530 on, while providing harsh punishments for the able-bodied, the law allowed those who had suffered losses by fire or at sea, and poor soldiers and sailors returning from wars, to be licensed to travel and beg within certain geographical limits, or along specified routes home. University vice-chancellors could even license scholars to beg during vacations (Aydelotte, 1913: 24). It was those moving and begging without licenses who were to be whipped or stocked, then forced to labour in their own parish. With a view to ensuring that 'idlers' met their just deserts, the Privy Council issued directions to Justices of the Peace in all the shires requiring them to set up watches and punish vagabonds, then give them passports 'discretely written and sealed so as to be difficult to counterfeit' and direct them home (Aydelotte, 1913: 64).

We might further note that it was the ambition to prevent the free movement of an unwanted population (vagabonds and vagrants) that led to their forcible transportation to the colonies. The system of passes and patrols adopted initially to control the movement of indentured servants and debtors, as well as transported criminals and slaves in the colonies in the seventeenth century (later developed to restrain the mobility of larger slave populations), replicated those previously employed at home to manage the movement of the poor and 'indigent' (Hadden, 2001; Waldstreicher, 2004). This apparatus of control has been updated and chattel slaves are no longer its object. But its basic principles, mechanisms and violent disregard for human life remain unchanged.

## Blocking escape: fast forward

Dwindling opportunities for legally authorized international migration has prompted the expansion and diversification of markets for clandestine migration services (Alpes, 2011; Kempadoo et al., 2005). These markets are widely viewed by state actors as constituting a significant and serious threat to state sovereignty and security, but they are not all compared to the transatlantic slave trade. As noted in Chapter 1, the UN Convention on Transnational Organized Crime maintained the statist division between 'good' (state authorized) and 'bad' (unauthorized) movement, but added a new twist by subdividing the 'bad' into 'smuggling' and 'trafficking', with only the latter being described as a form of 'modern slavery'. 'Trafficking', as much as 'smuggling' is an illegal activity, but 'trafficked persons' are said not to be complicit in the crime. Because they are 'victims', they are deemed entitled to certain forms of protection and assistance, in the same way that those who seek or have been granted asylum are understood to warrant protective treatment that is not available to other categories of migrant.

The moral obligation to fight the contemporary equivalent of the transatlantic slave trade is frequently presented as the justification for stepping up efforts to prevent unauthorized movement *per se*. The measures employed to this end in Europe, North America and Australia since the 1990s have been increasingly high-tech, but they are also familiar. In place of slave patrols comprised of men with horses and dogs, unmanned aerial vehicles (UAVs) or drones are used to monitor the borders of the United States and Europe, 'providing aerial surveillance support for border agents by investigating sensor activity in remote areas... allowing the boots on the ground force to best allocate their resources and efforts' (Unmanned, 2012). In the 2000s, new surveillance systems, such as SIVE (*sistema integrado de vigilancia exterior*) that 'combines radar, high-tech cameras, and patrols' (Andersson, 2014a: 85), were introduced to monitor Southern Europe's coastlines, along with

X-ray technology used to scan commercial trucks at ports 'to detect carbon dioxide and heart beats, thus indicating the presence of migrants' (Albahari, 2006: 10).

In a move reminiscent of the system of fines and confiscations imposed on sea captains who helped slaves to escape from the American South, the 1990s witnessed European Union (EU) states introducing 'sanctions against carriers transporting passengers without the proper documents'. In France, for example, fines of FF10,000 per person were imposed on firms that conveyed undocumented migrants onto French territory (Samers, 2003: 563). From 2005, the EU stepped up its fight against all forms of 'illegal immigration' through the strengthening and integration of such carrier sanctions, shifting 'the burden of responsibility for irregular migration to the businesses' (Düvell and Vollmer, 2011: 9). Just as defending the property rights of slave owners in slave states of the United States demanded federal action in the form of laws concerning the rendition of fugitive slaves, so defending EU member states' sovereignty in terms of controlling who is admitted on their territory is understood to require federal measures and cross union cooperation in relation to border control. In 2000, the Eurodac fingerprint system was introduced, which enables all EU member states (EUMS) 'to identify asylum applicants and persons who have been apprehended in connection with an irregular crossing of an external border of the Union or of the territory of another EUMS' (Duvell and Vollmer, 2011: 10), a technology that would no doubt have been much appreciated by Elizabethan Justices as an aid to monitoring and dispensing justice to vagabonds, just as slave states would surely have welcomed the surveillance technologies described above, along with all the other features of the European Union's 'electronic curtain'.

From the 2000s, the European Union also began externalizing its 'immigration control and Schengen border enforcement to "gatekeepers" and "buffer states" through bilateral agreements, visa regimes, carrier sanctions, military training and the establishment of migration detention facilities' (Albahari, 2006: 20). In essence, this means member states using their political and economic power to encourage non-EU neighbours (especially North and West African states) to undertake certain control functions on their behalf. This includes migrant-holding and 'processessing' (as, for instance, in the Italian government's unofficial involvement in the mid-2000s in 'financing the construction of three detention camps in Libya as well as deportations of "irregular" migrants from Libya further to Sub-Saharan Africa and Egypt', Andrijasevic, 2006: 121). It also means extending the reach of the new technologies of surveillance and expanding 'transnational policing networks around the figure of the illegal immigrant' – One such high-tech venture funded by the EU, the Seahorse Project, 'had by 2010 pulled in Spain, Portugal, Mauritania, Cape Verde, Senegal, the Gambia, Guinea-Bissau and Morocco' (Andersson, 2014a: 82).

Next we might note that, as Slave Codes historically obliged all white citizens to police the movement of slaves, so increasingly in the UK, the entire community is being mustered to monitor unauthorized movement, with employers, universities and now private landlords all under a legal obligation to check the status of migrants and report those suspected of living in the country without authorization, or breaking the terms on which they have been permitted to enter. Perhaps the next step will be to institute an organization similar to the Malaysian Volunteer Corps, RELA, which was in 2005 granted powers to arrest irregular migrants, and now has over two-and-a-half million registered members:

> From 1 March 2005 to 31 December 2009, RELA personnel arrested 111,852 immigrants . . . There have been many complaints about the way that RELA conduct raids, with reports of them destroying valid identity documents and using unnecessary violence. Non-citizens have reported extortion, stealing and manhandling during arrests.
>
> (Nah, 2012: 500)

It is also noteworthy that the Immigration Act in Malaysia was amended in 2002, 'introducing whipping of between one to six strokes for those who enter Malaysia illegally . . . as well as for those who employ more than five non-citizens without a valid Pass' (Nah, 2012: 500).

Corporal punishments are not administered to irregular migrants in the EU, the United States or Australia. But their border policies are often deadly. The IOM (2014) recently issued a report estimating that more than 40,000 migrants had died between 2000 and 2013 in the course of 'irregular' movement, nearly 6,000 along the US–Mexico border (see also O'Leary, 2008), and 22,000 on the borders of the EU, mostly in the Mediterranean sea. Between 1993 and 2012, the organization United for Intercultural Action documented 17,306 deaths of refugees and migrants attributable 'to border militarisation, asylum laws, detention policies, deportations and carrier sanctions' in Europe (UNITED, 2012); between 2000 and 2014, the Australian Border Deaths Database recorded 1,969 deaths at the Australian frontier (Border Crossing Observatory, 2015). Clearly, as with estimates about the scale of 'trafficking', estimates of deaths related to border controls need to be treated with caution.

However, determining whether or not a person is dead does not require subjective judgement in the way that determining whether or not a person is a VoT does, and it is incontrovertibly the case that the border securitization policies described above, enacted with the goal of preventing unauthorized migrants and asylum seekers from entering the territory of the EU, Australia and the United States, have lethal consequences – and are known to have lethal consequences – but are pursued nonetheless (Albahari, 2006: 20).

The loss of life is often blamed on 'traffickers' and 'smugglers' (of which more below), but state actors are sometimes directly responsible, as in the recent case of the 11 migrants who drowned in February 2014 after Spanish police fired rubber bullets at the rickety boat in which they were making their way from Morocco to the Spanish enclave of Ceuta (Amnesty International, 2014). United for Intercultural Action estimates that in Europe, almost 10 per cent of the deaths of irregular migrants they list can be attributed to police or border guard actions (UNITED, 2012). In October 2014, the British Government announced that the UK would no longer contribute to search and rescue operations in the Mediterranean. Its spokespeople defended the move as necessary to deter 'illegal' migrants from embarking on treacherous voyages, a proposition, Ruben Andersson (2014b) commented, 'as absurd as removing seatbelts in cars to make drivers more risk-averse ... Maritime "migration management" now reeks with the politics of death'. The hypocrisy is made all the more repulsive, and all the starker, when this move is set alongside the same government's much vaunted concern with the fate of 'modern slaves'. If 'trafficking' is today's slave trade, why are the migrants who drown in the Mediterranean not the contemporary equivalents of the slaves thrown overboard by the crew of the slave ship *Zong* in 1781 (Rupprecht, 2007)? Migrants' agency moves conveniently in and out of politicians' sight, it seems.

The project of preventing unauthorized migration is fundamentally incompatible with that of protecting and promoting human rights, and this is so even where concern is limited to a small number of groups whose particular 'vulnerabilities' are recognized as entitling them to special protection, namely, VoTs, children and asylum seekers. At the point of departure, the so-called smuggled and the so-called trafficked all want to move, and they include amongst their number children and people fleeing persecution and seeking refuge on grounds that are deemed legitimate in relevant international law. The current border regime operates indiscriminately on all these groups. Those who are children, asylum seekers and 'potential victims of trafficking' (and one person may be all three), as well as those who are not, drown in the Mediterranean, suffocate in lorries, are blown apart by landmines, fall under the trains to which they cling and die of thirst in deserts. Their deaths are not the result of acts of private individuals operating a slave trade similar to the transatlantic trade, but rather a consequence of the powers claimed by contemporary states over human mobility. Dominant discourse on 'trafficking' also disregards other ways in which the state is a source of harm to large numbers of migrants.

## State-sponsored violence: detention and deportation

Immigration detention refers to 'the deprivation of liberty of noncitizens under aliens' legislation because of their status' and, though not new, it is today being used on an unprecedented scale (Grant, 2011: 69). Immigration detainees do not feature in the new abolitionists' talk of 'modern slaves', yet, like many of the victims of the US penal system described in the previous chapter, they could be said to meet the criteria that the new abolitionists state constitute 'slavery'. They did not choose and cannot 'walk away' from the situation they are in, and they are under the potentially violent control of those who hold them. In Canada, for example:

> Detainees are held in secure facilities with surveillance cameras, guards and metal detectors. The holding centers are equipped with segregation units and solitary confinement for detainees deemed 'uncooperative'... Prohibitive rules abound... Shackles, handcuffs, and leg irons are standard protocol for transportation.
>
> (Walia and Tagore, 2012: 76)

That immigration detainees are vulnerable to physical violence as well as to sexual and racial abuse at the hands of their captors in the UK, the United States, Canada and Australia, as well as elsewhere in the world, is now well documented (Doherty, 2015a, 2015b; HRW, 2010; HRW, 2014; Townsend, 2013). Immigration detainees are frequently held in remote and isolated locations, and moved between such locations without warning, making it difficult for families, friends and lawyers to maintain contact with them (Mountz, 2012). The effects of such 'dispersal' policies are to alienate the detainee from her or his community, family and support networks. Migrants held in civil detention in the United States have no right to a government-appointed attorney. The organization Just Detention states that only about 16 per cent have legal representation and observes that the Department of Homeland Security, which oversees the detention of immigrants, also proceeds to determine their legal status and whether or not they are to be deported: 'If this were taking place within the criminal justice system, it would be as if the jailors of a man awaiting trial were then to serve as his judge and jury' (Kaiser and Stannow, 2011). In the UK, too, a country that proportionally confines the most asylum seekers for the longest periods of time in all of Europe, migrants held in detention have fewer rights and protections than do citizen offenders (Bosworth and Guild, 2008). And just as one of the horrors of the system of transatlantic slavery (and that of the workhouse) was the wrenching apart of families, so immigration detention and the practices of deportation routinely destroy family life (Golash-Boza, 2012; Rosas, 2012; see also Madziva, 2010).

The illegalization of particular forms of movement has, in general, become a vast industry (Andersson, 2014a) and within this, depriving non-citizens of their liberty is an activity that generates significant profits for the many private companies involved in the provision of 'security' services and the construction and management of immigration detention centres. Immigration detention is an important segment of the 'prison industrial complex', and in the US alone, migrants' rights organizations estimate that it generates profits of US$5 billion per year (Cuentame, 2012). In the context of high demand generated by the crackdown on 'illegal immigration' under the Bush regime from 2004 on, Corrections Corporation of America, the US' leading private prison company, 'has been able to charge as much as $95 per detainee per day in some facilities' (Feltz and Baksh, 2012: 145).

In the UK, as well, the management of detention centres (as well as prisons) is increasingly outsourced to global private security companies such as G4S and Serco. Indeed, G4S, Serco, Sodexo, and other private security firms have come to dominate detention, transport and escort services for irregular migrants and asylum seekers (and in 2010, 773 complaints were lodged against G4S by immigration detainees including 48 claims of assault) (Grayson, 2012). Without bodies to hold and process, there would be no profit for these private companies to secure, and since immigration detainees function as the raw materials of this 'labour process', they are arguably subject to 'severe economic exploitation'. Some immigration detainees are, in addition, subject to labour exploitation. In the UK, migrants whose immigration status denies them any and all access to the labour market, and who may in fact end up in detention because they have not complied with this rule, can – once detained – 'be paid to work in the detention centre that is holding them' (Anderson, 2013: 78). The labour they perform is of the type that, when undertaken in prison, Zatz (2008: 870) terms 'prison house-work'. They serve food, clean and launder, paint rooms and generally contribute to 'the provision of services internal to the detention centre, most of which are managed by large corporations', and pay rates are either £1.00 per hour, for routine work, or £1.25 for specified projects (Anderson, 2013: 78). A 2014 Corporate Watch report suggests that by employing detainees at these well-below minimum wage rates, Serco, G4S, Mitie and GEO could have saved themselves more than £2.8 million (Rawlinson, 2014). Similarly, in the United States it is reported that the use of immigration detainees' labour 'saves the government and the private companies US$40 million or more a year by allowing them to avoid paying outside contractors the $7.25 federal minimum wage' (Urbina, 2014). Some detainees are paid 13 cents an hour, others 'held at county jails work for free, or are paid with sodas or candy bars, while also providing services like meal preparation for other government institutions' (Urbina, 2014).

Release from detention rarely spells anything like freedom. Some-times it implies deportation – often referred to as 'administrative removal' or 'repatriation' in immigration speak, but in reality usually a form of forced movement across borders (Anderson, 2013; Andersson, 2014a), and one that can also have deadly results (as, for example, in the case of the growing number of 'young Honduran males who are attacked, killed or simply disappear after being deported from the United States or Mexico', UNHCR, 2015). In the UK, immigration detainees are frequently released rather than deported, often due to the Home Office's inability to complete the administrative procedures nec-essary for removal. Axel Klein and Lucy Williams (2012) note that most former detainees remain destitute and without entitlement or resolu-tion of their immigration cases, and are often required to wear electronic tags (mostly around their ankles) as a condition of release. The tag is an uncomfortable, unbreakable plastic ring, 'remotely connected to a con-trol box inside a bedroom that is linked to a telephone centre', again operated by private contractors (2012: 746).

This 'electronic wizardry' has, Klein and Williams argue, 'created a physical mark of distinction reminiscent of pre-modern acts of ritual shaming,' one that 'adds insult to the far more degrading denial of basic rights'. The rights from which released detainees are excluded include freedom of movement (curfew regimes 'bind people to particular houses'); freedom to work (they are not even allowed to work as volun-teers); and freedom to manage their own maintenance and affairs – they are not allowed to find ways to make savings from the 'meagre income strictly earmarked for subsistence' (Klein and Williams, 2012: 747). Citing Meillassoux, Klein and Williams observe that the former detainee, like the slave, is not only 'marked by an original, indelible defect which weighs endlessly upon his destiny', but also reduced to the bare life of physical survival as described by Agamben (1995). They continue:

> the status of the undocumented immigrant is similar to the Roman concept of homo sacer, as a person outside the protection of the law. Even more than homo sacer, we think that a useful analogy is found in the Middle Ages' legal concept of 'civil death' or 'attainder' (the corruption of the blood). Civil death is the emulation of natural death through depriving mostly convicts of rights to transmit property or title or to perform any civic function.
>
> (2012: 750)

As with the laws of Southern slave states that could simultaneously recognize slaves as willing selves as regards criminal culpability *and* as objects of property, former immigration detainees are affected by the disabling power 'inherent in a legal action that invents a personality only to exclude it' (Dayan, 2010: 43; cited in Klein and Williams, 2012: 749). They are recognized as human beings in the sense that UK law admits a duty on the part of the state to keep them physically alive (as opposed to treating them in the manner of stray dogs), but refused the core elements of the bundle of rights and freedoms that make flesh and blood human beings into persons in contemporary UK society. As Klein and Williams (2012: 750) conclude:

> The creation of this particular class of people with a social and legal position that contains elements of slavery and civil death has profound implications for social relations in the UK and for our understandings of the role of the state. The air of England may still be too pure for slaves, but it is rank enough to strip away the civil rights of some and lock them into a permanent state of structural exclusion.

Klein and Williams are not arguing that former immigration detainees *are* 'modern slaves', and neither would I wish to describe immigration detainees and/or unauthorized migrants as such. As John Park (2013) observes, comparing contemporary unauthorized migration to slavery, or twenty-first-century 'illegal' migrants to nineteenth-century chattel slaves would 'tend to become a voluminous and ultimately ridiculous exercise. The forced migration of millions of Africans, their enslavement over several generations, and the many attendant horrors of American slavery are distinct historical realities that militate against any such comparison'. Indeed, this is precisely the problem that those who compare what they describe as 'trafficking' to the transatlantic slave trade run into. My point is rather that it is as easy, if not easier, to identify similarities between the condition of irregular migrants and immigration detainees and that of transatlantic slaves as it is to identify parallels between the situation of transatlantic slaves and those dubbed 'modern slaves' by the new abolitionists. Yet issues such as the economic value extracted from immigration detainees, the state-authorized restraints on migrants' rights and freedoms and violence against migrants sponsored by liberal states do not feature on the new abolitionist campaign agenda.

## Slavers, smugglers and saints

The project of preventing unauthorized migration entails the indiscriminate criminalization of all those who assist in it, and in dominant discourse on 'trafficking as a modern slave trade', immorality and criminality is uniformly attributed to all those who assist with irregular travel. This is logical from the perspective of strengthening the state's right to control admission onto its territory. It is not logical if our primary concern is with human rights. It is certainly true that intensification of border control alongside a dramatic reduction of the opportunities available for legal and safe migration has created conditions that can be lucratively exploited. Fees for clandestine migration services are often very high and it is clear that some of those who exploit the politically constructed vulnerability of irregular migrants are, by pretty much any standard, violent criminals. Migrants from Central American countries making their way through Mexico to the United States; and Eritreans seeking to move through Sudan and thence to Israel, for instance, are at risk of kidnap by groups who then hold them hostage and force them to beg family and friends for large amounts of money (Lijnders and Robinson, 2013; Tiano and Murphy-Aguilar, 2012).

But not *all* those who promise help to clandestine migrants are vicious gangsters. Some of those who provide services or assistance do so for entirely altruistic reasons, as in the case of *Las Patronas*, a charitable organization in Mexico set up by women to assist those making the perilous journey through Central America sitting on the roofs of freight trains, hoping to make it to the United States. *Las Patronas* cook for the migrants and throw them packages containing food and drink at a point on the line where the trains slow (Grant, 2014). Similarly, the organization No More Deaths provides food, water and information to migrants attempting to make the desert crossing into the United States, doing so for moral and humanitarian reasons, not for profit. Others may charge fees and gain financially from facilitating migrants' movement, but without employing any violence or trickery. They may, in fact, have a mixture of motives. Albahari (2006: 23) quotes a fisherman in Otranto who told him:

> Why shouldn't I help these disgraziati? [miserables] This is the only way they have to reach the coast and Italy, so I'm providing a service they are grateful for. I ask a little money for the fuel and the risk. You know, the risk of being stopped by a patrol. But in the end, life at sea is dangerous anyway, for me as well as for these refugees.

Those who organize movement may also be people who are trying to get by in circumstances just as difficult as those facing the migrants they assist and exploit. Keo's (2013: 84) study of people imprisoned for 'trafficking' offences in Cambodia, for instance, found that '80 percent of the 427 individuals incarcerated for human trafficking in six prisons between 1997 and 2007 were female', and in a sample of 199 detained traffickers in 2008, 71.4 per cent were females. Keo also found that about 80 per cent of his sample 'were poor, had very limited education, were or had been married, and had large families with five to eight children' (2013: 84).

Those who offer assistance with unauthorized movement span the entire moral spectrum, then. Again, this resonates much more closely with the historical experience of those who sought to escape transatlantic slavery than it does with enslaved Africans' experience of the Middle Passage. Fugitive American slaves, like those who today migrate by irregular channels, were defined by their 'illegality': 'federal law and state rules both described runaway slaves as a legal and political problem until they were returned to their rightful place, their southern masters' (Park, 2013: 3). Those who facilitated their escape were also criminalized. Some of these 'criminals' were well organized – especially the abolitionists, including fugitive slaves, who at enormous personal risk operated what was known as the 'Underground Railroad', and sometimes even ventured into slave states to reach slaves and guide them to safety (Henson, 2008; Still, 2007).

But not everyone who assisted fugitive slaves did so for purely altruistic reasons. Some charged for their services. Slaves attempting the difficult journey to Mexico, for example, were sometimes assisted by

Mexicans living in Texas, also in difficult circumstances, often having crossed the border themselves in the other direction in order to escape a situation of debt peonage in Mexico: 'Running slaves to Mexico was an odd job that migrant Mexicans in West Texas took on at tremendous personal risk, but a few did – putting themselves "at the command of the slave for a small bribe"' (Nichols, 2013: 424). In some cases, those who offered slaves assistance went on to cheat and betray them, or to sell them into indentured servitude in Mexico (Tyler, 1972). In other regions too, slaves could be exploited by those who gave them shelter on their journey, or sold back into slavery in exchange for a reward. They therefore took great risks by placing their trust in a third party (Bibb, 2008; Brown, 1847; Twelvetrees, 1863).

Today, the extraordinary courage and altruism of the women and men who operated the Underground Railway is popularly celebrated, including by our political leaders. In the United States in 2013, official materials were produced to honour Harriet Tubman a century after her death, for instance. In these materials, she is described as 'an American hero who represents the values and principles that this nation was founded on. Born into slavery, Tubman escaped in 1849, yet returned to help others find their freedom' (Florida Department of Education, 2013). She is not described as a 'Human Smuggler'. Yet were Tubman to engage in similar activities today, this is precisely the legal and discursive terrain on which she would find herself.

## Conclusion

Contemporary states' efforts to combat 'trafficking' go hand in glove with their wider actions against 'illegal' migration. But they are invariably presented and discussed as if born of a desire to protect human rights. Possibly the finest example of the contradictions of this discourse is to be found in the US State Department's *Trafficking in Persons* (TIP) Report 2013 country profile for North Korea. The report tells us that North Korea 'is a source country for men, women, and children who are subjected to forced labor, forced marriage, and sex trafficking'. But within North Korea, it notes, forced labour in prison camps 'is part of an established system of political repression', and in such camps:

> all prisoners, including children, are subject to forced labor, including logging, mining, and farming for long hours under harsh conditions. Reports indicate that political prisoners endure severe conditions, including little food or medical care, and brutal punishments; many

are not expected to survive. Many prisoners fall ill or die due to harsh labor conditions, inadequate food, beatings, lack of medical care, and unhygienic conditions.

This sounds very much like the experience of many transatlantic slaves, and as though even an escape that had to be paid for through a time-limited period of coerced labour in almost equally dreadful conditions would be extremely desirable, and potentially life-saving, for many North Koreans.[1] But the TIP Report moves to upbraid the North Korean authorities for being insufficiently attentive to the problem of 'trafficking'. It then remarks:

> While internal conditions in the DPRK have prompted many North Koreans to flee the country in the past, which has made them vulnerable to human trafficking, border security increased during the reporting period, which led to a decrease in the rate of refugees resettled in the Republic of Korea. Nevertheless, there was no evidence that the DPRK government attempted to prevent human trafficking by screening migrants along the border.

That the US State Department should enjoin what it elsewhere describes as a pariah state to more intensively screen migrants along its border, and seemingly welcome its increased border security because, in reducing the numbers of people able to escape, this measure also reduced 'vulnerability to human trafficking', perhaps says everything that needs to be said about the sheer absurdity of anti-trafficking policy and practice from a human rights perspective. If the State Department was to embark on a historical exercise in TIP reporting, it would perhaps have equally strong words for the Southern slave states of, say, 1850, whose failure to entirely seal off all avenues for unauthorized border crossings and seaboard escape left absconding chattel slaves 'vulnerable to human trafficking'.

The measures employed by contemporary states in an effort to immobilize would-be migrants and drive out those who succeed in entering or remaining on their territory without authorization have nothing to do with protecting human rights. They are also ineffective as regards their true objectives. For all the money spent on border surveillance and enforcement, and its staggering human cost, the people who make 'illegal' border crossings constitute but a tiny fraction of 'illegal' migrants in most states. In the UK, for example, 'Illegal entrance is probably a relatively unusual means of becoming an illegal immigrant... Far more typical is entering legally on a visitor or student visa, for example, and staying longer than one has permission for ("overstaying")' (Anderson, 2013: 122). In Spain, 'fewer than 1 percent of those entering the country since 1990 have done so by means of irregular boat migration', Ruben Andersson notes, and 'the majority of Europe's irregular migrants are visa overstayers... The political impact of the "boat people" approaching Europe's southern borders... greatly surpasses their actual numbers' (2014a: 5).

The function served by the brutal and often deadly measures described above is as much spectacular as material (Anderson, 2013; Andersson, 2014a; De Genova, 2013). Governments find it politically expedient to present an image of themselves as able to control and defend the borders of the state, as 'tough on immigration', but the truth is that contemporary states and the elites whose interests they represent can no more afford to close down their borders and hunt down every 'illegal' migrant than transatlantic slaveholders could afford to hold all their slaves securely shackled in dungeons. Human mobility is essential to economic, political and cultural survival and development in today's world, and lines must always be left open to facilitate the forms of movement that are regarded as desirable. Even North Korea has not entirely sealed its border with China, which is what makes escape possible despite the state's efforts to control border crossings. This returns us to the fact that historically, the legal controls over slaves' mobility in the New World, and over that of the poor in England, were designed not only to contain or prevent certain forms of movement but, just as importantly, to facilitate others. This was a double, not a single, project for the state. The following chapter explores discourse on 'forced labour', 'trafficking' and 'modern slavery' against the movement of 'temporary migrant workers' that is sanctioned by states.

# 6
# State Authorized Mobility, Slavery and Forced Labour

When 'human trafficking' first entered the policy stage as an urgent global problem, the emphasis was very much upon the sex sector as the key locus of coercive, violent and exploitative employment relations. Over the past decade, attention has broadened to include what is described as 'labour trafficking' more generally, often discussed by new abolitionists under the heading 'forced labour'. This is a problem said to affect every region of the world and a wide range of sectors, and there is a good deal of research to demonstrate the occurrence of severe labour abuses against migrant workers (internal and international), including violence and confinement, as well as retention of documents and non-payment or the clawing back of wages through exorbitant charges for accommodation, travel, food and so on, in manufacturing, construction, Artisanal and Small Mining (ASM), logging, hospitality, agriculture, fishing, domestic, care and cleaning work, as well as sex work (e.g., ILO, 2005, 2013; Standing, 2011; Dwyer et al., 2011). Cases that have recently grabbed the world's media attention include that of the Bangladeshi strawberry pickers in Greece who were shot by their 'overseers' in 2013 when they attempted to demand the six months' back wages owing to them (Baboulias, 2013), and the condition migrants (mostly from Myanmar, Cambodia and the Lao People's Democratic Republic) working in Thailand's fishing industry, where abuse can even extend to torture and murder to deter and punish escape from captivity (EJF, 2012; HRW, 2010).

The thousands of mostly Nepalese and Indian construction workers present in Qatar as the country readies itself to host the World Cup in 2022 have also been much in the news lately. In 2013, an investigation by the *Guardian* newspaper revealed that the latter were living in overcrowded, filthy hostels, some had had their passports and other documents confiscated, had not been paid, and had been denied access to free drinking water in the desert heat, and had in some cases been violently assaulted when they complained about their treatment (Pattison, 2013). An International Trade Union Confederation report states that 191 Nepalese workers died in 2013 working in Qatar, bringing the total to have died since 2010 (when Qatar won the right to host the World Cup) to 400. Between 2011 and 2013, almost 700 Indian nationals died working in Qatar (Doward, 2014; ITUC, 2014: 14).

Extending the focus of concern to such workers generates a number of conceptual and political problems for anti-trafficking activists and new abolitionists, however. When 'trafficking' is discussed as entailing the forcible movement of women and girls into prostitution, those who fall prey to it are readily imagined as victims, objects and slaves by the general public and by politicians across the political spectrum. Their gender and age means they are already popularly viewed as lacking agency, and prostitution is already popularly viewed as debasing, so that 'sex trafficking' appears to many as a fate 'worse than death' (Peters, 2013). Adult men who undertake 'ordinary', socially sanctioned and 'manly' jobs are much more difficult to squeeze into the mantle of victimhood, and in Western liberal societies, adult males from poorer nations who seek to improve their material situation and life-chances through migration are more likely to be imaginatively dressed in the garb of that new folk-devil, 'the economic migrant', than wrapped in sympathy. Their suffering needs to be extreme and exceptional for them to appear as non-agential objects, the 'supplicant slaves' of anti-slavery iconography (Trodd, 2013).

The emphasis on extreme and exceptional suffering in dominant discourse on 'labour trafficking', 'forced labour' and 'modern slavery' may be an effective means of exciting public concern about those affected but, as I hope to show in this chapter, it also depoliticizes the problems at issue. The anti-slavery movement of the nineteenth century also reflected and produced a vision of the slave as object and 'thing' through its stress on the extreme physical suffering of slaves in its visual and textual imagery of chains, ropes, handcuffs, bars, scourged backs and slave ships (Kempadoo, 2015; Trodd, 2013; Wood, 2010). However, it promulgated this vision with a view to mobilizing political action against chattel slavery as a legal institution, not merely with a view to rescuing individual slaves who were particularly violently abused, or to ameliorating the most inhuman aspects of the system. Today's abolitionists are far less certain about the connections between what they dub 'labour trafficking' or 'forced labour' and the broader systems of labour exploitation in which they are found. Indeed, their primary focus is on the morality of individual employers, creditors or labour-brokers who violently abuse workers, not the structures and systems within which they operate, which are only very selectively questioned. In this respect, they have more in common with the early European critics of transatlantic slavery who called for the amelioration rather than abolition of slavery (see Fergus, 2013), than with their anti-slavery forebears.

## 'Forced labour' and its boundary troubles

The narrow focus on prostitution in 'trafficking' discourse at the millennium was immediately questioned by groups such as the Asian Migrant Centre (2000) and the ILO, that were more generally concerned with labour and human rights. Observing that workers, especially migrant workers, in many other and more economically significant sectors, also often endured extremely harsh and exploitative conditions of labour, and heavy constraints on their freedom of choice and movement, they sought both to extend concerns about 'trafficking' to other forms of work, and to widen the focus of political and policy interest to rights violations experienced by workers whether or not they were 'trafficked'. The ILO launched a global campaign against 'forced labour' and its 2005 report, titled *A Global Alliance against Forced Labour*, estimated that a minimum of 12.3 million people globally were subject to forced labour, of whom around a third were affected by forms of forced labour imposed by the state for economic, political or other purposes, the remainder being forced to work by private actors.

Whilst working with the definition of 'forced labour' originally provided in the ILO Forced Labour Convention of 1930 (Lerche, 2007: 427), the ILO report also fleshed out the definition by identifying a range of possible elements in contemporary expressions of forced labour, including:

- Threats of actual physical or sexual violence.
- Restriction of movement of the worker or confinement to a very limited area.
- Debt bondage, where the worker works to pay off debt. The employer may provide food and accommodation at such inflated prices that it is extremely difficult for the worker to escape the debt.
- Withholding wages or refusing to pay the worker.
- Retention of passports and identity documents.
- Threat of denunciation to the authorities (Dwyer et al., 2011: 5).

As another composite conceptual category, comprised of several different possible elements, not all of which have to present at the same time,
and each of which presents its own definitional problems, the term
'forced labour' is dogged by many of the same difficulties as those that
surround the terms 'trafficking' and 'modern slavery' (Anderson and
Rogaly, 2005; Lerche, 2007; Rogaly, 2008). To classify as 'forced labourers' only those who have not offered themselves voluntarily for work
leaves us with the problem discussed in Chapter 3, namely that contract
can initiate very different relations depending on the regime of rules
that surround it, and in the absence of alternative options, people will
consent to all manner of contracts. Indeed, under certain circumstances,
people may voluntarily offer themselves for work that they know might
imply most or all of the elements of 'forced labour' identified by the ILO,
just as historically there are examples of contexts in which people have
been driven to sell themselves into slavery, to avoid starvation and/or
secure protection from political violence (Patterson, 1982: 130).

Further difficulties arise from the fact that the unpleasant experiences
the ILO groups under the heading 'forced labour' vary in degree as
well as type. This problem is partly recognized by the ILO (2005: 8),
which acknowledges that 'the line dividing forced labour in the strict
legal sense of the term from extremely poor working conditions can
at times be very difficult to distinguish' (see also Dwyer et al., 2011;
Skrivankova, 2010). What tends to be missing even from these more
nuanced accounts is the fact that, as Anderson and Rogaly (2005) have
argued, since workers do not fall neatly into two distinct categories,
determining where on the spectrum the line between 'forced' and 'voluntary' labour lies is a matter of political judgment, and one that must
be made in the context of wide variations between countries and economic sectors in terms of what are socially and legally constructed as
acceptable employment practices.

New abolitionists do not waste time on such conceptual problems,
but simply subsume the term 'forced labour' under the category 'modern slavery'. So, for example, Kevin Bales (2005: 58) states that forced
labour meets his three criteria of slavery (loss of free will; appropriation of labour-power; violence or the threat of violence), and other new
abolitionists follow suit. (We can, in fact, add to the methodological critique of the *Modern Slavery Index* by noting that while violence or its
threat must be present for a worker to meet Walk Free's definition of
'slavery', it need not necessarily be one of the penalties used to menace
a worker who has not voluntarily offered her services in order for that
worker to count as a 'forced labourer' under the ILO definition. Despite

the difference in definitions, Walk Free incorporates the ILO's estimates of the global population of 'forced labourers' into its own estimate of 'modern slaves'.)

Another boundary trouble concerns the non-correspondence between the 'voluntary' versus 'forced' labour binary, and the conceptual and policy division between legal and illegal migration. The ILO report argued that where 'forced labour' involving migrants was concerned, the problem could not be entirely subsumed under the heading of 'trafficking', since even migrants who 'enter destination countries of their own volition, perhaps with the assistance of friends and family members who are already there...can still be highly vulnerable to forced labour exploitation' (2005: 47). The report nonetheless retained a strong emphasis on 'forced labour' as an outcome of irregular migration, and this focus is shared by the new abolitionists (although as will be seen, there are some exceptions to this general rule). It is certainly true that cases in which workers experience the constellation of coercive and exploitative practices that are described as 'forced labour' often do involve people who, in popular parlance, would be termed 'illegal immigrants'. This is not least because, as the ILO (2005) points out, irregular immigration status makes workers reluctant to report maltreatment to the authorities for fear of summary deportation, and the threat of reporting them to the authorities can be used by employers to control illegal migrants.

Anti-immigration politicians respond to evidence on the situation of those made vulnerable to abuse and exploitation by their irregular immigration status by calling for stronger measures to prevent 'illegal immigration' and harsher punishments for those who facilitate their travel and exploit them (e.g., May, 2013). But others identify anti-immigration sentiment and the policies it fosters as part of the problem, not the solution. Taran and Geonimi (2003: 5) of the ILO, for example, point out that where trade and finance were deregulated in the last decade of the twentieth century, immigration policies became more restrictive in industrialized countries and also in many developing countries. In the context of continuing demand for cheap labour, they observe, such immigration law places an obstacle between high demand and strong supply, and thereby creates 'a potentially lucrative market for services of getting the supply to where the demand is'. Bales (2005: 166) likewise comments on the barriers that immigration policies can erect between the supply of, and demand for, workers, observing that the extension of legal opportunities for labour migration 'would mean that potential trafficking victims would be less likely to rely on traffickers ... [to] find them work abroad', and this in turn 'would lessen demand in the destination country for illegally supplied labour by forcing it to compete with legally supplied labour'.

Though convincing on some levels, this analysis can sometimes reflect, or at least encourage, the assumption that both supply and demand for 'cheap labour' are products of the workings of a purely economic logic. It also glosses over the fact that migrants who are *legally* present and working in the destination country (and indeed citizen-workers, of which more later) can also be subject to coercive, violent and exploitative employment relations. In fact, what at the time of writing are seen as exemplary cases of 'forced labour' actually often involve migrant workers who have moved through state authorized channels (construction workers in Qatar), and workforces that include a mix of authorized and illegal migrants (workers in the Thai fishing industry). Susceptibility to ill treatment can be as much a consequence of measures set in place by states to *allow* the movement of workers as of those enacted to prevent it.

The legal/illegal binary that features so prominently in political and popular discourse on migration does not actually map onto a division between migrants who are protected from 'forced labour' and migrants who are vulnerable to it. Nor, in fact, does such a binary reflect any policy reality, for immigration laws around the world do not construct a simple either/or line between legal and illegal movement, but rather an ever-proliferating profusion of legal statuses (Anderson, 2013). These statuses often generate a staggeringly complicated range of different terms upon which a migrant may legally remain on the territory, terms with which any given individual can, at different moments in time, be fully compliant, semi-compliant or non-compliant (Ruhs and Anderson, 2010). Bridget Anderson notes that 'illegality has tended to be theorized as *absence* of status' (2013: 86, original emphasis), whereas, as Nicolas De Genova (2002) has famously argued, illegality is actually *produced* by immigration controls. 'Such insights need to be developed into an examination of how immigration controls produce status more generally, in order to analyse the types of *legality* so produced, and the impact of these on migrants' positions in labour markets', Anderson (2013: 86) argues. With this in mind, I want to turn to the political construction of markets in the labour-power of temporary migrant workers.

## The market for migrants' labour-power

In liberal thought, political life – the state, the law, civil society (the realm in which human beings are constituted as 'persons'), and economic life – the market (the realm in which persons act to produce and exchange commodities or 'things') appear as two separate realms. But in reality, economic and political life, or market and state, are mutually imbricated, and the idea that they are separate is precisely that, an idea. As David Graeber puts it, 'States created markets. Markets require states. Neither could continue without the other, at least, in anything like the forms we would recognize today' (2011: 71). This point applies to New World slave markets as much as to any other, which is why exclusive attention to the ways in which human beings were constructed as 'things' in slavery, and failure to attend to the ways in which states produced and endorsed the power of slaveholders, yields such a thin description of the phenomenon. It also applies to labour markets, including markets for the commodified labour-power of migrant workers.

The term 'migration' presents definitional and conceptual problems almost as great as those implied by the term 'slavery' (Cohen, 1987) and, as noted in the previous chapter, the ways in which the vast panoply of forms of movement in which human beings today engage are imagined, classified, interpreted and represented are rooted in states' concerns to control human mobility. The policy division between those wishing to move to improve their economic situation, and those escaping war or political persecution, for example, fits with the liberal model of the market as separate from state and civil society, but not with the lived experience of those who move – 'Even at the most obvious level, conflict zones are usually not good places for economic as well as political survival' (Anderson, 2013: 54). Moreover, what is classed as 'economic migration' is invariably shaped by political forces, both national and global.

As noted in Chapter 3, the pursuit of neoliberal economic reforms by many governments, often at the behest of the International Monetary Fund (IMF) and the World Bank, has strongly impacted on the options available to people for economic survival, especially in the developing world (Lerche, 2007; Quintana, 2004; Sassen, 2010). This politically orchestrated restructuring of the economic order has contributed to (albeit not 'pushed' or 'driven') many people's decisions to leave home, either temporarily or on a more permanent basis. Structural adjustment measures have also provided debtor governments with a strong economic interest in their citizens' emigration. That is to say, remittances from migrants increasingly substitute the social welfare that states are no longer able to provide. Migrant remittances to developing countries reached almost US$80 billion in 2002, exceeding the net foreign direct investment for the first time (Kapur, 2005: 28). By 2010, recorded remittances alone received by developing countries far exceeded the volume of official aid flows and constituted 'more than 10 percent of Gross Domestic Product (GDP) in many developing countries' (World Bank, 2011). Though the sending of remittances is often regarded in a positive light, it can have serious costs for the individual migrant under pressure to remit (see Datta et al., 2007).

Commentary on 'labour migration' often identifies demand for workers in destination countries as a 'pull' factor. According to the Organization for Security and Co-operation in Europe (OSCE), for example, labour migration is crucial 'in enabling industrialized countries to meet economic, labour market and productivity challenges in a globalized economy', and 'serves as an instrument for adjusting the skills, age and sectoral composition of national and regional labour markets' (2006: 12). Demographic changes are also held to account, in part, for demand for migrant workers in both the industrialized world and relatively more economically developed countries of the developing world, since birth rates were declining in many such countries at the millennium (Thailand is a case in point, Martin, 2007).

Although some migrants from developing countries move to undertake highly skilled work (think, for example, of the dependence of industrialized countries' health services upon doctors and other highly skilled medical workers from the developing world), the majority are found at the bottom of the employment ladder 'and often do the dirty, dangerous and difficult – "3-D" – jobs' (ILO, 2004: 10). This is so whether people migrate to work in affluent, industrialized countries or in relatively more prosperous developing countries. A simple 'push-pull' economic model of migration might suggest that this is explained by economic factors alone – rising levels of economic activity in certain countries generates more '3D' jobs, while demographic changes restrict the supply of local workers, so demand for migrant labour increases. Workers in less developed countries or regions are 'pulled' by the opportunities for relatively higher paid employment. Yet this assumes not just that less developed countries with fewer and worse paid employment opportunities are, like the poor, 'always with us' (as opposed to being products of particular global political arrangements), but also that '3D' jobs simply exist. Against this, it can be argued that the danger, difficulty and dirtiness of most forms of work are powerfully shaped by politics, in particular, by workplace and wider class struggles.

As Harry Braverman's (1974) seminal study of the degradation of work showed, employers' efforts to wring as much value as possible out of the commodified labour-power they purchased led to changes to the organization of the labour process that transformed the technical content of many jobs. This provoked resistance which, in a period when organized labour occupied a relatively strong bargaining hand, was accommodated in various ways, including by improving the employment package surrounding low skill work undertaken by worker citizens (Smith, 2006). But what is gained can also be lost. As part of the shift away from welfare capitalism and towards a more neoliberal regime since the 1980s, both public and private sector employers have been replacing the directly employed workers who once enjoyed a 'standard' package of employment rights, benefits and protections, with subcontract, agency, franchise or self-employed workers (sometimes but not always temporary migrants) (Collins, 1990; O'Connell Davidson, 1993). Their more precarious employment situation 'encourages' them to work harder and longer (which often makes their job more dangerous), in worse (often dirtier) conditions, for the same or often lower wages. Many jobs have thus become not only more dirty, dangerous and difficult, but also more insecure (Costello and Freedland, 2014; Schlosser, 2001; TUC, 2008).

This brings to mind analyses provided by those who have drawn on the concept of a 'reserve army of labour' to explain when and why demand for migrant workers emerges (Castles and Kosack, 1973; Cohen, 1987; Phizacklea and Miles, 1980). The concept was employed by nineteenth-century British labour activists and adopted by both Karl Marx and Karl Polanyi 'to denote the surplus labouring population of the unemployed and under-employed, whose existence they regarded as a necessary product of capitalist accumulation and the state's class policies' (Farris, 2015: 3). Migration sociologists of the 1970s and '80s applied the concept to labour migrants, who provided, they argued, 'a quantitatively and qualitatively flexible labour force for capitalists, which divides and weakens working class organization and drives down the value of labour power' (Samers, 2003: 557). They also pointed to a further advantage from the perspective of capital in the industrialized countries that make use of migrant labour, namely that the cost of biologically reproducing, nourishing, housing, educating and training potential workers is born in the country of origin. In the case of migrant workers who are only temporarily present, during the prime of their working lives, the costs of caring for them in old age and infirmity also fall upon the home country. All this has the potential to 'eliminate, or at least substantially reduce, the cost of the social wage' (Cohen, 1987: 125–6). The fact that demand for migrant workers has fallen following recession lends support to this view although, as Sara Farris

(2015: 121) notes, migrant women in the care–domestic sector have been less affected by the economic crisis in Western Europe, suggesting that 'female migrant labour, mostly employed in the reproductive sector' has been reconfigured as '"regular" rather than a reserve army of labour'.

The 'reserve army' thesis identifies the ways in which divisions between propertyless labourers can be manipulated to the advantage of capital, but the representation of migrants as cheap and biddable workers has not always been challenged by actors in the organized labour movement, or in labour politics more generally. Leading figures of the British Labour Party today, for instance, often dress anti-migrant sentiment in the language of the imperative to protect the hard-won rights of the worker citizen, and such thinking has a long and sorry history both in Europe and in white settler nations. Indeed, the move to introduce restrictive immigration legislation in Australia in the 1880s (discussed in Chapter 4) followed a strike by white seamen protesting against moves by a shipping company to replace its existing workforce with Asian labour 'at half the cost' (Lake, 2014: 97). It was described, in 1879, as 'a strike against the yellow man', but as Marilyn Lake notes, the construction of 'the Chinese as inherently cheap labor' was contested by contemporary Chinese Australians. In an 1879 booklet, three Chinese community leaders remarked that '"Human nature [was] human nature all the world over," and "the Chinaman [was] just as fond of money, and just as eager to earn as much as he can, as the most grasping of his competitors"' (Lake, 2014: 98).

A migrant worker is not innately more flexible, less desirous of good wages and working conditions, or less willing to join a union than a local worker, nor do all those who move abroad to work 'naturally' or necessarily wish to return to their place of origin at the end of their working lives. The temporary migrant workforce, and its economic value to employers, is minted and underwritten by states. Without the state's assertion of a right to control movement across its borders, no such workforce would exist.

## Immigration regimes and the production of 'aliens'

In exercising their 'right' to determine whether or not to admit strangers, and through their immigration law, directing what Benjamin Faneuil Hunt described as 'the terms upon which those who are admitted shall remain' (Wong, 2009: 197), states assign different legal statuses that set varying limits on all elements of the bundle 'of claims, privileges, immunities, liabilities and obligations with respect to others' that make up social status (Finley, 1964: 247). In most countries, a migrant's immigration status will have repercussions in terms of, to paraphrase Moses Finley's list (1964: 247–8), her or his claims to property; immunity from or liability to detention, deportation and certain forms of punishment; privileges and liabilities in judicial process; privileges in the area of the family; privileges of social mobility (such as acquiring permanent leave to remain or citizenship); privileges and duties in the political and military spheres. It also has implications for the authorized migrant's freedoms in relation to the labour market.

The immigration policies of countries that depend heavily on migrant labour typically provide aspiring migrants with only temporary authorization to work in the destination country. Depending on the country and on the particular type of work permit they are issued, a variety of further restrictions on their rights and freedoms are imposed. Some countries attach conditions to work permits that deny migrant workers the right to marry, become pregnant, or engage in 'immoral or undesirable' activities (HRW, 2005). More commonly, authorized labour migrants may be prevented from bringing their children and partners into the country, even when this implies years of family separation; they may be denied legal rights to join trades unions and excluded from employment legislation that provides other workers' rights and protections, and even when they are not formally refused the right to unionize, other restrictions imposed on temporary migrant workers' freedoms can make it extremely hard for them to organize collectively (Anderson, 2013).

One of the main ways in which states seek to ensure that admittance onto their territory will not allow temporary migrant workers to claim or enjoy the freedoms that (in theory) accrue to citizens is by ensuring that their immigration status attaches them, in various ways, to the employer that sponsors them. The *kafala* system, employed in the Gulf Cooperation Council States and Lebanon, provides one example of this. This system, based on a tradition that requires the foreign worker to have a sponsor (*kafeel*) in order to enter the country, binds migrant workers to their employers. It is notorious for the extensive powers it affords the employer and the heavy restrictions it imposes on migrant workers, including – and of special significance for thinking through similarities with slavery – the prohibition of any mobility on the part of the worker without the sanction of the kafeel (Johnson 2012). Workers not only cannot move between employers, but also cannot leave the country, without the kafeel's approval.

Over the years, there have been many reports of violence (including torture, rape and murder), exploitation and other abuse by sponsors under the *kafala* system (HRW, 2005, 2006; Mahdavi, 2011). The abuse suffered by many of the migrant construction workers in Qatar that was noted at the start of the chapter, and their inability collectively to challenge the appalling and deadly conditions in which they work, is widely attributed to the restrictions licensed by the *kafala* system (ITUC, 2014). The *kafala* system has been widely condemned. It is frequently described as a form of modern slavery by human rights activists and trades unionists, the ILO presses for its reform and Walk Free is currently running a campaign demanding that FIFA calls 'for an end to the exploitative kafala system in its current form in Qatar, specifically by allowing workers to freely change jobs and leave the country without their employer's permission' (Walk Free, 2014). Nevertheless, though the *kafala* system has a high profile in campaigns against 'forced labour' and 'modern slavery', Gulf states are not alone in imposing heavy restraints on the freedoms of migrant workers.

The H-2 programme in the United States is another example of a scheme that has been censured, including by new abolitionists (see Bales and Soodalter, 2009). Around 106,000 'guestworkers' were brought into the country in 2011 under this programme, approximately half of whom entered agricultural work, the other half being placed in jobs in forestry, seafood processing, landscaping, construction and other non-agricultural industries. A 2013 report from the Southern Poverty Law Center (SPLC) observes that:

> far from being treated like 'guests,' these workers are systematically exploited and abused. Unlike U.S. citizens, guestworkers do not enjoy the most fundamental protection of a competitive labor market – the ability to change jobs if they are mistreated. Instead, they are bound to the employers who 'import' them. If guestworkers complain about abuses, they face deportation, blacklisting or other retaliation.
>
> (SPLC, 2013: 1)

As under the *kafala* system, workers are tied to the employer who sponsors their visa and, without access to legal resources, SPLC states they are routinely accommodated in squalid conditions, required to work excessively long hours, denied medical benefits for on-the-job-injuries, cheated of wages, overcharged for housing, telephone services and other costs and forced to remain under threat of deportation (see also Hill, 2011).

Although some specific visa programmes are singled out for concern, the fact is that most countries that rely on migrant labour – including Canada, Australia, the UK, Japan and Malaysia, as well as the United States and countries of the Gulf States – operate visa systems that bind workers to a sponsor, requiring them to work at a specific job for a pre-specified employer for a fixed period (Anderson, 2013; Baines and Sharma, 2002; Huong, 2010; Standing, 2011). Workers under such visa systems are vulnerable to exactly the same kinds of abuse as has been reported in the case of the H-2 visa, and the *kafala* system. Whether enacted in the European Union, Australia or the United States, in Singapore, Malaysia, Taiwan or Thailand, the objective of guest worker programmes and temporary work visas, like that of the *kafala* system, is 'to ensure that migrant workers are temporally transient and spatially fixed' (Lan, 2007: 258). Such programmes are designed to permit the physical movement of human beings across geopolitical borders (such that their labour-power is available for the benefit of employers and the national economy), but at the same time prevent the human beings in whom that labour-power inheres from securing the rights, benefits and protections that worker citizens might enjoy. Or, we might say, such measures are designed to allow the temporary migrant worker's labour-power to be bought and consumed as a 'thing', without having to acknowledge that worker as a 'person'. Their aim is to prevent such migrants from rooting themselves in, or belonging to the community in the way that citizens (and sometimes migrants with different immigration statuses) belong, in other words to fix them as 'aliens' and outsiders.

It might be expected that this, of itself, would sound alarm bells for anyone concerned with slavery. After all, as Claude Meillassoux argued, the slave is above all an alien, legally and/or socially prevented from becoming 'kin' (1991: 35, see also Hartman, 2007: 5). And yet the new abolitionists balk at denouncing the discriminatory constraints on freedom implied by immigration controls outright – indeed, given their more general insistence that 'modern slavery' is exceptional to contemporary global capitalism, and that no industry or economy is dependent on 'slavery' (Bales, 2007a), the line between migrant workers in 'modern slavery' and temporary migrant labour schemes *per se* is vitally important to them. The 'work demanded of some migrant workers can be manifested as slavery under certain conditions', Bales (2005: 57–8) tells us, but it would be incorrect to define 'abusive treatment of migrant workers' *per se* as slavery, since loss of free will, appropriation of labour-power, and violence or its are not *necessarily* combined features of *all* migrant workers' experience. Providing the employer does not actively prevent the migrant from choosing to quit and go home, she is free. As Free the Slaves puts it:

Sweatshop workers and migrant laborers are exploited by being paid very little, forced to work long hours and often abused at their workplace. Slaves are subjected to all these conditions, but additionally they have lost their free will – they cannot walk away. Most slaves are paid nothing at all, and the physical and psychological violence used against them is so complete that they cannot escape their slavery.

(FTS, 2007–2014b)

But does the absence of violent obstacles to quitting and returning home really equate to being free to 'walk away'? A focus on debt suggests not.

## Migrant debtors and 'debt bondage'

'Debt bondage' is described by the ILO as one of the mechanisms through which 'forced labour' is exacted, and it also figures in new abolitionist discourse as a form of 'modern slavery'. In general, when 'debt bondage' is discussed in relation to migration, the focus is on movement through irregular channels, and on 'trafficking', especially 'sex trafficking'. It is also very much upon situations in which indebted migrants are prevented from quitting an abusive and exploitative situation by an individual (or network of collaborating individuals) who is simultaneously creditor and employer. Little attention is paid to the fact that aspiring migrants' efforts to cover the costs associated with movement, whether through irregular or authorized channels, can generate one or more of a number of different forms of debt to a variety of different third parties – including spouses, lovers, friends, parents or other relatives; money-lenders; brokers/recruiting agents and subagents; banks; and sponsors (see, for example, Anderson and Rogaly, 2005; Chu, 2010; Kegan, 2011; Marshall and Thatun, 2005; Wu et al., 2010), leaving many migrants standing in the midst of what Nicolas Lainez (2016) describes as a 'constellation of debts'.

Huong's (2010: 895) discussion of the web of obligations into which Vietnamese workers are drawn by the triple contracts they must enter (with recruiter, state/bank and employer) to get temporary employment in Malaysia likewise reveals the limitations of the new abolitionist model of migrant workers as divisible into the 'slaves' who are bonded to one individual, and those who are free to walk away. Indebtedness *per se* can operate as a restraint on workers' freedom to quit employment and debt is a routine, rather than an exceptional, feature of migration (O'Connell Davidson, 2013). More troublesome still, debt is routine precisely because of the immigration regimes that states set in place to control and manage migratory flows. Just as those who seek to move across borders illegally often require the assistance of third parties – some of whom charge enormous fees and/or abuse or cheat the migrants they promise to help – so the vast, unwieldy bureaucracies attached to authorized movement are often impossible for would-be migrants to negotiate without assistance. This, along with other barriers that make it difficult or impossible for migrants independently to access the labour market, opens up lucrative opportunities for third parties who are in a position to arrange movement and organize employment.

The potential for such fees to expose legally sanctioned labour migrants to the risk of abuse and exploitation is widely recognized by organizations and groups concerned with the rights of migrant workers. It is sometimes even referred to as 'institutionalized trafficking' (see ILO, 2011). In fact, the 2007 TIP report even commented on the problem of debt bondage and involuntary servitude among some groups of migrant workers legally present abroad, remarking on the 'intentional imposition of exploitative and often illegal costs and debts on these laborers in the source country or state, often with the complicity and/or support of labor agencies and employers in the destination country or state' (cited in Plant, 2008). Attention to such illegal costs and debts highlights the artificiality of the legal/illegal migration dyad (the same migratory process may involve both legal and illegal elements, Anderson and O'Connell Davidson, 2003). But it is also important to note that licensed recruitment agencies in migrant-sending countries and placement agencies in migrant-receiving countries can often perfectly legally charge migrants fees for brokering their migration. And even though regulation sometimes includes a cap on some of the fees that can be charged to workers, officially sanctioned recruitment fees in some countries are equivalent to four or five months' salary, and it is legal to withhold a substantial portion of wages pending the worker's return home. In other words, it is not just illegal fees, but also legal costs imposed on labourers that can be extremely high (O'Connell Davidson, 2013). When coupled with compound interest on loans advanced to pay them, they too can mean that migrants are never able to repay their debt or find their remittances seriously eroded.

The market for the services of licensed recruitment and placement agencies is in large part a by-product of states' efforts to ensure that migrant labour is available as an instrument to ensure a flexible supply of cheap workers for jobs that are unattractive to citizen workers, but at the same time to prevent the permanent settlement of migrant workers, especially those without personal wealth or recognized professional qualifications. Lan (2007) provides a particularly compelling analysis of how Taiwan's adoption of a quota system that regulates both the numbers of migrant workers and their distribution in selected occupations and industries, leads to a very profitable market in brokering migrant labour, and one that results in migrant workers becoming deeply mired in debt.

These politically constructed markets turn vast numbers of migrants, not an exceptional minority, into debtors. And debt is an obstacle to quitting and returning home even when the debt is not to the employer, but to a money lender, a family member, or a recruitment agent (or all three), because for most migrants who are heavily indebted, there is absolutely no chance of being able to earn enough to repay or even service such debt at home. In this context, the immigration rules that tie workers to a sponsor and deny them free movement in the labour market in themselves constitute a significant barrier to being able to freely 'walk away' from an unwanted or abusive employment relation. Before considering the powers that the state delegates to employers who sponsor migrant workers in more detail, I want to reiterate the problems with the 'can or cannot walk away' formula as a means of drawing the political line between 'forced' and 'voluntary' labour by briefly considering a group of workers who are, sometimes for long periods, physically prevented from walking away even from the most severe exploitation and violence.

## Labour abuse at sea

There are differences between sectors and workplaces in terms of the possibilities for minimizing the danger, dirtiness and difficulty of jobs, even in political climates most favourable to unionization. Fishing provides one example of '3D' work that presents huge challenges in this respect. The sea is a hostile environment for humans, and fishing at sea is always and everywhere a very dangerous occupation (Acheson, 1981). Working conditions are poor, with fishing crews typically working very long hours, often under extreme conditions of cold and wet, and often over long periods away at sea, with little opportunity for sleep, leisure or privacy. In addition, there has always been significant risk of 'fatal accidents as a result of ships foundering, men falling overboard or being injured by winches and fishing gear' (Schilling, 1966: 405).

The physical perils of fishing work are not entirely fixed and unalterable, however. Regulatory controls make a difference. In the 1960s, for instance, there was a substantial gap between the fatal accident rate for workers on British trawlers (33 per 10,000) and those working on Norwegian trawlers (six per 10,000), a discrepancy explained by the more extensive safety regulations 'designed to protect men from falling overboard and from injury by machinery and equipment' that were applied in the Norwegian fishing industry (Schilling, 1966: 406). More recently, Lindøe (2007) has compared occupational health and safety in the Norwegian fishing and offshore oil industries, observing that though the work settings are similar in many respects, the latter provides a significantly safer working environment, despite efforts to implement health and safety regulation in fishing designed on the same principles as the offshore industry. The problem, Lindøe (2007) argues, is partly that employment units in fishing are far smaller than in offshore oil, with most vessels operated by a small crew or even by a single fisherman, and maritime inspectors visit only a third of the smaller vessels; and partly that where the oil industry is dominated by huge corporations with the resources to invest in safety (and economic incentives to do so), fishing is not. Many of those involved in the industry can neither afford new vessels, nor to invest in modernizing old vessels or in training or new equipment. As critical, where the workforce in the offshore oil industry is almost entirely unionized, and unions therefore enjoy a strong bargaining position in relation to management and have played a decisive role in developing safety regulations, there is no tradition in the Norwegian fishing industry for using industrial relations in the development of better safety standards:

> Most of the vessel owners and the fishermen are members of the same union. Often, they have close relationships. On small vessels, they also share the same risks and face the same hazards. As a consequence, there has not been any critical counterpart regarding worker safety.
>
> (Lindøe, 2007: 29)

This connects to a tendency towards egalitarian relations amongst crew members on fishing boats that was, until recently, more widely reported around the world, and also expressed in 'the shares system' whereby fishermen were paid a portion of the catch, rather than a flat fee or wage (Acheson, 1981: 278). The relative lack of 'workplace' hierarchy was often highly prized by fisherman who, in the 1970s, frequently expressed a strong commitment to their occupation despite (perhaps partly because of) its difficulties and dangers. They stressed that they liked fishing because of the 'independence', 'challenge', 'lack of regimentation' as well as the income (Acheson, 1981: 296).

Fishing has traditionally appealed to a 'self-selected group of very unusual men' (Schilling, 1966: 405) and, because of its peculiar hazards and rigours, plus the long periods of absence from home it can imply, this group has always been small. Labour recruitment has therefore long presented a particular problem in this industry and in much of the world, fishermen have tended to come to the work through kinship networks (Acheson, 1981). Unsurprisingly then, the recent and massive expansion in global demand for cheap seafood has led to significant labour shortages, especially in places where vessels are poorly equipped and working practices most unsafe, and where fishermen have to spend long periods at sea because fish stocks have been so seriously depleted by over-fishing. Thailand is one such context. Though the fishing industry has grown more important to the Thai economy since the millennium (it now contributes approximately 1.2 per cent of annual GDP, and 'the total value of Thailand's fish exports rank third globally, with as US$7.13 billion annual value in 2010' (ILO, 2013a: 14)), fishing and fish processing work has become less attractive to Thai nationals (Martin, 2007).

Demographic change, in tandem with wider earning opportunities for Thai nationals generated by the country's 'tiger economy' and greater opportunities to migrate to work in relatively more affluent countries in the region mean that even relatively poor and unskilled Thai people are often in a position to turn down offers of employment in the fishing industry (Yang, 2007). Thai fishers who do 'currently work within the industry do not wish to see their children pursue fishing as an occupation because it is considered difficult and dangerous work, with an unsteady income, and a low social status' (ILO, 2013a: 28). The Thai fishing industry is thus heavily dependent on migrant workers and, even so, is still experiencing a significant labour shortage. As a result, some employers and brokers are resorting to deception, corruption and coercion to recruit and retain workers, extending to instances of boys and men being drugged and physically forced aboard vessels and extreme, even lethal, violence to deter or punish escape (EJF, 2012; Hodal et al., 2014). Even those who have consented to the work can find that once on board:

> boat captains will often seize and hold their passports and work permits, preventing them from leaving situations in which their rights

are abused. If forced to go into debt with a broker over registration fees, workers may find themselves in situations of debt bondage, and will have to work without remuneration until the debt is paid.

(ILO, 2013a: 27)

It is important to remember that not *all* workers are affected by such practices – 17 per cent of 596 fishery workers in a recent ILO (2013b) survey reported they were working against their will, for example. However, there is a clear link between the shortage of workers willing to take on such dangerous and difficult work for such low wages, and the abusive practices found in the industry. (Thailand's military government's reaction to revelations about the extent and severity of such abuse was to propose the use of convict labour in fishing – proposals that were subsequently withdrawn following an outcry from human rights groups (O'Toole, 2015).)

The Thai fishing industry is by no means unique as a site of such labour abuse, as Rebecca Surtees' (2015) interview research with 46 Ukrainian seafarers and fishers held captive on boats and seafood processing platforms in the waters of Russia, Turkey and South Korea between 2005 and 2010 illustrates. The Ukrainian men she interviewed had sought work in ways usual in the industry (through personal contacts or newspaper advertisements), ways in which those of them who were experienced seafarers had found decent work in the past. They were, in other words, active agents seeking maritime employment and not the naïve innocents that feature in 'anti-trafficking' campaign materials. It was only once they boarded their vessels (normally after long journeys to distant ports, or in some cases, after being transported by boat out to sea to board unlicensed ships) that they realized what was happening to them. One interviewee described the experience as follows:

We were taken on to a boat to go to sea and embarked on a ship that did not have any sign and name on it... When the boat went, we were told by those who were on board that they were working 24 hours a day, almost without sleep, no money paid, and also that it was impossible to leave since the ship never entered port.

(2015: 65)

Out at sea for periods of months or even years, completely isolated, the men were driven to work seven days a week, 18 to 22 hours each day, under the most appalling conditions, by those who supervised and controlled them, sometimes by means of violence. Their contact with land and other vessels was minimal. Another interviewee said, 'When we were in slavery on that old clunker they would not let us enter the port because some seafarers who worked before us tried to escape', and when the ship did dock, 'They would usually have dogs around so that it would not be possible to go ashore at all'. Though coast guards do conduct routine inspections at sea, such inspections are not plentiful and frequent enough to reach every vessel, and even when a vessel is inspected, it is senior officers rather than lower ranking crew members who are interviewed. In ports, too, seafarers and fishers 'do not generally come into contact with port authorities, particularly if they are prevented from leaving their vessel' (Surtees, 2015: 68).

Isolation – the very characteristic of fishing work that can, in some circumstances, lend itself to solidarity and egalitarianism – is also precisely the feature of the work that leaves workers terrifyingly vulnerable to abuse. Once aboard a vessel, the seaman or fisher is as much at the mercy of the employer as the transatlantic slave was at the mercy of the slaveholder and his drivers, and this is so partly for reasons that are beyond politics: the ocean really is a vast and lonely expanse. However, the fact that so many vessels are so far out at sea is not a given. It is a political construct not merely in the sense of negotiations over fishing rights, but also in the sense that massive, industrial-scale fishing and fish processing is not occurring to meet a 'natural' or fixed level of demand for seafood in the contemporary world, but rather to feed demand for *cheap* seafood that can be met profitably by the top global retailers (Thailand annually ships around 500,000 tonnes of prawns into the global market through multinational food companies to be sold by leading supermarkets, for example (Hodal et al., 2014)). The dramatic growth of this market has been made possible by new technologies in fishing, fish processing, and transportation, and technologies also exist that could, in theory, be used to make fishing vessels at sea less isolated and more visible (think of the technology currently being deployed to detect migrants making 'illegal' sea crossings). The principles of much more effective health and safety regulation for fishing are known (Lindøe, 2007), and seafarers' exposure to the risk of the kind of labour abuse described above could be substantially reduced by greater spending on, and improvements to, routine inspections and law enforcement – spending that could easily be supported given the billions of dollars in profits generated by the fishing industry each year.

It is not inevitable that people are coerced into fishing labour and held captive on vessels, but it is extremely difficult to mobilize effectively against such abuse. This is partly because whilst the demand for seafood (and so for labourers on fishing vessels) is driven by the huge multinational players, these players do not organize the labour processes that generate the seafood. Instead, the retailers and their food company suppliers (again, mostly large multinationals) stand at the apex of long global supply chains that widen out to a profusion of subcontractors and small employers at the base. Risks and costs are passed down the line, to be carried by the small employers, hence this is where extreme labour abuse typically occurs, apparently several degrees removed from the large, multinational buyers (Ruhmkorf, 2015). The factory-farmed prawns from Thailand that appear on supermarket shelves in Europe and North America are, for example, fed with 'trash fish' trawled far out in international waters, and workers involved in the latter are more vulnerable than those engaged in farming prawns (Hodal et al., 2014).

Long and complicated supply chains make it much easier for those at the top to evade responsibility for safety and labour standards at the bottom, especially when those supply chains cross national borders. Fishers and seafarers like those described above are at risk in part because, on the one hand, 'labour regulation is national but the market place is global, and governments (of all persuasions) are prepared to sacrifice the labour standards of their citizens', and of migrant workers, in the competition for trade and investment (Wilshaw, 2015), while on the other hand, governments of the home states of the multinational enterprises that are driving the 'race to the bottom' are unwilling to make those enterprises criminally responsible for human rights abuses in their global supply chains (Ruhmkorf, 2015). In the absence of state intervention to either protect workers or constrain employers, the ship at sea is very much as Frederick Douglass described the Southern plantation – unapproachable feudal fiefdoms, secluded, untouched by the laws and institutions of the state (Gilroy, 1993: 59). Or, we might equally say, the absence of effective governance leaves the fishing vessel literally as well as figuratively a 'hidden abode' of capitalist production, a place of work where employers who chose to do so can formulate their autocratic power over their workers purely as an emanation of their own wills (Marx, 1954).

The workers held captive by abusive employers are not robbed of their free will. Like transatlantic slaves, they remain 'willing selves', and could choose suicide over compliance. Perhaps through the eyes of thirteenth-century Christian Formalists, like Thomas Aquinas, those fishers who do not attempt to swim away could be said to remain aboard voluntarily, but few in the twenty-first century would describe a choice taken between certain death, and one other alternative, as freely made. Whilst fishers who are subject to labour abuse are out at sea, there is probably near unanimous consensus that they 'cannot walk away'. However, when vessels do go into port, the possibilities for leaving increase, and at this point other factors inhibiting flight often come into play. For example, if identity documents have been confiscated or debts have been taken on in the course of recruitment, compliance can still look preferable to the alternatives. We move onto territory where direct and irresistible force exercised by individuals begins to blend with the more indirect, dull compulsion of markets to produce continuums of different forms of pressure. Here, the question of what type and degree of restraint can be said to prevent a worker from 'walking away' becomes a matter of political and moral judgment. And this is the terrain where most migrant workers facing labour abuse are found.

## Sponsors and the ship of state

The visa systems that tie temporary migrant workers to their sponsors exist to fix migrants as outsiders even when physically they are present on the territory of the state, paying taxes, and contributing to its economic viability. Though immigration controls imply a bureaucratic burden and other restrictions that can be unwelcome to some employers, they can also work very much to the advantage of others. In the UK, for example, non-citizens who enter to work require a 'certificate of sponsorship' from their employer that can be withdrawn at any time, so that 'many workers subject to immigration control are effectively on fixed-term contracts that may be terminated at the employer's discretion' (Anderson, 2013: 88). If the employer does withdraw sponsorship, the migrant has 60 days to find another authorized sponsor or leave the UK, so that the termination of these contracts has implications beyond the workplace. To this extent, migrants on work-related visas are dependent on the goodwill of their employer for their right to remain in the UK, and such measures equip employers with 'additional means of control' (Anderson, 2013: 89).

In some sectors, domestic and care work being particular examples, demand for migrant labour is not simply demand for workers willing to undertake at low wages jobs that are constructed as '3D', but also demand for workers who cannot simply up and leave these jobs at will. In the case of fishing, especially where it involves long periods spent at sea, the ocean itself constitutes an insuperable barrier to upping and leaving. But in the case of domestic workers – whose utility to the employer (like some transatlantic slaves' utility to slaveholders) may in part lie in being sent on errands and who, even if locked into the home may have access to a telephone or other means of calling for help – many countries' immigration controls accomplish the same ends. The advantages of such controls from the employer's perspective are well captured in the words of a Dutch woman that Bridget Anderson and I interviewed in 2001 in the course of research on employers' demand for migrant domestic workers. She explained to us that Singapore (where she had previously lived) had by far the best system for employing migrant domestic workers, for there it was possible to employ Filipino women who were often very well educated and spoke good English, yet were never 'too assertive' or difficult in any way:

> because they are so dependent on you. In Singapore, the system is wonderfully organized from an employer's perspective. The employer holds the Filipino maid's passport, and the maid has to pay to leave. The employer pays the government, it's all official, but the maid is totally dependant on the employer... they can't just quit.
>
> (O'Connell Davidson, 2010: 251)

In the UK, visa regulations concerning domestic workers were changed from 2012 such that non-EU migrants would only be able to enter as domestic workers (and even then only for a six-month period) when accompanying their employer. They are not entitled to change employer, and must leave the UK with their employer if the employer leaves (Anderson, 2013: 175). Around 15,000 migrant domestic workers enter Britain each year under these rules (Leghtas and Roberts, 2015), accompanying wealthy employers, mostly from the Gulf region, and as there is no system of workplace monitoring or governance structure to enforce minimum labour standards that apply to domestic work in private households, these workers enter an abode as hidden from state oversight as a vessel at sea, if not more so. That domestic workers are vulnerable to abuse and exploitation of the type described by the UK government as 'modern slavery', and that the current visa regulations institutionalize such vulnerability by binding workers to their sponsors, is well documented (Anderson, 2013; HRW, 2015). Yet in March 2015, the government opposed an amendment to the Modern Slavery Bill that would allow domestic workers the freedom to remedy their situation by quitting and finding an alternative employer. It is interesting to set this against the fact that the same government also rejected a proposal to include in the Modern Slavery Bill provisions making it a criminal offence for forced labour to exist anywhere in the supply chains of multinational enterprises, instead 'introducing new duties on companies to report on what they are doing to prevent forced labour in their supply chains' (Ruhmkorf, 2015). Huge and powerful corporations are thus only required to make and report efforts to avoid exploiting 'modern slaves' and are not criminally liable for the failure of such efforts; individual migrant domestic workers cannot make and report their own efforts to avoid 'modern slavery', but must somehow find a way to bring their appalling treatment to the attention of the authorities (for which, by way of a thank you, the authorities will likely deport them).

More generally we should note that migrants' rights campaigners have long argued that where employers are legally required to hold the identity documents of the migrant workers they sponsor, the migrant is unable freely to quit their employment. Many countries have responded to these concerns by outlawing this practice (including in the United Arab Emirates, though abusive labour practices are reported to persist there, according to Malit and Youha, 2013) and in the UK, sponsors are forbidden from confiscating documents. They are, however, obliged to comply with various rules and regulations concerning the recruitment of workers, and also have an ongoing duty to monitor their migrant employees. Employers are instructed that if a sponsored migrant fails to arrive on the first day of work, or 'is absent from work for more than ten consecutive working days without permission', they must 'report this within ten working days of the 10th day of absence' (Gov.Uk, 2014). Failure to comply with immigration rules and sponsor duties can lead to civil penalties, criminal prosecution and/or withdrawal of a sponsor licence and removal from the sponsorship register, leaving the employer unable to bring sponsored migrant workers to the UK or continue to employ existing sponsored migrants. Employers are advised to:

> monitor your employees' immigration status, keep copies of relevant documents for each employee, including passport and right to work information, track and record employees' attendance, keep employee contact details up to date, report to UKVI if there is a problem, eg your employee stops coming to work.
>
> (Gov.UK, 2014)

There are strong echoes of the way in which slave states historically deputed certain of its own powers to slaveholders in such a way as to imply not merely rights over their slaves, but obligations to control and contain them such that the boundary between slavery and freedom remained impermeable. It is true that in the case of contemporary employers in the UK, the responsibility being delegated is only one of surveillance: employers are legally obliged to report migrants who may, potentially, have absconded or otherwise infracted immigration rules, and not to physically prevent them from so doing. Nonetheless, the delegation of that responsibility implies an extra-economic dimension to the relation between employer and employee that does not exist in employment relations with other workers. In addition to the dependency implied by the employment relation, the sponsor is also designated the role of front line actor in the state's efforts to restrict the temporary migrant's freedom of movement. That some employer-sponsors are over-zealous in their performance of this role seems rather less than surprising, especially given the fact that the primary focus of state control is on preventing the infraction of immigration law, as opposed to the violation of migrant workers' rights.

Were we to apply the analogy between the state and the patriarchal head of household as used by Hunt, it seems that temporary migrant workers are not, in fact, welcomed into the 'home', but invited *only* into 'the hidden abode' of production. Perhaps a better analogy would be with a ship, onto which temporary migrant workers are permitted to board on condition they remain confined in the engine rooms or galley. Here, they must work for individuals who not only enjoy, as employers, a power of command over their labour-power (and so over their persons) but are also, as sponsors, assigned by the state a duty to keep watch over them, ready to alert the state actors who enjoy a monopoly on use of force should they attempt to leave the bowels of the ship and move freely around it. In this respect, employers' interests and states' desire to fix non-nationals as outsiders are neatly dovetailed.

As already noted, the new abolitionists are not entirely blind to problems presented by the immigration rules and programmes that restrict the freedoms of temporary migrant workers. In light of abuse in the Thai fishing industry, Walk Free's (2014) country report on Thailand goes so far as to recommend that the Thai government should ratify the International Convention on Migrant Workers and Members of their Family. It does not make the same recommendation to the governments of the United States, Australia or the United Kingdom, however, even though many cases of abuse and exploitation of migrant workers have been discovered on their territories, and even though they, like Thailand, have not yet ratified it. (Indeed, this worthy but hardly radical Convention 'took 23 years to come into force, the longest of any of the ten core international human rights instruments, and has registered the slowest rate of ratification', and none of the major developed countries that are destinations for migrant workers have yet ratified it (UNOG, 2014).)

Contemporary states claim the 'perfect right' of receiving or excluding strangers and setting the terms of admittance, and this goes unchallenged not only by the new abolitionists and most mainstream organizations campaigning against 'forced labour', but also by the Convention on the Rights of Migrant Workers and their Families. Yet in claiming this as a right, states also grant themselves the right to deny some individuals the freedom that is otherwise regarded by liberals as the most fundamental to free wage labour, namely the liberty to 'park' their labour where they will (Smith, 2006), and to make their entry and stay on the territory conditional upon a private relationship with the employer who sponsors them. In so doing, they turn the experience of temporary migrant workers (especially those who are heavily indebted) into a lottery, just as the experience of slaves confined as dependants within the private household or plantation was a lottery. If workers are fortunate enough to end up with a decent and humane sponsor, all may be well. If they are unlucky, then like the seafarers and fishers interviewed by Surtees, they find themselves facing invidious choices, up to and including the choice between compliance and death.

In practice, however, very few of the migrants described by campaigners as 'forced labourers' are prevented from walking away by overwhelming physical force or insuperable physical obstacles such as those faced by fishers at sea. It is the fear or knowledge of what they would walk *into*, given their immigration status and the impossibility of repaying migration-related debts should they be forced to return home, that constricts their mobility. Indeed, as Mark Johnson's (2012) research on Filipino migrant domestic workers in Saudi Arabia reveals, running away from legal sponsors to work illegally in the informal economy is a strategy by which some migrants, subject to the kind of legally sanctioned bondage described above, manage to secure greater personal freedom, and to pay off their debts and remit money to dependants, albeit under constant threat of detection and deportation (see also Lan, 2007; Mahdavi, 2011). If 'losing free will' is what defines the 'modern slave', are we to take it that migrants who do manage to escape abusive employers were not really 'modern slaves' in the first place? In which case, were the transatlantic slaves who managed to escape their captivity not really 'slaves' either?

## Slavery, citizenship and freedom

What the new abolitionists describe as 'modern slavery' (e.g., cases in which temporary migrant workers are beaten, held captive, starved, threatened with death, tortured or murdered by employers) cannot be addressed in isolation from the situation of the many low skilled, temporary labour migrants who are 'exploited by being paid very little, forced to work long hours and often abused at their workplace' (FTS, 2007–2014b), because the same systemic features contribute to temporary labour migrants' vulnerability to abuse and exploitation in both its routine and exceptional forms. As Chapter 4 argued, these systemic features link back to measures devised to manage raced-migration following the abolition of slavery and contain many echoes of the ways in which slave and colonial states historically sought to manage and control the movement of populations deemed outsiders and subpersons. However, even if this history is acknowledged, it does not follow that an anti-slavery framework can help to advance the rights and freedoms of labour migrants.

Taking chattel slavery as a comparator for the experience of migrant workers, no matter how abused and exploited, deflects attention from the active desire for movement and for work, and so from the structural factors that make individuals vulnerable both as migrants and as workers. If we focus on, say, migrant strawberry pickers, construction workers or domestic workers as *workers*, a campaign for measures to prevent their employers from withholding their wages, locking them up, and shooting, beating or raping them, looks far from radical. As a minimum labour standard, this is a very low bar indeed. And if we focus on them as *migrants*, campaigns to assure them the bare bourgeois freedom to quit a job and return home look equally insipid. In fact, freedom from what is dubbed 'modern slavery' sounds rather like Judge Lumpkin's 1853 previously cited description of the meaning of manumission – something that confers 'no other right but that of freedom from the dominion of the master, and the limited liberty of locomotion' and not 'any of the powers, civil or political, incident to *citizenship*' (Tushnet, 1981: 150, emphasis original).

Viewed in this light, the solution to the problems discussed in this chapter may appear to lie in the extension of the powers incident to citizenship to any and all persons present on the territory of the state. I agree that preventing states from discriminating on the basis of nationality and insisting that they recognize all human beings on their territory as morally equal 'persons' would represent a huge leap forward.

The energy and resources currently devoted to the fight against 'modern slavery' would be far better spent, I think, on advocating for this end. But the civil and political powers of citizenship are not enough, as is clear if we return to thinking about economic life.

This chapter has focused on migrant workers who are subject to immigration controls, but other workers can also find themselves in extremely harsh situations from which they cannot freely retract. This is illustrated by many cases in EU countries involving migrants from other EU nations who do have the right to move and work but who nonetheless suffer severe labour exploitation and abuse (Anderson and Rogaly, 2005; Clark, 2013; Harris, 2013). Moreover, most of the ASM and other informal sector workers discussed in Chapter 3 are nationals of the countries where they are subject to the experiences described as 'forced labour' and 'modern slavery', as well as serious abuse and exploitation that is seen to fall short of these categories, and citizens of affluent, industrialized countries are not unassailable. The TUC (2008) estimates around two million workers in the UK are in what it describes as 'vulnerable employment', defined as 'precarious work that places people at risk of continuing poverty and injustice resulting from an imbalance of power in the employer-worker relationship', only some of whom are migrants. Indeed, Bridget Anderson (2013) has argued that the citizen/migrant binary is just as questionable as the other oppositional couplings that structure dominant liberal thought. It is perfectly possible to hold or acquire formal citizenship without also gaining admission to what she terms 'the community of value' and, by the same token, members of the most privileged elites occupy a largely transnational space – it is not only, or always primarily, by dint of their nationality or citizenship that they are able to arrogate the liberties they enjoy. Money can buy citizenship, and also some excellent substitutes.

The problem is not simply that immigration and citizenship law has generated a system of 'global apartheid', but also, Nandita Sharma (2006: 142) argues, that far from operating as a progressive force within nations, 'citizenship has constructed complex and layered levels of inequalities' in terms of access to sustenance, health and educational services, justice, protection and freedom. Because restraints on freedom are produced and mediated by multiple systems of domination (class, race, caste, age, gender as well as nationality) and because economic and political life are not separate but always and inevitably tightly knotted together, the lack of citizenship can operate to deny some human beings liberal liberties without its presence offering any guarantee of equality, inclusion or protection. This is a fact attested by the experience of emancipated slaves and their descendants in the United States. It is also made plain by a consideration of restrictions on women's freedoms, historically and today, which is the focus of the following chapter.

# 7
## Slaves and Wives: A Question of Consent?

In 1807, the English parliament outlawed the slave trade and, in 1838, it ended chattel slavery in its colonies. But in the modern liberty-loving England of 1847, we find a report in the *Stamford Mercury* of a woman being sold at public auction in Lincolnshire:

> On Wednesday... it was announced by the crye, that the wife of Geo. Wray, of Barrow... would be offered for sale by auction in the Barton market-place at 11 o'clock;... punctually to the time the salesman made his appearance with the lady, the latter having a new halter tied round her waist. Amidst the shouts of the lookers on, the lot was put up, and... knocked down to Wm. Harwood, waterman, for the sum of one shilling, three-halfpence to be returned 'for luck'. Harwood walked off arm in arm with his smiling bargain, with as much coolness as if he had purchased a new coat or hat.
>
> (Thompson, 1991: 417)

The practice of wife sales was not common, but neither is this case unique. In his research on the phenomenon, E. P. Thompson found documentary evidence of 218 cases, between 1760 and 1880 (1991: 409). Thompson's research reminds us that the narrative in which the transition to modern, market societies proceeds as a story of liberation, and in which 'slavery' is inimical to a liberal social order, rests upon selective amnesia in relation to gender as well as race. White women's experience, as well as that of paupers, propertyless labourers, and 'people of colour', is necessarily absent from such stories, for the great watersheds in white men's history – the French and American revolutions, the industrial revolution, the English 1832 Representation of the People Act – did not signal momentous change for their womenfolk. Indeed, just as the retrospective application of the new abolitionists' definition of 'slavery' would find the economies of industrializing Europe and America from the seventeenth through to the nineteenth century heavily dependent on the labour of 'modern slaves' as well as chattel slaves, so it would lead us to conclude that 'modern slavery' was the lot of most white wives (and in fact, the analogy between marriage and slavery was widely drawn by white nineteenth-century feminists seeking to challenge their own disenfranchisement and legal erasure as persons).

Even in those countries where women's political struggles for rights to vote, reforms to property and divorce laws and a series of other measures to address discrimination in civil and economic life have been successful, men and women's economic, social and political standing has still not been completely equalized. Still today, we live in a world in which gender inequalities are the norm, and these inequalities are often both expressed in, and maintained by, violence against women. Commenting on a case that attracted worldwide media attention and provoked political protest in India, that of the gang rape of a 23-year-old student in New Delhi in 2012, an attack so brutal that the young woman died soon afterwards, Srila Roy (2013) observes:

> [India] is a country in which rape is used as mode of policing women's access to public spaces, as a tool of disciplining lower caste women and putting women of minority communities 'in their place,' as part of the privilege enjoyed by married men (marital rape is not recognized in Indian law), and the legal impunity bestowed on the Indian army in conflict zones.

Such violence is not a problem 'of the developing South (attributable to "tradition" and/or "culture")', she continues, but a truth 'prevalent everywhere', including in liberal industrialized countries like the United States and the United Kingdom where rape is also 'rendered everyday and not extraordinary. Routine, not exceptional'.

Roy's point is not that every woman is or expects to be raped, but rather that sexual violence against women is sufficiently commonplace as to excite interest, and demand explanation, only when it takes a particularly extreme form, or when it is perpetrated against particular kinds of victim – the very young or very old, the 'respectable' as opposed to the 'whore' and so on. The rape and murder of two young women, aged 18 and 19, in Florida in September 2014 (Gomez, 2014), did not provoke the same media and public response as the Delhi rape either globally or nationally, for example. This was not least because the black teenage victims worked as exotic dancers, a fact that was seemingly widely understood to render their violent deaths explicable, even if still regrettable.

If violence against women in public spaces is unexceptional, so too is violence against them in their homes. Though efforts to index the global prevalence of domestic violence present methodological challenges similar to those presented by efforts to estimate the incidence of 'forced labour', 'trafficking' or 'modern slavery' globally (see Merry, 2012), there is nonetheless evidence to suggest that it is hardly an extraordinary occurrence. For instance, interview data from 24,097 women gathered between 2000 and 2003 through standardized population-based household surveys in ten countries (Bangladesh, Brazil, Ethiopia, Japan, Namibia, Peru, Samoa, Serbia and Montenegro, Thailand and the United Republic of Tanzania), found that in all but one setting 'women were at far greater risk of physical or sexual violence by a partner than from violence by other people' (Garcia-Moreno et al., 2006: 1260). Data on nearly 500,000 homicides from 66 countries analysed in 2013 revealed that partners are responsible for 38.6 per cent of all murders of women compared with 6.3 per cent of murders of men (Stockl et al., 2013).

Whatever feelings such statistics may stir in readers, I doubt that surprise is one of them, for we all grow up in societies where violence within the home, primarily (but not exclusively) perpetrated by men, and against women and children, is simultaneously regarded as unfortunate, yet unremarkable except in its most extreme expression. In Britain, the murder of women by their partners or husbands rarely makes headline news (Viner, 2005), and attacks and aggressions that fall short of killing or maiming the victim are not considered newsworthy at all, unless those involved happen to be famous (see, for example, Moore, 2013). Moreover, in the economically developed as well as the developing world, gender norms concerning domestic labour are such that most women who experience violence or its threat are also expected to perform the labour necessary to the reproduction of their household.

We are thus looking at a world in which significant numbers of women experience two of the three elements that the new abolitionists hold are at the core of 'modern slavery', that is to say, labour exploitation and violence or its threat, and this chapter begins by considering the difficulties that this presents for new abolitionists and policy makers who seek to draw a line between wives who are 'modern slaves' and wives who are not. It then revisits three problems within new abolitionist discourse that have already been discussed in relation to servitude and wage labour, this time through the lens of gender. First, the chapter returns to the question of whether contract and consent can represent a solution to the problem of domination, noting that in the context of gender inequalities that enforce women's dependence on men, even 'voluntary', consensual heterosexual marriage of the type endorsed by new abolitionists is not actually an arrangement that rules out the possibility of violent domination and labour exploitation from which a wife cannot walk away.

Second, it revisits questions about what is obscured in analogies between chattel slavery and other systems of domination. It argues that the comparison between marriage and slavery (whether applied to all heterosexual marriage, as by some feminist thinkers, or just to particularly coercive and violent marriages, as by new abolitionists) does not help us to understand why non-slave women's freedoms have, historically and today, been so heavily restricted. These restraints are borne of a desire to control women's sexuality in such a way as to preserve their capacity to reproduce human beings imagined as kin, community members or citizens, not aliens, outsiders or slaves. To explain (and so to challenge) these restrictions on freedom, we need to think about the ways in which wives are *not* like slaves, the chapter argues. Moreover, as with other systems of domination, patriarchy does not actually transform women into 'things' or 'objects', or evacuate them of will. A third concern of the chapter is thus with the choices that women make as willing – if highly constrained – selves. Acknowledging agency as always extant and inalienable not only allows us to recognize the fact that women can be complicit with patriarchy, but also that women's standing in relation to the markets that are commonly read as slavery-like is ambiguous. This is highlighted by E. P. Thompson's analysis of wife sales, to which I briefly return at the end of the chapter.

## Forced marriage and modern slavery

Forced, servile, early and child marriage are amongst the many phenomena discussed under the rubric of 'modern slavery', and in policy, media and campaigning discourse they are typically represented as a 'cultural problem' that affects women and girls in 'traditional' societies of the developing world, and ethnic minority women in Western liberal countries. In this dominant discourse, consent is used to mark the moral boundary between the 'good' marriage on the one hand, and all forms of slavery-like marriage on the other. The United Nations Universal Declaration of Human Rights provides that '[m]arriage shall be entered into only with the free and full consent of the intending spouse' (art. 16(2)), and the 1956 Supplementary Convention on slavery identifies three slavery-like institutions or practices to which women can be subjected in the context of marriage, prohibiting any institution or practice whereby women are promised, given, exchanged, transferred or bequeathed in marriage 'without the right to refuse' (Weissbrodt and ASI, 2002). Neither the involvement of parents or families in arranging a marriage, nor the presence of an economic element in the arrangement, is marked as slavery-like by the Supplementary Convention – it 'is not the payment which is an abuse but its occurrence in a forced or non-consensual marriage' (Weissbrodt and Anti-Slavery International, 2002). This is an important proviso given that economic exchange has long been, and remains, an important feature of marriage (as in, for instance, dowry, bride price, groom price, bride service or other gifts and settlements made by parents of bride or groom upon marriage). Providing she agreed to the arrangement, then, a daughter could, in theory, be given in marriage to settle a debt without this constituting a slavery-like practice under the Supplementary Convention definition.

The absence of consent is also stressed in guidance on 'forced marriage' offered by the UK's Foreign & Commonwealth Office and Home Office (2013) – 'A forced marriage is where one or both people do not (or in cases of people with learning disabilities, cannot) consent to the marriage and pressure or abuse is used'. The pressures that are seen to constitute force or invalidate consent are listed as:

> physical (including threats, actual physical violence and sexual violence) or emotional and psychological (for example, when someone is made to feel like they're bringing shame on their family). Financial abuse (taking your wages or not giving you any money) can also be a factor.
>
> (FCO and Home Office, 2013)

The Australian parliament passed legislation in 2013 to criminalize forced marriage, again defining it as marriage entered into without the free and full consent of one or both parties as a result of threats, deception or coercion, which includes any of the following: force; duress; detention; psychological oppression; abuse of power; and taking advantage of a person's vulnerability (Anti-Slavery Australia, 2013). Early and child marriage are regarded as by definition non-consensual, since children are considered legally incapable of entering into contracts. However, though Article 2 of the 1962 Convention on Consent to

Marriage, Minimum Age for Marriage and Registration of Marriages requires state parties to 'take legislative action to specify a minimum age for marriage', it 'does not itself specify any minimum age' (Weissbrodt and ASI, 2002). There are differences between countries in terms of the age below which marriage is unlawful, and though the UN Convention on the Rights of the Child, 1989, defines a 'child' as a person below the age of 18, many countries – including the UK and the USA – allow those under 18 to marry with parental or juridical consent.

This emphasis on consent as marking the line between marriages that are free and those that are a form of modern slavery is reproduced in new abolitionist writings and campaign materials. In its 'International pledge to commit to making the ending of forced marriage a global priority', Walk Free invites us to sign up to the statement: 'I believe marriage should be a partnership between two consenting adults. That no man, woman or child should ever be forced, bullied, sold or trapped into a marriage'. According to Free the Slaves, forced marriage is a form of slavery that 'can and should be addressed within the framework of the anti-slavery movement' (FTS, 2013b: 9). But how easy is it to draw a clear line between 'forced' and 'voluntary' marriage in the contemporary world, and does the consensual/non-consensual boundary actually map onto a line between coercive, violent and exploitative relations and equal, consenting partnerships?

## Crossed lines: consent and subordination

In a TEDx talk, Kevin Bales (2010) explains that when he speaks of 'modern slavery', he is 'talking about real slavery. This is not about lousy marriages, this is not about jobs that suck. This is about people who cannot walk away, people who are forced to work without pay, people who are operating 24/7 under a threat of violence and have no pay'. If this is so, then the line between 'forced' marriages and those that are entered voluntarily does not necessarily correspond to the line between wives who are 'slaves' and those who are not. After all, it is possible for a woman to be emotionally and psychologically pressured into entering and remaining in a marriage that she does not want (e.g., by parents who tell her that she will bring shame on the family by refusing to marry, or by leaving her husband), and yet be free from both violence and labour exploitation within the home. A forced marriage could initiate a marriage that is, in Bales' terms, merely 'lousy', and not actually 'slavery'. Conversely, women who *do* give full and free consent to marriage or cohabitating partnerships can end up exploited, controlled by violence or its threat, and unable freely to leave the relationship.

This non-correspondence between the concept of 'forced marriage' and that of 'slavery' within marriage more generally is evident in a Free the Slaves report on the Democratic Republic of the Congo (DRC or Congo). Here, the report notes, many women and girls are victims of forced marriage:

> It can begin through abduction and rape. It can be arranged by fathers to repay debts. These brides enter marriage against their will. They are forced to provide labor without compensation. They cannot pursue their own life goals. And they cannot escape.
>
> (FTS, 2013b: 6)

In addition, they are subject to violence, its threat, or other psychological coercion, and therefore 'meet the definition of slavery' (FTS, 2013b: 9). However, the report's authors also note that in eastern DRC, there is 'a local context of marriage that normalizes the subservience of wives and even their physical abuse, whether the marriage is consensual or not', raising 'the question of whether one can consent to a marriage which, once entered, may become a relationship of enforced servitude that cannot be freely exited' (2013b: 9). But rather than moving from here to acknowledge that the forced/voluntary binary cannot grasp the realities of women's experience of unfreedom in the context of marriage, the report's authors extend the notion of 'forced marriage' forward in time, such that it is now said to apply 'not only at the moment of marriage – the wedding day – but also once the marital relationship is underway, including the reasonable means of exit, if any' (2013b: 9). Thus, while the report leads in with talk of abduction, rape, and women being in effect 'sold' to repay their fathers' debts, it soon moves to describing the experience of wives more generally. Married women and girls in the DRC, we are told, are often:

> exploited by being forced into sex, domestic servitude, or other labor. They often suffer, with high-risk pregnancies, limited healthcare and physical and emotional abuse. Crucially, they are allowed to make few if any independent decisions about their futures. These women and girls are not free to leave. Many have children whom they would lose if they left. Many have no means of survival since they lack education and skills. In addition, their families would not support them were they to return to their parents' home; since leaving a forced

marriage arranged by their families would be considered a shame to the entire family. Often, they are held physically against their will, and/or fear they would be hurt or killed if they left. Many of the girls and women [in the study]...had lost hope. As such, psychological control was enough to imprison them.

(FTS, 2013b: 9)

Now rather than foregrounding consent in their determination of whether or not a wife is a 'slave', they seemingly shift·to follow Bales and Soodalter's (2009: 13) recommendation that, 'When we aren't sure if someone is, in fact, a slave, we can ask one basic question: "Can this person walk away?"' But even a cursory glance at the legal and social position of wives in the contemporary world reveals the inadequacy of this piece of advice. Indeed, were we to systematically apply it to wives in the contemporary world, then Walk Free's estimate of around 36 million modern slaves would look woefully short of the mark.

Around 49 per cent of Nigeria's estimated population of 168 million (UN Data, 2015), for instance, is female, and many also suffer with high-risk pregnancies, limited healthcare and physical and emotional abuse. They live in a country where a tripartite legal system consisting of statutory, customary as well as sharia laws in the northern states, equips husbands with the powers that are described in new abolitionist writings as those of ownership. The Penal Code of Northern Nigeria grants husbands permission to beat their wives for the purpose of correction, providing the violence does not result in 'grievous hurt' (s. 55), while under Sharia law, the husband can withdraw maintenance if his wife refuses sexual intercourse (Africa4Womensrights, 2015). In addition, there are no sanctions against marital rape in the Penal Codes; a wife must in some cases seek her husband's permission to obtain a passport or to travel outside the country; and male heads of household generally control decisions regarding property (SIGI, 2012).

Consider the United Arab Emirates, where the female population (of approximately 2.7 million in 2013) is governed by a legal regime which constructs wives as minors under the authority and control of their husbands, denies them full rights to bodily integrity and rights freely to retract from marriage. Article 39 of the Personal Status Code (2005) makes a woman's male guardian and her prospective husband the parties to the marital contract, albeit that the validity of the contract is contingent upon the woman's approval and signature. The code does not recognize marital rape (and even though rape outside marriage is criminalized, fear of being accused of adultery – a crime which can be punished by flogging and death by stoning – acts as a strong disincentive to reporting it), and under Article 56, 'wives are required to obey their husbands, take care of the house and raise the children' (IFHR, 2010). Women can only access divorce through the 'Khul' procedure, under which they must renounce all their 'financial rights under the marriage contract, most notably, her dowry or mahr', and women's custody rights in relation to children are severely restricted (IFHR, 2010). Though Article 29 of the Constitution guarantees all UAE citizens freedom of movement and residence within the limits of the law:

> women must have the authorisation of their male guardians to travel abroad. An Emirati man has the right to seize the passports of his wife and daughters and can even request that the Immigration authorities prohibit their departure out of the UAE. Fathers and husbands have the legal authority to forbid their wives and daughters from working outside the home.
>
> (IFHR, 2010)

Last but not least, 'Under Article 71 of the Personal Status Code, women who leave their husbands can be ordered to return to the marital home. There have been several such recent court decisions' (IFHR, 2010). Elements of these laws can be found in many other countries, including other Gulf States, Egypt, Iran, Afghanistan, Nepal and Pakistan, so that many millions of the world's women, especially those who lack the resources to surmount extensive legal and financial obstacles, cannot walk away from unwanted or abusive marriages. Moreover, the social stigma that Free the Slaves describes as discouraging wives in the DRC from leaving their husbands also operates to some degree in many – perhaps even most – countries today (SIGI, 2012). To this we might add that laws criminalizing homosexuality (with punishments up to and including the death penalty) as well as often extreme violence against gay and transsexual people, make it difficult to describe either men or women who enter into heterosexual marriages or partnerships as exercising a free *choice* (Chalabi, 2013; Rich, 1980).

In Western popular and media debate, such laws and the attitudes towards women they enshrine are typically presented as expressions of pre-modern, or 'traditional' or 'backward' cultures, and often imagined as linked in particular to Islam. And yet a similar legal framework historically operated in modern, liberal, Judaeo-Christian societies, and its vestiges still remain. In this respect, Elizabeth Cady Stanton's introduction to the 1887 edition of *The History of Woman Suffrage* has a remarkably contemporary ring. 'American men may quiet their consciences with the delusion that no such injustice exists in this country as in Eastern nations', she observed, 'yet the same principle that degrades [woman] in Turkey, insults her in this republic' (Stanton et al., 1887). Until the mid-nineteenth century in the United States and the late nineteenth century in Britain, the common law doctrine of coverture worked to make 'husband and wife... one person in law, so that the legal existence of the woman was suspended during the marriage, or incorporated into that of the husband' (Brace, 2007: 39). It was the husband who, as head of household, enjoyed the status of civil citizenship.

Until the enactment of the Married Women's Property Acts, 'followed by a series of other measures, all fought for intensely', white wives were legally disabled in relation to property (Lister, 1997: 67). Like chattel slaves of America's Southern states, they could own nothing, possess nothing, acquire nothing in their own right. Husbands also had a legal right to the sexual use of their wives' bodies. They were exempt from prosecution for raping women to whom they were married, an immunity said to date back to judge Sir Matthew Hale's ruling in the seventeenth century that: 'A husband cannot be guilty of rape committed by himself upon his lawful wife, for by their mutual matrimonial consent and contract the wife hath given up herself in this kind unto her husband, which she cannot retract' (cited in Painter, 1991). The husband had a claim to his wife's obedience and her labour, a claim that was legally enforceable by violence; he had the power to permanently separate his wife from her children should he think fit to do so; and wives could not testify against their husbands in a court of law, as slaves could not testify against their owners or any white person. 'The legal and civil position of a wife resembled that of a slave', Carole Pateman (1988: 119) observes, noting that English wives could even be sold at public auction.

In modern, liberal societies, then, husbands were once granted in law and custom the rights to use, management, and disposal that Bales (2012: 283) identifies as indicative of ownership today. And this was no temporary or short-lived blind spot. In 1970, 'the Ohio Supreme Court held that a wife was "at most a superior servant to her husband... only chattel with no personality, no property, and no legally recognized feelings or rights"' (Hoff, 2007: 51). In the UK in 1985, a man who had 'killed his wife after she mocked the size of his penis, comparing it unfavourably with that of another lover' was acquitted of murder, and ultimately had his prison sentence 'reduced to four years after the Court of Appeal ruled: "To taunt a man about his lack of sexual inclination or prowess does involve striking at his character and personality at its most vulnerable"' (Maybin, 2014). In 2005 Lord Chief Justice, Lord Phillips, found it necessary to draft new guidelines on the sentencing of men found guilty of murdering their wives in order to explain to judges 'that nagging, or a man's discovery that his wife was unfaithful, did not justify a lighter sentence' (Viner, 2005). It was not until 1993 that marital rape was criminalized in the United States, just two years after five Law Lords in the UK had ruled against husbands' immunity from charges of raping their wives, declaring that marriage was (finally) no longer a relationship 'in which the wife was to be the subservient chattel of the husband' (cited in Painter, 1991).

Given that it took until the millennium for law makers to reach this conclusion, we should perhaps not be surprised by the fact that significant numbers of men in liberal societies still find it acceptable to exercise violent control over their wives or partners. In the UK, for example, the Office for National Statistics estimated that between 2012 and 2013, around 1.2 million women suffered domestic abuse (Home Office, 2014). Though women in the UK are in theory offered legal protection against such violence, social, psychological, financial and indeed legal barriers to escaping abusive relationships remain. The barriers are particularly high for poorer women (and the Legal Aid, Sentencing and Punishment of Offer Act 2012 has now raised the bar higher by making the legal aid that would allow women to 'walk away' from a violent and exploitative husband or partner even harder to access, O'Hara, 2014), and for migrant women whose immigration status is dependent on maintaining a relationship with the husband or partner. Just as systems of sponsorship can afford employers a great deal of power over temporary migrant workers, so immigration regulations that impose a 'spousal probationary period' of five years to protect the state against the possibility of 'bogus marriages' leave migrant spouses in a very vulnerable position in relation to the EU partners or spouses who sponsor their entry and right to remain. As Bridget Anderson comments, immigration controls 'help shape the constraining conditions within which power and force operate, and in this way could be said to "force" spouses to remain in unhappy marriages in order to keep their residency' (2013: 68).

For the moment, however, the key point is that a context of marriage that 'normalizes the subservience of wives and even their physical abuse' is not unique to the DRC, or a special feature of Muslim cultures, nor is it found only in countries in the developing world. And it was exactly such a context of marriage that led many feminist thinkers from the eighteenth century on to describe the condition of white European and American women as analogous to that of chattel slaves.

# Woman and slave

The metaphoric linking of women and slaves found in Mary Wollstonecraft's (1975, 2004) work became ubiquitous white feminist writings in the nineteenth century, especially in America:

'A woman,' Elizabeth Cady Stanton explains to the Woman's Rights Convention of 1856, 'has no name! She is Mrs. John or James, Peter or Paul, just as she changes masters; like the Southern slave, she takes the name of her owner.' The image of the slave evoked not simply the loss of 'liberty' but the loss of all claims to self-possession.

(Sanchez-Eppler, 1988: 31)

It was, indeed, often white feminists' 'opposition to arbitrary male power and the notion that they were their husband's property' that led to their involvement in the anti-slavery movement (Blackburn, 2011: 377). The similarities between the condition of white women and that of chattel slaves that were so obvious to those in the 'Woman Suffrage Movement' were far from visible to other nineteenth-century abolitionists, however. When American women arrived as representatives of anti-slavery organizations at the World Anti-Slavery Convention in London in 1840, they discovered that 'women formed no part of the constituent elements of the moral world' (Stanton et al., 1887). After lengthy debate amongst the male delegates, a vote was taken and by an overwhelming majority it was determined that women should be excluded as delegates of the convention, and allowed merely to observe from behind the bar (Hall, 2003, Stanton et al., 1887;).

That anti-slavery sentiment was as easily allied to profound gender conservatism as it was to feminism is also illustrated by the history of slave emancipation in the New World. In fact, the design of citizenship for freed slaves could be described as a testament to the power of Pateman's critique of liberal social contract theory, in which she argues that behind the social contract (a story of freedom) lies the sexual contract (a story of subjection), and that civil freedom 'is a masculine attribute' built upon the 'patriarchal right over women' (1988: 2). Consider abolition in the French colonies in 1848, for example. As Myriam Cottias (2008: 188) explains, from the time of the French Revolution, the patriarchal family had been regarded as the basic institution of society, 'allied to two other concepts, those of work and property'. To reorder slave societies in such a way as to include freed slaves as members of the community with civic responsibilities, 'abolitionists and republicans assumed the task of re-establishing masculine power through founding nuclear families that they considered to be the universally acknowledged fundamental unit of civic society' (Cottias, 2008: 191). Thus, the former distinction between free and enslaved was eradicated, but women were excluded from the vote, one of the primary rights of a citizen. Civil freedom had a gender, and it was male (see also Amy Dru Stanley's, 1998, brilliant exegesis of the ambiguities of emancipation for enslaved women in the United States). The self-mastery of the citizen implied mastery not merely of himself, but also of his wife and children.

If we think only about the fact that propertied white men occupied a position of mastery in relation to all the dependants in their households, the analogy between white wives and chattel slaves may look powerful. But its limits become clear if we broaden our focus. Despite sharing many legal disabilities with chattel slaves, nineteenth-century white American and European women were not constructed as aliens or outsiders, nor were they marked by the 'chronic, inalienable, dishonour' of the slave (Brace, 2004; Patterson, 1982: 12; Ware, 1992). Though unprotected from violence in the private sphere of the home, they were not routinely and systematically subjected to extreme and spectacular forms of violence as were chattel slaves (Paton, 2004), in fact in slave states, they were amongst those who perpetrated and/or ordered brutal violence against slaves (Ball, 2014; Beckles, 1993; Camp, 2004; Douglass, 1986; Mason, 1893; Prince, 2004). White women may not have been full and equal political subjects of modern, liberal societies of the eighteenth and nineteenth centuries, but they nonetheless belonged to the political community (Brace, 2004). As the remainder of this chapter aims to show, the restraints on wives' freedoms past and present reflect the inferior and unequal terms on which they were and are *included* in the social order, which is to say, they are rooted in the ways in which wives are *unlike*, not like, chattel slaves.

## Split lives: productive and reproductive labour, market and home, husbands and wives

One very obvious contrast between the experience of white wives and that of chattel slaves historically concerns their relation to, and role in, the processes through which the societies in which they lived produced and reproduced themselves on a daily and generational basis. Most (though not all) New World slaves were forced to labour to produce goods that their owners then sold across markets – cotton, rice, sugar cane, indigo, tobacco, coffee, ginger and so on. As a general rule, wives were not forced into this kind of labour by their husbands. In fact, the history of the movement towards modernity is one in which white women were progressively excluded from for-market production processes. In England, from the thirteenth century, the unity of production and reproduction that had typified feudal economies began to be undermined by the growing use of 'money payments (money rents, money taxes)' Sylvia Federici (2004: 28) argues. Increasingly, she continues, 'production-for-market was defined as a value-creating activity, whereas the reproduction of the worker began to be considered as valueless from an economic viewpoint and even ceased to be considered as work' (2004: 75).

The extremely and spectacularly violent persecution of women as witches took place alongside this splitting of productive and reproductive activity, and its gendering as 'male' and 'female' respectively. Women's sexuality and reproductive powers were one of the central foci of those who persecuted and tried 'witches', and a number of feminist scholars argue that the witch hunts played an important role in producing 'Woman as a different species, a being *suis generis*, more carnal and perverted by nature' (Federici, 2004: 192; Mies, 1986). The waged work available to those so constituted as 'women' was more poorly paid than that of their male counterparts, and became increasingly restricted with industrialization, not least because the development of industrial capitalism led to the centralization of production processes. The labour involved in producing goods for sale across markets gradually moved from the homesteads where it had initially taken place under 'putting out' and other systems of domestic production, into ever-larger factories. As a result, 'home' and 'place of paid work' were progressively separated out, and increasingly through the nineteenth century, they were imaginatively reconstructed as oppositional and gendered realms – the former woman's domain and the site of 'reproductive' labour, the latter men's domain and the site of 'productive' labour (McClintock, 1995). Alongside this, a new, bourgeois model of the family as 'a combination of co-residence and blood-relationship based on the patriarchal principle' was being generalized (Meis, 1986: 105).

Proletarian men came to collaborate with propertied men in the project of establishing modern, patriarchal homes and families, and their associated social and sexual division of labour (Hartmann, 1997). In Britain, by the 1840s, male trade unionists were articulating demands for a 'family wage', and expressing hopes that 'the day is not distant when the husband will be able to provide for his wife and family, without sending the former to endure the drudgery of a cotton mill'

(*Ten Hours' Advocate*, 1846, quoted in Hartmann, 1997: 105). In the United States too (albeit slightly later in the century), the American Federation of Labor (AFL) advocated against women's presence in the labour market, and explicitly called for labour legislation that would support 'the construction of a family model of male-breadwinning and female-homemaking':

> We stand for the principle that it is wrong to permit any of the female sex of our country to be forced to work, as we believe that the man should be provided with a fair wage in order to keep his female relatives from going to work.
>
> (Barzilay, 2012: 132)

Such dreams dovetailed neatly with liberal reformers' insistence that industrial work was harmful for women as well as for children. Indeed, campaigns ostensibly borne of concern about child labour often resulted in legislation to exclude women from certain forms of work, or to restrict women's working hours (Valverde, 1988). In such campaigns, even proponents of *laissez faire* could be found pressing for measures to preserve 'society' against the effects of self-regulating markets. Though state intervention in adult labour markets was unthinkable, children under 13 years of age were imagined as 'let out to hire' by their parents, not as entering into labour contracts as sovereign selves. The argument was extended to women by reformers who posited that legislative inter-ference with the labour of adult women was both conscionable and necessary, since 'not only are [women] much less free agents, but they are physically more incapable' (Leonard Horner, quoted in Valverde, 1988: 627).

Efforts to exclude women from paid employment drew upon and strengthened what E. P. Thompson (1991: 400) describes as the 'marriage of convenience' between Puritanism and industrial capitalism, which had worked to 'reform' popular culture from above. Such 'reform' had been strongly resisted in the eighteenth century, but ultimately this was a marriage that both helped to discipline the labouring poor into the habits of time-keeping, industry, thrift, temperance and responsibil-ity required for capitalist development, and to consolidate certain ideas about gender and sexuality. In particular, it bolstered and further pop-ularized the vigorous and violent condemnation of 'all non-productive, non-procreative forms of female sexuality', that had been mobilized in the witch hunts of the sixteenth and seventeenth centuries (Federici, 2004: 192), and that was central to white women's inclusion in the 'private', domestic realm of home and family. This brings us to a second sharp difference between the experience and condition of chattel slaves, and that of white wives.

## Objects, gifts, commodities and sociality

Marcel Mauss's (2002) classic anthropological text on 'the gift' argues that in societies where capitalist markets are absent, 'principles and practices of exchange are enacted by means of a traffic in gifts', and 'giving, receiving, and reciprocating gifts expresses, affirms, and in fact creates a social link between the participants' (Best, 2004: 82). For Mauss, as in orthodox sociological theory and in popular, everyday thought in liberal societies, gift exchange is quite unlike commodity exchange. Where the latter is instantaneous and impersonal (buyer and seller discharge all their obligations to one another the moment that the goods and the money change hands), gift-giving generates lasting social connections, for it 'instantiates an obligation to reciprocate' (Best, 2004: 82). Put another way, where commodity exchange is imagined to establish equivalence between *things*, gift exchange is seen as productive of relations between *persons* (Graeber, 2009: 110).

Levi-Strauss (1967) famously held that in what he termed 'primitive' societies, marriages are a form of gift exchange, and one that has particularly profound consequences, since it forms the basis of kinship. The exchange relation that constitutes marriage, he said, 'is not established between a man and a woman, but between two groups of men...the woman figures only as one of the objects of exchange, not as one of the partners' (1967: 134, cited in Tabet, 2012: 47). The woman is 'a conduit of a relationship rather than a partner to it', and 'it is the partners, not the presents...who are the beneficiaries of the product of such exchanges – social organization' (Rubin, 1997: 37). Modernity did not spell an end to the social construction and regulation of marriage as gift exchange. Hoff (2007: 49) notes that in America, 'from the colonial period until well into the first half of the nineteenth century, marriage was commonly an arranged, economic matter, with daughters passing from the economic control of parents to husbands', and the same was true in European countries.

In one respect, the women so transacted resembled chattel slaves. They were given, object-like, by their fathers and to husbands who, through marriage, acquired certain property rights in them. However, since the wife was constructed as a vehicle for kinship relations between groups of men, she was a very different sort of exchange object than the slave who was sold as a commodity, or even given as a gift. Unlike the slave, the wife was an object invested with the 'quasi-mystical power of social linkage' (Rubin, 1997: 37). Like the social equivalent of a conductor that allows the flow of electrical current in one or more directions, her capacity for motherhood extended these powers forward in time, such that she not only connected two existing sets of kin to each other, but also projected these connections into future generations. Their conductivity made white wives socially and politically valuable in ways that slaves were not. Indeed, as Pateman (1992) points out, though constructed as men's subordinates in the private sphere, and denied equality in the public sphere of economic and political life, white women have never been *completely* excluded from 'civil society'. They have long been understood to have a political contribution to make and a political duty to perform, and 'Their political duty (like their exclusion from citizenship) derives from their difference from men, notably their capacity for motherhood' (Pateman, 1992: 19). The political community depends fundamentally for its existence on women, for 'Only women can give physical life to new citizens, who, in their turn, give life to a democratic political order' (1992: 29).

The capacity for motherhood offered enslaved women in the New World no such route into inclusion and belonging. Except in the case of Puerto Rico, Cuba and Brazil in the second half of the nineteenth century, where 'free-womb' laws decreed 'that the children henceforth born to slave mothers would be free once they reached their mid-twenties' (Blackburn, 2011: 20),the status of children born of enslaved women in the New World followed that of their mothers. In the US South, miscegenation laws further functioned to 'protect the property of white males' (Lott, 1999: 44). Whether an enslaved female became pregnant as a result of rape or of a sexual encounter of her own choosing, by a white or black male, or by a husband or not, the child would simply add to her owner's stock of slaves. The economic value that attached to slave women's reproductive capacities varied over time and place. In some contexts, especially prior to the abolition of the slave trade, many slaveholders found it expedient to work enslaved women to infertility or even death (Campbell et al., 2008: 7). But even when their power to beget children was valued, it was valued for the material and pecuniary advantage it yielded the slaveholder, and/or for its contribution to the maintenance of the social order in which slaves were subordinated to the will of slaveholders (Beckles, 1987, 1993).

Whether male or female, chattel slaves had no legally or socially recognized right to a private, domestic existence. Though sometimes permitted to go through marriage ceremonies, they could not trade with each other loyalty and obedience for protection and economic support, or vice versa. In general, the male slave was in no position to support his enslaved wife or lover, or protect her from violence on the part of the slaveholder or anyone else, and the enslaved woman was unable to reserve her reproductive labour and capacities for her enslaved husband or partner. The sale of a slave did not generate lasting social connections between the white seller and buyer, and even when slaves were gifted by one owner to another, the exchange generated only a relationship of reciprocity, not one of kinship. Enslaved women had no recognized powers of social conductivity – they were legally alienated from kin backwards and forwards in time. As Vincent Brown (2009) reminds us, this absence of formal recognition did not prevent the enslaved from devising means by which to maintain connections to their ancestors and forge ties of kinship (see also Adams, 2007; Camp, 2004; Wong, 2009), but it does mark an overwhelming difference between white and enslaved women in the same societies.

In sum, in the period of transatlantic slavery, white women occupied a position that was simultaneously similar and dissimilar to that of chattel slaves, and similar and dissimilar to that of white men. And it is their dissimilarities from both that helps to explain the persistent restraints on their freedom in the contemporary world.

## The ambiguities of freedom

Much of the violence that was noted earlier in this chapter perpetrated against women of all racial and ethnic groups has its origins in the value attached to women as objects of *gift* (not commodity) exchange. Wherever a model of community formation within which men establish links with each other through the exchange of women pertains, female sexuality is constituted as both valuable and threatening to the boundaries of community (Chow, 1999; Rubin, 1997). The exchange of women as gifts facilitates the reproduction of a racial or ethnic community and its status hierarchies but, since women are not actually objects, only treated as such, their potential sexual agency is extremely dangerous. They could refuse:

> their traditional position as 'gifts', as the conduits and vehicles that facilitate social relations and enable group identity, [and] actually *give themselves*. By giving themselves, such women enter social relationships as active partners in the production of meanings rather than simply as the bearers of those meanings.
>
> (Chow, 1999: 47–8)

A gift that gives itself ceases to be a gift and thereby undermines the possibility of forging connections through gift exchange. This helps to explain why parents (mothers as well as fathers) have traditionally been and often still remain concerned to impose, and even to violently enforce, rigid controls on their daughters' freedom of movement and action, lest they 'ruin' themselves, or rather their value as objects of gift exchange. This in turn explains why girls and women who are not visibly under the control of a husband or patriarchal family (those who, depending on particular country context, dare to walk alone at night, to use public transport, to wear the 'wrong' clothes, to openly identify as lesbian, to work as an exotic dancer) are perceived as 'fair game' for rape and murder. If they will not acquiesce to their role as objects of gift exchange, they must live in fear of being forcibly reduced to objects of violence.

Again, these are ideas 'traditional' in Western liberal as well as other societies, as illustrated – amongst other things – by the language of 'ruin' and so-called shotgun weddings, or forced marriages, in twentieth-century Europe, Australia and North America (see, for example, Robertson, 2002). It is also important to note that while ostensibly addressing the ordering of the 'public' realm of the market, labour legislation in Europe and America that led to the expulsion of white women from many areas of employment in the nineteenth and first half of the twentieth century was strongly allied not just to a vision of women's place as in the home, but also to a desire to protect their 'sexual honour'. Demands for women to be 'freed' from the need to undertake paid work were threaded through with references to sexual 'decency', 'respectability' and 'true' womanhood. We see this in the widespread talk in nineteenth-century England of women being 'withdrawn from their domestic duties' by paid employment, and concerns that once so withdrawn, they would behave as men, meeting together 'to drink, sing, and smoke', as Lord Ashley put it in the House of Lords debate on the 1844 Act to limit women's hours of work in the mills (Valverde, 1988: 627). It is there too in the association between women's paid employment, family disintegration and prostitution that was a recurring theme in early twentieth-century American debates on working women (Barzilay, 2012), and in the use of the term 'working woman' as a euphemism for 'prostitute'. The conceptual oppositions of reproductive and productive labour, home and market, and virtuous and public woman left female domestic workers, as well as sex workers, in a particularly ambiguous position (Anderson, 2000; Hairong, 2008; McClintock, 1995), something of continuing relevance for such workers, for debates on 'trafficking' and for the possibilities of labour law (Kotiswaran, 2014a).

The gendered division between public, market life and private, domestic life was consolidated by the form of worker citizenship that was secured through class struggle in the twentieth century. Social protection against the labour market was not allocated to men and women alike, but rather in ways that reinforced women's dependence on men. This was another double movement, then. Women who belonged to the community were *excluded* from what was being constructed as the public realm of productive labour (meaning, the realm in which labour-power is sold across a market in order to produce goods and services for sale across markets), but *included* in what was being constructed as the private, domestic realm (Pateman, 1998). Here they performed (or supervised, depending on class position) the labour necessary to the reproduction, on a daily and generational basis, of the human beings who act in markets – such as the workers, employers, consumers and investors.

Women did not cease to *work*, nor was their labour irrelevant or peripheral to the functioning of capitalist economies (Anderson, 2000; De Beauvoir, 1972). It was their unpaid labour that ensured reproductive processes were managed with greater 'frugality' and 'parsimony' amongst free workers than by any slaveholder, as Adam Smith (1986: 184) had it. Women worked, but their 'reproductive' labour-power was not constructed as a disembodied commodity with a market value. It was instead socially imagined as inseparable from the person performing such labour, an expression of woman's very essence. As such, it was simultaneously devalued and idealized, or rather, made invisible as labour and idealized as a natural function (McClintock, 1995).

'The married woman is a slave whom one must be able to set on a throne', Balzac once remarked (quoted in Simone de Beauvoir, 1972: 142), and the idealization of women's socially and politically constructed difference, which continues to be imaginatively located in their supposed natural capacities for mothering and home-making, makes the subservient position of wives ambiguous. So powerful is the fiction of gender that many women are themselves deeply invested in it as an organizing principle of social life. In the past and still today, some of the staunchest defenders of gender and the patriarchal family form are women, eager to claim their seat on the throne. This again differentiates gender from slavery as a system of domination, and has long represented a conundrum for feminists. Even those heterosexual women who are not active cheerleaders of patriarchy often regard a highly unequal distribution of labour within the home as a symbiotic, rather than an exploitative, arrangement. And of course, it may often be true that an unequal arrangement is chosen and desired by, and brings psychic satisfaction to, both parties. A relationship managed and audited to ensure that each partner gives and receives identically and in equal proportion hardly sounds utopian. But all of this makes questions about freedom and marriage far more complicated than it appears in talk of 'forced marriage' as 'modern slavery'.

## Promises, promises: the limits of contract

After describing how the 'local context' in the DRC renders wives subordinate to their husbands, the Free the Slaves' report on 'forced marriage' states that there is also:

> a less malignant marital tradition in the DRC that places value on the wife as a person who deserves to be loved, cherished, and protected, as expressed poignantly by one villager... 'I give you my daughter to protect,' the man said, explaining what a father says to his son-in-law upon his daughter's marriage. 'Through you, let her experience love like she experienced from me'.
>
> (2013b: 10)

Since the daughter is as much an object when gifted from father to husband as she is when transacted to pay a debt, or abducted, the difference between this and a more 'malignant' marital tradition lies in the husband's promise to love, cherish and protect the wife. But what is the worth of a well-intentioned promise in relation to a person who is socially and politically positioned as subservient and powerless? The same question applies in relation to marriage in industrialized, liberal societies. Marriage is the legal seal on a promise to love and cherish exchanged between two consenting adults. It is described as a contract. And yet, as Hoff (2007: 49) points out, unlike a standard contract, the marriage contract is unwritten and its terms are not defined, so that 'Ostensibly, neither party knows exactly what provisions they are agreeing to'. It follows that even when consent is freely and fully given, it is unclear to what, precisely, the parties to the marriage contract have consented.

Marriage is not, in fact, a contract, but an institution – a patriarchal institution established for the purposes I have discussed above – and further contractualism is therefore no solution to the dilemmas it presents (Hoff, 2007: 50; Pateman, 1988). The limits to specification that leave non-contractual elements to most contracts (Durkheim, 1984) are even more exaggerated in relation to a life-long emotional–sexual–economic relationship. Who knows how time will alter either party's circumstances and level of physical, economic, emotional or psychological dependence? Who knows what aspects of an individual's personality will be brought out by the demands of parenthood, or the stress of some misfortune? Who knows whether either party will really be able to love the other in ten, 20 or 40 years time? Neither the well-intentioned promise of a husband on receipt of the gift of a woman, nor a marriage contract entered freely and voluntarily, offers any *guarantee* that the woman will not experience labour and sexual exploitation, and violence or its threat.

Women are made vulnerable to all three elements of what the new abolitionists term 'modern slavery' by their artificially constructed dependence on men. Social, cultural and economic barriers to independent existence and/or to sexual–emotional relationships other than marriage, and/or to equal consensual sexual enjoyment outside marriage leave the majority of women in the contemporary world with no real alternative to heterosexual marriage. The same barriers mean that very few women are in a position simply, and without consequence, to 'walk away' from unwanted or even violent marriages.

'There are few things more fundamental in life than marriage. It is the foundation of family. It provides legal and cultural structure for society', Free the Slaves (2013b: 9) tells us. Like their nineteenth-century forebears, they portray the patriarchal marriage and family form as 'a potent force for good in the world' (Ashworth, 1992: 196). Yet the evidence presented above suggests rather the opposite. To imagine a world in which women were *really* free to 'walk away' (and so a world in which practices such as bride kidnap, abduction, sale and other direct physical coercion of women and girls into marriage were rendered pointless), we would have to imagine a world in which women – both citizen and migrant – enjoy full and equal access to the means of life, education, housing and social protection from the market; full and equal access to mobility, justice, divorce, contraception, abortion and child care; a world in which women are no longer imagined as conduits for men's social relationships, and in which relations between men and women are no longer conceived as naturally hierarchical. We would, in short, have to imagine a world in which gender has been emptied of social and political significance. The new abolitionism is not a movement in pursuit of such a world. More than this, its uncritical acceptance of dominant constructions of gender and the binaries of liberal thought works to produce a lens through which women's efforts to free themselves of certain restraints, and exercise greater control over their own lives, can appear as 'slavery'.

## Consent and its conjuring tricks

The wife sales in England mentioned at the start of this chapter, E. P. Thompson observes, were vociferously condemned by middle-class nineteenth-century moral reformers in part because – they said – they resembled chattel slavery. Yet such sales took place in a context where divorce was unavailable and certain proprieties and norms involving the defence of the institution of marriage or of the family household strongly constrained working class women's ability to 'walk away' from unwanted marriages and pursue relationships with partners of their choice. The wife sale represented a public rite through which divorce could be effected and remarriage/cohabitation sanctioned by the community. Thompson's research revealed that while there were undoubtedly cases in which the wives concerned were victims of their husbands' desire simply to be rid of them, women were not necessarily passive objects of exchange. Rather, sales were frequently to the wife's lover and not necessarily to the advantage of the husband. Women often actively assented to the exchange, as illustrated by one news report of a case in which a husband attempted to back out of a sale midway through, and the wife angrily insisted, 'Let be, yer rogue. I will be sold. I wants a change' (1991: 462).

Thompson agreed unreservedly that the sale of wives 'took place in a society in which the law, the church, economy and custom placed women in an inferior or (formally) powerless position'; that they were rituals intended to degrade the women concerned; and that 'Even if we redefine the wife sale as divorce-with-consent it was an exchange of a woman between two men and not of a man between two women' (1991: 458–9). But what he found so striking and important about the historical data he retrieved and examined was that women of the labouring poor were nonetheless sometimes able to work this cultural form in ways that 'contradicted its intention', and that allowed them to pursue their own, actively chosen ends (1991: 461). In the absence of reforms to divorce laws, whose interests were served by the clampdown on this custom?

Funny tricks can be played with contract and consent. Through the eyes of nineteenth-century middle-class moralists, women's consent to marriage was meaningful despite the fact they occupied an inferior and formally powerless social position. In other words, women looked like subjects when they agreed to subordinate themselves to the will of a master. But when they sought to retract from that arrangement through the ritual of a wife sale – the only mechanism available to them by which to do so – the possibility of consent and agency vanished from view, and they were perceivable *only* as objects and slaves. There are echoes of the double character of the slave in this shifting between the attribution and refusal of women's agency. In the case of slaves, that shift allowed for human beings to be legally constructed as both objects of property and agents of crimes, and so invariably for their violent domination and perpetual alienage, whereas in the case of women (and children), object-hood can be associated with protection and inclusion, as well as with violence. Nonetheless, women's construction as ephemeral figures, capable of assuming the aspect of person or thing, depending on the purposes of the beholder, often leaves them at a particular disadvantage. This is well illustrated by discourse on, and responses to, what is dubbed 'sex trafficking', to be considered in the following chapter.

# 8
# Happy Endings?

In the first half of the nineteenth century, American proslavery thinkers often worked with a trope of wage labour as wage slavery (Cobden, 1854; Greenberg, 1996), as illustrated in the following extract from a letter published in the *Southern Literary Messenger* in 1843:

> One portion of the community always has, and always will live upon the labor of the other portion. In this respect, therefore, the African slave and the European operative stand upon a common platform... The only question with the operative is – what *form* his slavery shall assume? Shall he be the slave of a *master*, whose interest will nurture him in infancy, and whose humanity will provide for him in old age; or shall he be the slave of the *community*, which... bequeaths to him, in the decline of his days, as a remuneration for a life of... unremitting toil... the happy alternative of starvation, or the parish?
>
> (cited in Cunliffe, 1979: 7, emphasis original)

The letter casts both slavery and wage labour in terms of a taken-for-granted and highly unequal power relation between two classes (the class that labours, and the class that lives on the labour of others), one that appears as a form of asymmetric gift exchange. Through its author's eyes, the difference between chattel and wage slavery is that, in the case of the former, slaves are acknowledged as dependants, and private slaveholders graciously provide for them as such from cradle to grave, in exchange for which slaves can be expected to offer labour, obedience, and loyalty. In the system of wage slavery, by contrast, that dependence is refused and wage slaves are left to fend for themselves in an extremely hostile environment. If they are too sick or too old to work, the only alternative to starvation is the humiliation of public charity. In this account, the wrongness of *wage* slavery as a system is that it is wrenches labour from its bed in (hierarchically structured) networks of personal or human dependencies, leaving anonymous labourers without any protection save the paltry offerings of the parish.

As a justification for the institution of chattel slavery, the proslavery argument is clearly mendacious. But proslavery writers' characterization of the system of wage labour in England in the 1840s does not look so wide of the mark. The industrial revolution had by then 'brought about a shift to urban commerce that made vast populations of wage labourers rely on markets for food, housing, and all their basic needs' (Hart and Hann, 2009: 3). When in 1837, extraordinary weather conditions led to the failure of harvests, accompanied by a severe economic downturn, England entered the 'hungry forties'. Mortality is believed to have been higher in most English industrial towns in the 1830s and 1840s 'than it had been at any point in the previous 100 years of their development' (Szreter, 2005). Protesters described the absence of state intervention to ameliorate this situation as 'social murder' (Engels, 1973: 122).

Meanwhile, the New Poor Law of 1834 (called the 'New Starvation Law' by its critics) had reformed the system of poor-relief such that while the administrative units responsible could not actually refuse relief to those who applied for it, they could require applicants to enter the workhouse to secure it. 'Workhouses rose throughout the country like a chain of alien military forts, and the poor were seized like prisoners of war', and on entering the workhouse, husbands were separated from wives, children from parents (Anstruther, 1984: 20). They were effectively imprisoned, forced to labour without pay, and disciplined by means of violence (Losurdo, 2011). Nor were starvation and the parish always an 'either/or' option.

One well-publicized scandal concerned the inmates of a workhouse in Andover, Hampshire, who were compelled to undertake the labour of crushing bones for use as manure, a form of labour sanctioned by the Poor Law Commissioners in many workhouses across England. The establishment was run 'like a penal settlement' and in 1846, it was revealed that the inmates were so close to starvation that there were fights amongst them 'in the bone-yard for any bone, however stinking, to which adhered a particle of meat' (Anstruther, 1984: 22). The meaning of being so entirely cut adrift from any person with both the power and an obligation to protect and sustain you is well captured in a ditty, cited by Ansthruther (1984: 22), that children chanted as the coffins of dead inmates were drawn from the Andover Workhouse:

Rattle his bones
Over the stones
He's only a pauper
Whom nobody owns.

In this children's rhyme, the notion of 'ownership' is deployed to refer to a social rather than a property relation, reminding us that this is a term with multiple meanings, even in modern, liberal societies. Even today, to speak of someone being 'disowned' by family or friends is to describe a profound rejection, a severing of ties by means of which that person was once woven into a protective social fabric; people still speak of 'belonging' to a family, a community, an ethnic group, a club, without meaning that they are possessed as property. To 'own' can mean to admit, acknowledge or take responsibility for a deed or person (even for a problem in contemporary management-speak). In other words, historically and today in liberal societies, the term 'ownership' can be used not just to refer to a form of individual proprietorship that implies exclusive control, including the right to disposal, as described by Bales (2012), but also to a form of social inclusion or belonging, associated with rights as well as obligations. And while the idea of powers of property ownership being exercised over a human being is appalling, so too is the idea of a human being socially disowned, belonging nowhere, cast adrift, divested of any claim to protection or care (as the exile of Frederick Douglass' grandmother illustrates). Proslavery thinkers' representation of the former as a means by which to avoid the latter is very obviously self-interested, but the idea that the paupers who lived and died in the workhouse at Andover were free because they were not *de jure* slaves looks just as unsatisfactory.

'Freedom' is a concept just as elusive as 'slavery' (Patterson, 1991; Stevenson, 2012). Though widely represented in liberal societies as the absence of certain controls and restraints, a vision implicitly reproduced in the name of the organization 'Walk Free' and in the new abolitionist emphasis on the inability to 'walk away' as the defining feature of slavery, to imagine 'freedom' as negatively constituted by release from physical bondage reflects a very narrow and particular vision of human sociality. Claude Meillassoux (1991: 23) notes that E. Beneviste's (1969: 324) semantic analysis of the social origins of the term 'freedom' reveals that 'it refers to membership of an ethnic stock described by a metaphor taken from plant growth. This membership confers a privilege which is unknown to the alien and the slave'. Thus, Meillassoux continues:

Free men (the free-born, the gentles) are those *'who were born and have developed together'* ... The alien, *a contrario*, is he who did not grow up in the interstices of the social and economic networks which situate a man with respect to others.

(1991: 23, original emphasis)

Through this lens, it is belonging, rather than independence, that appears as slavery's opposite (see also Hartman, 2007).

However, human belonging also holds its own internal contradictions. To be immobilized in relations of dependency within a community, family or marriage, can be a suffocating experience whether or not it includes violence and labour exploitation, and is something that people can desperately long to escape. Judith Butler has observed that dispossession carries a 'double valence and ... is difficult to understand until we see that we value it in one of its modalities and abhor and resist it in another' (Butler and Athanasiou, 2013: 3). The same might be said of dependency. Dependence is ambiguous in the sense captured by Marx's notion of the wage labourer's double freedom (i.e., independent of both master *and* access to the means of life); it is also ambiguous in the sense that being 'owned' as a dependant, or belonging to others, can be experienced *either* as profoundly freeing *or* profoundly oppressive, depending on the wider social circumstances and on the individuals involved.

More than this, the obligations and affective ties generated by dependencies can both be valued as affirmations of one's own humanity, *and* render one unable to escape relations of domination. Consider, for example, the fact that in nineteenth-century America, slaves who were taken by their owners into 'free' Northern states (unlike fugitives who escaped to those states) could legally claim their freedom, and thus in theory became free to 'walk away' the moment they crossed the border. But as Edlie Wong (2009) has shown, Southern slaveholders wishing to travel North often specifically chose enslaved mothers to accompany them, knowing that they were unlikely to 'walk free' when the price of so doing would be permanent separation from their children. More generally, enslaved people's emotional ties to their children, and also to spouses and parents, meant that flight from slavery, even if successful, promised an extremely ambiguous form of 'freedom', one frequently marked by loss, grief, guilt and loneliness (Brown, 1847; Camp, 2004; Henson, 2008).

All these ambiguities play out in the contemporary phenomena of concern to the new abolitionists, just as they played out in nineteenth-century readings of chattel slavery, wage labour and mar-riage. Paying particular attention to 'sex trafficking', this chapter reflects on how a focus on these ambiguities complicates each of the three criteria that the new abolitionists take as definitive of 'slav-ery' (involuntariness; severe exploitation; violence) as instruments for distinguishing between 'slave' and 'non-slave'.

## Sex trafficking

When, in the late 1970s, E. P. Thompson lectured on the history of the sale of wives in England, his research was not well received by some feminists in the audience. Reflecting on this, Thompson noted that they had perhaps attended in the expectation of 'a scholarly disquisi-tion on yet one more example of the miserable oppression of women', and so felt cheated by the lecture's actual focus on the 'small space for personal assertion' that such sales could afford the wife (1991: 458). That some feminists were so welded to a view of women as always and only abject victims of patriarchy that they preferred to accept the view of wife sales promulgated by the (mostly male) nineteenth-century middle-class moralists who condemned it as slavery, than to counte-nance Thompson's reading of its ambiguities, will come as no surprise to anyone familiar with debates and activism on prostitution and 'sex trafficking' over the past 20 years. The school of feminist thought that propounded this view in the late 1970s and 1980s, namely radical feminism, also identified prostitution as a form of patriarchal violence against women, and female prostitutes as the quintessential victims of patriarchy (Barry, 1984; Dworkin, 1987). The lobby groups inspired to fight against prostitution by radical feminist ideas, such as the Coalition Against Trafficking in Women (CATW) founded in 1988, regarded pros-titution as 'sexual slavery' even before 'trafficking' came to be viewed as an urgent global problem. For them, a woman could no more give mean-ingful consent to her own objectification through prostitution than she could consent to be sold as a wife or a slave, and they therefore campaigned for the abolition of prostitution (Leidholdt and Raymond, 1990).

Growing political interest in 'human trafficking' in the 1990s offered a means through which to mainstream their understanding of sex com-merce as fundamentally wrong, and groups like CATW joined forces with religious groups that also opposed prostitution *per se* to press for measures to suppress and outlaw commercial sex. 'Trafficking' became the focal point of what Ron Weitzer (2007) has described as a 'moral crusade' against the sex industry. Those engaged in this crusade are very much concerned with the structural forces that lie behind female prostitution and find it unthinkable that women or girls could exercise agency within it. Indeed, 'sex trafficking' (especially 'child sex trafficking') is often depicted as a crime more monstrous than murder, and frequently described as 'unimaginable', even though imagination seems to play an important role in its construction as a social problem (see, for example David Feingold's, 2010, incisive critique of law enforcement officers' and journalists' credulity with regard to tales of online auctions of virgins and the like). Certainly, 'sex trafficking' – and also 'child slavery' – are topics that apparently have the power to dull the critical faculties of even the sharpest minds. Orlando Patterson is a case in point. In a skilful critique of Kevin Bales' work, he observes that Bales' definition of slavery is so wide and so loose that it:

> embraces not only the vast majority of bondsmen and exploited agricultural laborers in poor countries, but a substantial proportion of women in traditional societies around the world. Why stop at 27 million slaves? Using his definition, at least 150 million of the 359.8 million desperately poor women aged 15–64 in India, at least a half of the 49.5 million women, 15–64, in Pakistan, and the overwhelming majority of the 8.6 million women, 15–64, in Afghanistan must be considered slaves. We are already up to 183 million, and I have not yet started counting exploited men who are unable, through force or economic necessity, to escape their harsh labor conditions.
>
> (2012: 373)

However, Patterson takes Bales to task for the many factual, methodological and conceptual errors in his work in order to argue that 'there are at least 8.98 million genuine slaves in the world today. That is 8.98 million too many and quite enough to encourage and promote abolitionist activism' (2012: 359). Patterson arrives at his own figure of 8.98 million contemporary slaves by adding to an estimated 1.6 million in traditional forms of slavery an estimate of 5.7 million children 'in slavery' and 1.6 million women in what he terms 'commercial sexual slavery'. The children are mostly those estimated to be involved in 'worst forms of child labour', which Patterson accepts as slavery because, he says, children are always in this condition as a result of choices made by adults, controlled by adults, and often isolated from their families (assertions that, as seen in Chapter 3, are challenged by Okyere's research on children in artisanal gold mining and also by other research to be noted later). So far as women in 'sexual slavery' are concerned, Patterson cites a study of Ukrainian women in prostitution in Greece (its lead author is a member of CATW) which describes them as isolated by 'their poor grasp of the local language and their illegal status in the host country. A typical isolation strategy is to trick or coerce a woman into surrendering her passport making her, in effect, a "non-person"' (Hughes and Denisova, 2003; cited in Patterson, 2012: 355). The isolation so produced is, according to Patterson, the closest modern equivalent to the natal alienation of the traditional slave. But as there is ample research evidence to show that large numbers of exploited of migrant workers, male and female, across a range of sectors, are similarly isolated and stripped of identity documents, the question Patterson poses Bales might equally be put to him. Why stop at 1.6 million? What is so special about migrant *sex* workers?

Many commentators' view of prostitution as exceptional is informed by the literature produced by feminists campaigning for its abolition (see, for example, Jeffreys, 1997), in which it appears as a uniformly dismal, violent and oppressive institution. However, there is a very large body of academic research on sex commerce around the world, which reveals, perhaps above all else, immense diversity in terms of its social organization and the power relations it involves. In addition to reminding us that men and transsexuals, as well as women and children, are present in the commercial sex trade, this research shows that the degree of control that individuals who sell sexual services (whether or not they are migrants) exercise over whether, when, how often and on what terms they work, varies according to a range of factors. These include the particular economic pressures operating on them; the contractual form of the sexual–economic exchanges they enter into; and the specific legal, institutional, social, political and ideological context in which they work (see, for example, Bernstein, 2007a; Ditmore et al., 2010; Kelly, 2008; Mahdavi, 2011; O'Connell Davidson, 2005; Oso, 2002; Sánchez Taylor, 2001; Sanders, 2005; Shah, 2014).

Nonetheless, prostitution remains a profoundly stigmatized activity; one that, even when not actually criminalized, has nowhere been fully incorporated into the formal, capitalist economy and regulated as an employment sector in the same way as other forms of service work. In Europe, for example, regardless of how prostitution law is framed, self-employment remains the norm in the sex sector, and most sex work takes place in the informal economy beyond reach of any form of employment regulation or labour protection (Cruz, 2013). The concealed and informal nature of sex work can certainly work to the advantage of the unscrupulous employers and also law enforcement agents and other criminals seeking to cream off a slice of the profits of sex businesses in exchange for 'protection'. But the 'underground' character and ambiguous standing of prostitution as a form of work, alongside the fact that it is a means of earning that need not imply any start-up costs or training, are sources of its attraction to many workers, as well as potential sources of vulnerability (Day, 2007).

As part of an 'economy of makeshifts' that stands outside civil society (Brace, 2002: 334), prostitution has long represented, and continues to represent, an opportunity to earn money, often relatively good, money, for some of those who are excluded from civil society, and whose access to other, more formally organized and regulated labour markets is highly restricted or entirely denied. This includes those whose immigration status denies them the right to work, runaway teenagers and drug addicts, as well as poor women. Yet sex work is not only chosen by the excluded and marginalized – it can also appeal to those who have plenty of other options. And even amongst those who lack privilege, sex commerce may not be chosen primarily for economic reasons. It can also be attractive to those who actively wish to reject or flee the constraining norms of their particular society or community. It can be, and is, used by teenage boys and young men seeking to escape homophobic violence or rejection by family and community, as well as by those wishing to transcend the gender assigned to them at birth (Aggleton, 1999). It can also be used by women and girls seeking independence from sexual and gender norms that they find oppressive. Indeed, it can simultaneously represent the best or only earning opportunity open to an individual, *and* an activity expressing resistance to certain gender and sexual norms. I do not claim that this is the case for the majority of those who sell sexual services, but it is nonetheless part of the diversity of motivation and experience that needs to be recognized as falling under the umbrella of 'prostitution'.

Of special significance for debates on 'trafficking', sex commerce can be strategically used in order to do more than either subsist or escape. It can be a means through which to pursue and achieve migration projects, and through them actualize life-plans that would otherwise be unrealizable (Agustin, 2007; Andrijasevic, 2010). Take, for example, Nigerian women and girls who work off migration-related debt through street sex work in Italy, and who are often presented as exemplary victims of 'sex trafficking' (Kara, 2009). Violence – sometimes extreme – can feature in their experience, but it is not a consistent or universal element of relations between Nigerian debtor-migrants and their creditors (known as sponsors or Madams), and the powers that Madams exercise over the migrant are typically surrendered once the debt has been worked off, which generally takes between one and three years. At this point, former debtors often work for their former Madams supervising new debtor-migrants, and sometimes continue on to become Madams themselves (Carling, 2005; Cole and Booth, 2007; Testai, 2008).

This 'career' trajectory is not unique to migrant women from Nigeria. Sophie Day (2010: 824) reports that in London, migrant sex workers from many different countries of origin often initially 'worked in appalling conditions, with no English, and keeping little of their money. Yet, situations changed and it often took less than a year to become a manager in turn and send remittances home'. Her research, like many other rich and compelling ethnographies (Brennan, 2004; Cheng, 2010; Kempadoo, 2004; Lainez, 2016; Molland, 2012; Nencel, 2001; Shah, 2014; Zheng, 2009, to name but a few), reveals how difficult it is to fit 'sex work migration' into the binaries of trafficking/smuggling, slavery/freedom, victim/agent, or involuntary/voluntary action.

## Involuntariness

Slavery, according to Walk Free (2014), involves 'one person depriving another person of their freedom: their freedom to leave one job for another, their freedom to leave one workplace for another, their freedom to control their own body'. This may seem a straightforward definition when the person named 'slave' is deprived of these freedoms by means of chains or locked doors and barred windows (although as has been seen, it depends very much on whether the person depriving them of their freedom is authorized to do so by the state). But it becomes more complicated when an individual has consented to restrictions on their freedom. If a person voluntarily enters into a marriage and promises obedience and sexual fidelity to her husband, is she 'deprived' of the freedom to control her own body, or has she surrendered it? If an employment contract binds an employee to working out a period of three months' notice before leaving, is the employee 'deprived' of her freedom to leave one workplace for another during that time? What if she enters an agreement to work for three months to repay a debt? What if she agrees to work for three years in order to repay a debt? What if she agrees to work in prostitution for three years to pay off a debt?

To accept that it is, in principle, possible to agree to restrictions on freedom, and to voluntarily transfer control over aspects of the self (labour-power, sexuality) to another person, muddies the water between being 'free' and being 'deprived of freedom'. We are no longer able to speak in absolutes, but rather have to make judgments about the kind of restrictions to which people can legitimately be invited to consent. Additionally, these judgments are historically and contextually variable and contested. The restrictions on freedom implied by debt are particularly troublesome. Since monetized debt and markets in credit are as central to the operation of contemporary capitalism as wage labour, the new abolitionists need to draw a line between situations in which the restraints on freedom implied by debt are morally acceptable, and thus constitute restrictions that people can meaningfully consent to, and situations in which those restraints are intolerable, and so nullify consent. As has been seen, they attempt to do this through a focus on whether or not debt generates direct, hierarchical and potentially violent relations of dependency on a creditor (when it does, it is 'debt bondage').

Implicitly, then, debt is subdivided into two distinct forms: the 'good' type, which is organized as a commodity exchange by banks, building societies, student loan companies and so on, and which belongs to the realm of impersonal, contractual, market relations; and the 'bad' type that drags victims into inescapable and profoundly asymmetrical personal relationships of power in which they are deprived of freedom of movement and control over their bodies. But this distinction does not actually map onto the voluntary/involuntary binary. Debt that entails high levels of dependency upon a creditor and heavy restraints on freedom for a certain period of time can be actively chosen, as demonstrated by research on various forms of indentured labour historically and today, and on other contemporary systems through which migration debts are paid off by a period of labour closely controlled by the creditor at the point of destination.

Nigerian women and girls in sex work in Italy are a case in point. Because the relations of dependency established through this system of debt are time limited, and because this is in most cases a route to desired goal, the Madam/sponsor is often viewed 'as a potential benefactor rather than as a criminal... as hero than as villain by the aspiring immigrant' (Cole and Booth, 2007). Nigerian sex workers in Italy interviewed by Patrizia Testai (2008: 73) did not consider themselves as enslaved, or perceive the debt as fundamentally 'different from the debt that ordinary people incur in most parts of the world'. For many of the women concerned, even if the arrangement with the sponsor implies being unable to leave one job or employer for another, or to control their own body for a period of time, they are not 'deprived' of freedom but have rather entered into a bargain, a bargain that they often feel duty-bound to honour, as opposed to coerced into accepting. This helps to explain the cases in which women and girls who have been 'rescued' from 'debt-slavery' by anti-trafficking NGOs have subsequently run away from their 'rescuers' to return to their sponsors and fulfil the obligations they have taken on (Carling, 2005).

Though the 'bad' type of debt relation can be associated with violence and/or trickery, many creditors honour their agreements, so that 'bad' arrangements can lead to outcomes that are good, from the debtor's perspective. Conversely, impersonal systems of credit are no guarantee of protection against extremely coercive pressures. In the UK, for instance, banks, building societies and credit card companies are increasingly selling bad consumer debts to debt collection agencies, which then use aggressive, unethical and sometimes illegal methods to secure repayments, hounding debtors with constant and threatening letters, text messages and phone calls, including automated phone calls (McVeigh, 2009); bailiffs also have 'an appalling track record of abusing their existing powers against vulnerable people. They are often abusive and aggressive, and use threats of violence and prison to pressurise people into paying lump sums they cannot afford' (CAB, 2007; see also Kilgore, 2014). 'Good' debt arrangements can lead to very bad outcomes for the debtor.

The division between impersonal markets in credit, and debt that generates personal dependencies, does not perfectly correspond to a line between empowered and protected subjects autonomously pursuing their own ends, and victimized, hapless 'debt slaves', who have 'lost free will'. Nor does this division allow for the fact that impersonal debt can intersect with personal relations in such a way as to make 'walking away' an impossible choice for some workers, even in the absence of a creditor breathing down their necks. Consider, for example, a news report detailing the case of one of the Nepalese construction workers who died in Qatar in October 2013, a 23-year-old named Moktan. This young man came from a poor village and, according to the report, his elderly father had borrowed the equivalent of around £1,000 to pay for his passage and agency fees to Qatar, hoping that he would be able to assist the family by remitting some of his earnings back home:

The money was borrowed from a loan shark and was supposed to be reimbursed by Moktan's Qatari employer, but this did not happen. The family now fear that the loan shark will demand that Moktan's two sisters, aged 14 and 16, who were collateral for the loan, be sent to work in brothels in Mumbai to pay off the debt.

(Doward, 2014)

The creditor's contract was with the elderly father, not with Moktan, and the 'loan shark' did not exercise direct or personalistic power over Moktan while he was working in Qatar. Nonetheless, it seems probable that his father's debt would have weighed heavily on Moktan, operating as a pressure to act against his own will at least as strong as that which could be directly exerted over a debtor by a creditor. Even if he had not been bound by the constraints of the *kafala* system, would he have been free to walk away from the hazardous, and possibly also violent, working conditions he faced? And if his sisters do end up going to work in brothel prostitution in Mumbai to pay off the debt, how will their situation differ from his?

Debt exists on both sides of what is imagined as the public/private divide. In the public realm of the market, debt is framed as an impersonal object or 'thing' that can be precisely quantified, monetized, transferred, commodified and traded (Graeber, 2009). But in the private realm, even in contemporary liberal societies, debt is still recognized as a human and moral phenomenon. Here, it is read as referring to a diffuse set of personal obligations and as both expressive and generative of lasting relations of dependency between people. Most of us are debtors both in the sense of having taken on monetized debt to buy our homes and fund our various life projects, *and* in the sense of being obligated to other people. Many of us 'owe' our lives, or the lives of our loved ones, to the interventions of doctors, nurses, police officers, firefighters, or strangers who gave assistance at moments of dire trouble. As adults, most of us feel that we 'owe' something to those who fed and raised us as children, and that we 'owe' favours to friends, colleagues and acquaintances who help us out.

In none of these examples does debt have violent origins; nor does violence feature as a mode of enforcing the obligations they imply. Nonetheless, such debts typically carry sufficient moral weight to make people act against their own wills in the sense of doing things they would otherwise prefer not to do. This is true in relation to trivial matters, such as returning a child-care favour even when inconvenient to do so. It is also true in relation to very consequential matters. Returning to Moktan, if his sisters do end up in brothel prostitution in Mumbai, it will likely not only or even necessarily be due to any threat of violence from the 'loan shark', but also a result of the sisters' sense of obligation towards the elderly father who gifted them life and who will have no way in which to service his debts unless they accept the work. This illustrates how very different logics of debt can be at work even in a single instance of what is frequently described as 'debt slavery' (in this case, indentured prostitution), and testifies to the fact that the binaries of liberal thought (voluntary/involuntary, subject/object, public/private) do not reflect actual divisions between distinct fields of human experience.

At base, 'debt' describes a form of social glue, one that can hold people together in very different kinds of relationships and for varying periods of time. Debt is sociality and vice versa (Graeber, 2011), and sociality, along with the debts it implies, has many involuntary elements. We do not ask to be born, as some children have been known to complain. Drawing on Heidegger's concept of 'thrownness', John Park (2013: 3) notes that many of 'the most important circumstances and aspects of ourselves – our gender, our race, the families into which we're born, and even our core beliefs – are things that describe who we are, but are not the result of conscious choice'. Such '"thrownness" continues to shape political life', Park goes on, most obviously 'in the law of citizenship as most people are born "citizens" because they were born in a particular place, or they become citizens because their parents were also citizens' (2013: 3). For some, this implies unearned privilege, as Joseph Carens (1987: 252) famously argued: 'Citizenship in Western liberal democracies is the modern equivalent of feudal privilege – an inherited status that greatly enhances one's life chances'. But many un-chosen, involuntary aspects of self imply particular duties and obligations – or debts – that must be worked off in particular ways. According to where we happen to have been 'thrown', being marked 'female' at birth may imply an obligation to perform particular forms of labour or make sacrifices that are not required of those marked 'male'; being born a citizen may imply a duty to undertake a period of military service for the state.

To think of debt is to think of obligations, and we cannot state that all involuntary debts that generate personal dependencies imply a condition of 'slavery' without making almost all of us 'slaves'. David Graeber's work suggests that if we are interested in the roots of chattel slavery and other systems of domination in the modern, liberal world, it is the attempt to move from 'human economies' (those based on personal relations) to impersonal market systems that should concern us, as opposed to debt *per se*. This move had (and continues to have) 'profoundly jarring effects on the entire system of social production' and was linked to the 'spread of new forms of predatory violence' (Graeber, 2009: 125). The move also had profound consequences for the position of women and children in the social order, as seen in the previous chapter. And this is one very important reason why adding the criterion of severe economic exploitation to the definition of 'modern slavery' does not help to solve the problems generated by efforts to distinguish between slave and non-slave in the contemporary world.

## On being and not being exploited

In addition to the 'involuntariness' of their situation, 'modern slaves' are said to be subject to 'severe economic exploitation' (Craig et al., 2007: 12). Defining the term 'economic exploitation', let alone 'severe economic exploitation', is not for the fainthearted, since questions about what constitutes an exploitative employment practice are much disputed. In fact, they have historically been, and remain, a central focus of the organized labour movement's struggle to protect workers. There is variation between countries and variation between economic sectors in the same country in terms of what is socially and legally constructed as acceptable employment practice. In the absence of a global political consensus on minimum employment rights, and of cross-national and cross-sector norms regarding employment relations, it extremely difficult to come up with a neutral, universal yardstick against which 'exploitation' could be measured (Anderson and O'Connell Davidson, 2003). We are back on territory in which it is necessary to judge where, on a continuum and in different contexts, 'appropriate' exploitation ends and 'inappropriate' exploitation begins.

Undaunted, Kevin Bales (2007a) defines severe economic exploitation as the absence of a wage, or payment of wages in a form that either covers only the most basic necessities for daily survival, or that can be clawed back by the employer. This is not a definition that would satisfy those Marxists for whom exploitation is to be found in the gap between the price that attaches to a 'fair day's pay', and the value that is extracted from the worker's labour-power (Reiman, 1987), nor, indeed, can it accommodate the fact that *de jure* slaves were sometimes paid wages. The fact of payment does not signal the presence of freedom, Tom Brass (2010: 123) notes, 'as many examples of payments made to workers who were also chattel slaves, indentured labourers, debt peons and attached or bonded, all attest'.

Nor does talk of 'severe economic exploitation' help us to make sense of the fact that, in contexts where human, subsistence economies have been replaced by a social order in which markets play a central role in the production and distribution of material sustenance, access to markets becomes a source of (relative) freedom, as well as unfreedom. Where there is no functioning system of welfare to protect people *from* the market, those whose access *to* labour markets (or indeed credit markets) is curtailed by various legal and social barriers often find that, to paraphrase Joan Robinson (2006: 45), the misery of being exploited by capitalists, or exploiting oneself in informal economic activities, 'is nothing compared to the misery of not being exploited at all'. Such informal activities and debt relations can thus be valued – especially by women, teenagers and young people – either because they promise a kind of freedom from unwanted dependency on relatives, or because they allow the individuals concerned to fulfil their social obligations to the parents and/or children to whom they belong and who belong to them. As one interviewee in Skilbrei and Tveit's (2007: 50) research on Nigerian women in prostitution in Norway said:

> I support 16 people at home in Benin city, 14 younger sisters and brothers, my mother and my son. They all live in two rooms. I cannot go back, I have to help them … Now … they can eat three meals every day, and my brothers and sisters can go to school every day.

But equally, Pemunta's (2011: 167) study of Bayang and Ejagham women of Southwest Cameroon in the 1980s and '90s offers an example of how, in the face of economic upheavals and structural adjustment, women's engagement in both cross border trade and sex work offered a means not merely of subsistence, but also by which to challenge and reconfigure 'existing gendered norms of femininity and womanhood in the face of overwhelming community pressure to marry'. Similarly, research on the teenagers who appear in new abolitionist discourse as 'victims of trafficking' and 'child slaves' has repeatedly found that their desire for independence, and/or to independently contribute to their families' subsistence, often plays an important role in their decisions to leave home to work elsewhere. It also shows that, even when children have been subject to various forms of deception and abuse in the process of movement or in employment, they do not always regret that decision, and may still subjectively evaluate their current situation (described as 'slavery' by the new abolitionists) as preferable to their former condition at home (Bastia, 2005; Busza et al., 2004; Hashim and Thorsen, 2011; Howard, 2014; Howard and Morganti, 2015).

Nicolas Lainez (2016) has observed that the focus on certain forms of debt relation as a source of enslavement overlooks the 'emancipatory dimensions' of credit, and the same is true of other phenomena discussed under the heading of 'modern slavery'. While this can often stand as a testament to the bleakness of the options open to many people in the contemporary world, it also stands in marked contrast to evidence on transatlantic slavery, which does not suggest that those transported to the New World ever subjectively experienced chattel slavery as an improvement to their lot. Indeed, herein lies one of the most dangerous features of dominant discourse on 'trafficking'. To speak of particular forms of economic activity (e.g., prostitution) or particular types of debt relation, or particular economic activities undertaken by particular 'types' of person (e.g., 'worst forms of child labour') as 'modern slavery' encourages policy makers and others to overlook the fact that these activities and arrangements are simultaneously sites of potential abuse and exploitation *and* spaces for self-assertion. And because this fact is ignored, a raft of repressive measures has been enacted in many countries of the world in the name of suppressing markets and forms of action where 'slavery' is said to flourish. Measures to prevent children from migrating offer one example of this (Hirsch, 2013; Howard, 2014; O'Connell Davidson, 2011; Whitehead and Hashim, 2005), measures to suppress markets in commercial sex provide another. Which brings me to questions about the new abolitionists' highly selective attention to violence.

## On violence

Violence is afforded a privileged role in the making of 'modern slaves' by the new abolitionists, for violence or its threat is understood to indicate the presence of force, and so the absence of consent. And yet 'force' and 'violence' are slippery terms, and do not refer to an absolute or stable set of practices or experiences. The physical chastizement – up to and including beatings and whippings – of formally 'free' servants, labourers, members of the armed forces, and wives, has historically been legally authorized and still sometimes is in the case of wives. Bodily punishments inflicted on children in particular have long been, and still are, considered appropriate and legitimate disciplinary measures, rather than 'violence' (in the UK, Justice Secretary Chris Grayling recently stated that he smacked his own children when they were young and defended the right of parents to smack, for example, BBC, 2013).

When the new abolitionists emphasize violence as standing at the heart of slavery, they implicitly rely on a notion of *inappropriate* force, as opposed to force per se (Moravcsik, 1998: 173). This makes 'violence' a less straightforward litmus test with regard to identifying 'modern slavery' than it may at first appear. The new abolitionists need to include more than just brute acts of corporeal restraint and violence, otherwise they would be forced back to a Hobbesian definition of slavery. Craig et al. (2007: 13) therefore expand the concept of violence as follows:

> very often relationships of enslavement do not actually involve physical violence. However, the nature of the relationship – the nature of working and housing conditions, the withdrawal of important papers such as passports or ID documents, deceit and the abuse of power, the use of what are essentially thugs to maintain control – may make the threat of violence a real one and render the possibility of flight a remote one.
>
> (see also Weissbrodt and Anti-Slavery International, 2002: 7)

But the new abolitionists also wish to prevent the term from billowing out to cover 'the situation of people being forced into dangerous or difficult work by economic circumstances or other impersonal forces' (Craig et al., 2007: 13), and to exclude the use of force and the exercise of potentially violent control by actors authorized by the state (at least, by states they deem legitimate) in the context of prisons, immigration detention, and border control.

This means having to keep one eye very firmly shut while looking at prostitution, for the supposed rise of 'sex trafficking' has 'triggered the establishment of a vast network of laws designed to regulate cross-border movements through a criminal justice and law order approach' (Kapur, 2013: 18; Sharma, 2003), which has in turn prompted, or been used to justify, coercive interventions on the part of states that have led to the incarceration and/or deportation of very large numbers of women and children (Ahmed and Seshu, 2015; Bernstein, 2007b; O'Connell Davidson, 2006). In the United States, the moral panic surrounding 'sex trafficking' has extended to include US national teenagers, whose involvement with commercial sex has now been legally codified as 'domestic minor sex trafficking', and thus rebranded as 'modern slavery'. As Jennifer Musto (2015) observes, this can lead to young people acquiring criminal records through their 'protracted involvement in the justice system…Their status as victims may not protect them from the consequences of this, including limits on "future education, employment, housing, financial, and other life opportunities."'

The ambition to combat 'sex trafficking' has also been reworked to justify state sponsored violence against sex workers in the form of police raids on brothels. Though now framed as missions to 'rescue' VoTs, one sex worker in New York described her experience of such raids as follows:

They...bang on the door, they break the door, they come in with the guns out!...It's really horrible, sometimes if they are very angry, they don't let you get dressed. They take you in your work clothes....One never lets go of the fear. Being afraid never goes away. They provoke that.

(Sex Workers Project, 2009: 3)

The fact that sex workers are escorted by police officers, often in hand-cuffs, to police custody following such raids surely raises the question of who is being 'rescued' and from what through these actions, and the United States is far from alone in its use of force to 'rescue' women and girls from 'sex slavery'. Indeed, in 2005, the World Health Organiza-tion condemned the use of 'rescue raids' in several countries, including Indonesia and India, on grounds that they compromised the safety of sex workers (Ahmed and Seshu, 2014). And new abolitionist organiza-tions are sometimes front-line actors in interventions that, while osten-sibly designed to redeem 'slaves', indiscriminately impact on all sex workers and work to close down the space for self-assertion that sex com-merce can provide. In 2003, the International Justice Mission agitated for police action against a brothel in Chiang Mai, Thailand, prompting raids in which 43 women and girls were rounded up and then locked into two rooms of an orphanage by Public Welfare authorities. Though some said that they had indeed been forced into prostitution, others had chosen to work in the brothel and were indignant that they were being detained when they needed to make money for their families:

During the one hour each day when they were allowed outside the building, four girls soon slipped out the front gate and disappeared. A few nights later, 11 of them strung together sheets, shimmied down the second-floor window of the orphanage, and climbed over a con-crete and wire fence. Nine more ran away weeks later. During one of the escape attempts, a woman fell from a second-story window and was hospitalized with back injuries...Within one month following the raid, a total of 24 girls and women had run away from being saved.

(Jones, 2003)

Such '[s]cenes of Anglo men raiding brothels in Cambodia, India, Thailand, and other developing nations' became increasingly common after 'faith based human rights groups applied pressure on the Bush administration to more vigorously enforce the 2000 Trafficking Victims Protection Act (TVPA)', Gretchen Soderlund (2005: 68) remarks. The conditions into which the 'rescued' are transported through such raids can be, in effect, a form of imprisonment, and reports of their physical and sexual abuse and labour exploitation at the hands of their 'saviours' are not unknown (see also Crowhurst, 2012; Testai, 2008; Malucelli, 2006 on the treatment of women 'rescued' from street prostitution in Italy). As Anders Lisborg (2014: 23) notes, though there are examples of good practice, in his visits to shelters and 'victim protection facilities' in South Eastern Europe, South Asia and South East Asia, he found that:

> rigid restrictions and confinement are still being enforced in the name of protection . . . One shelter was strategically located on a small island and frequently shelters are characterized by high wall, iron bars in front of the windows, closed gates and guards – not only to keep possible intruders out but also to keep victims in.

It is the construction of women and children as non-agential that allows the movement from brothel prostitution into state or NGO-run institutions to be read as 'rescue', and the condition of being held behind bars as 'freedom' rather than 'captivity'. Imagined as lacking or robbed of 'free will', they can be 'slaves' (for slaves are held to be objects), but not 'captives' (for captives are viewed as subjects) (Shilliam, 2012).

Responses to 'sex trafficking' seemingly reflect a concern with the dangers that women and children 'adrift' from their true masters present to the social order, as much as with the dangers actually faced by individual women and children (including the threat of hunger and homelessness, for example). The parallels between the contemporary movement against 'sex trafficking' and the late nineteenth-/early twentieth-century movement against the 'traffic' in women for prostitution (dubbed 'white slavery') are striking (Agustin, 2007; Chapkis, 1997; Doezema, 2010), with the latter also having led to large numbers of women and girls being held against their will in institutions that resembled workhouses (Bartley, 2000). Indeed, more generally, state-led 'anti-trafficking' activity seems to continue, or at least echo, a wider history of state controls over populations deemed 'dangerous' because 'they will not adapt themselves to the community', as Nazi officials put it in the 1930s when explaining the need to monitor and control the residence and leisure activities of beggars, vagrants, prostitutes, drunkards, people with sexually transmitted diseases who evaded public health measures and other 'deviants' (Rodger, 2008: xiv).

Policy debate and practice on 'trafficking' is in line with the wider processes through which 'the worlds of welfare and criminal justice' are being brought together (Rodger, 2008: ix), and through which the criminal law is being used in the asylum process and against migrants more generally (Webber, 2006). And yet, we are told, the state's interest in combatting 'trafficking' is borne of a desire to protect human rights. Force, it seems, has become protection, just as war became peace, slavery freedom and ignorance strength, in George Orwell's *1984*.

## Beyond fairy-tale endings: modern slavery and freedom as politics

The overarching narrative guiding the reports, blogs, testimonies, and other materials presented on new abolitionist websites is one in which the suffering of the slave is terminated by emancipation. Rescue from 'modern slavery' is the happy ending that transports the victim-protagonist into an entirely different moral condition, a 'happy land, where things come right', where kids are kids, the sexually abused get therapy, workers get paid, and everyone can pursue their dreams. 'Finally, Rambho was rescued by . . . Free the Slaves' partner organization in northern India. Today Ramhbo is free and he plans to help his mother find a house. He also wants to make sure no other children become enslaved', concludes one of the 'survivor stories' on Free the Slaves' website, and 'Suddenly they were doing the same work but *making money. They immediately invested in their future. They sent their kids to school . . . They left hell* a while back. And have *no plans for a return visit*', ends another (FTS, 2014c, original emphasis).

Such stories do not attend to the social structures that limit the options open to people, thereby generating unenviable choices and cramping the space for self-expression. All the ambiguities of dependency, debt, and belonging, and of forms of market action that are simultaneously sites of potential abuse and spaces for self-assertion, are written out. The moral complexity of the different actors is similarly expunged. New abolitionist stories do not feature 'traffickers' who are themselves poor women, or victims who aspire to become 'traffickers', or young people who choose to migrate into harsh forms of manual labour because such labour migration affords them opportunities for sexual experiences they otherwise could not access, or police and NGO workers who sexually abuse, or beat and/or imprison the victims they 'rescue'. They are rather, as Sverre Molland (2012: 10) has argued in relation to discourse on 'sex trafficking' in the Mekong region, stories in which:

The victim is the perfect pawn representing total innocence and a total deprivation of agency. The traffickers are perfect villains, a pure form of evil with total control and the ability to adapt to market opportunities. And the marketplace where all this takes place is perfect – a classical liberal economic marketplace subject to only a handful of simple and predictable laws of cause and effect.

In fairy tales, Bruno Bettelheim observed:

A person is either good or bad, nothing in between. One brother is stupid, the other is clever. One sister is virtuous and industrious, the others are vile and lazy. One is beautiful, the others are ugly. One parent is all good, the other evil.

(1976: 9)

Similarly, the figures in new abolitionist stories of 'modern slavery' and 'trafficking' are stripped of ambivalence. And just as in fairy tales and romantic novels, marriage is the conclusion that resolves all of the heroine's suffering, conflict, loss and longing with which we have identified throughout the story, emancipation from slavery is the optimistic and emotionally satisfying ending that provides readers with closure.

Ray Fleming (1993: 30) notes that 'the fairytale conclusion in marriage and living "happily ever after" is often a reflection of a patriarchal value system that confirms the power of men in culture to equate their own interests and perspectives with universals'. The stories in which the happy ending for 'modern slaves' is incorporation into market society as consumers and 'respectable' wage labourers for the adults, and school or institutional care for the kids, likewise reflect a tendency for the interests and perspectives of the powerful to be equated with universals. More than this, the depiction of a world in which people are *either* abject, passive objects and slaves *or* freely contracting subjects, works to rescue the privileged Western audience from certain psychic anxieties. 'Hauntingly beautiful' images of the suffering bodies of pre-modern, non-agential, victimized Others, such as those produced by Lisa Kristine for example, provide a mirror in which modern liberal subjects find themselves reflected back not just twice as large, as Virginia Woolf had it, but also twice as free.

Kevin Bales likens 'modern slavery' to smallpox, a definite condition that 'we' can eradicate. The disease metaphor makes powerful rhetoric, but also disregards the serious divisions that exist between those who study slavery historically, as well as those who research the phenomena dubbed 'modern slavery'. There was consensus amongst medical scientists that smallpox was caused by infection with a virus (one that can be identified not merely in living victims of the disease but also in corpses). The medical science community agreed to name that virus 'variola', and also agreed it could be differentiated from other viruses, even from those in the same genus, family and subfamily. But, as has been seen, there is no equivalent consensus on the nature, defining characteristics and proper definition of 'slavery' amongst the community of researchers who study it. Walk Free's *Global Slavery Index* is not, therefore, like the work of epidemiologists mapping a disease; the International Justice Mission staff who 'raid and rescue' brothels are not like Médecins Sans Frontières staff treating victims of Ebola.

'Modern slavery' no longer exists, and none of the phenomena today described as such are the equivalent of transatlantic slavery. In the contemporary world, the term 'modern slavery' names not a thing, but a set of judgments and contentions about political authority, belonging, rights and obligations, about commodification, market and society, about what it means to be a person, and what it means to be free. As such, it *should* be a zone of political contestation. When claims are made that this or that phenomenon is like slavery, it *should* spark connections to current political debate and analysis, for instance, about whether all humankind has a right of locomotion, and what moral right states have to use overwhelming physical force against 'ordinary, peaceful people, seeking only the opportunity to build decent, secure lives for themselves and their families' (Carens, 1987: 251); about the continuing afterlife of racial slavery (Black Lives Matter, 2015; Sexton, 2010); about the continuing intersections of caste with class, gender and sexuality 'to create...patterns of exclusion, vulnerability, stigma, and disenfranchisement' (Nilsen and Roy, 2015: 2); about the legitimacy of the Prison Industrial Complex (Davis, 2003; Sudbury, 2005b); about the morality of debt – international and consumer debt, as well as personal (Graeber, 2011); about capitalism's continuing drive to enclose more and more of the common wealth through the commodification of water, health care, knowledge and education, such that democratic control of social resources is in effect surrendered to private individuals (Holmwood and Bhambra, 2012; Soron and Laxer, 2006); about rights to protection against the market, and how to assure such rights universally (Cruz, 2013; Weeks, 2011); about how to ensure that protections against markets do not reify divisions and inequalities based on gender, age and sexuality; about the exclusionary conception of the normative child that informs current policy and practice with regard to children's rights (Grier, 2004; O'Connell Davidson, 2011; Okyere, 2012); and much, much more.

But the new abolitionism does not foster connections to such debate and analysis. It selectively names certain forms of suffering as 'modern slavery', then constructs simplistic narratives about the roots of these problems in criminality or evil. In so doing, it abstracts the phenomena under discussion from their social and political moorings and propels them into the ether of morality, where they float as essential wrongs – as the stuff of fairy tales. The discourse of 'modern slavery' promulgated by the new abolitionists and gratefully seized by our political leaders is one that depoliticizes (Brown, 2006; Jacobsen and Stenvoll, 2010). It is a discourse that misses social structure and the violence that it does, and that mistakes freedom for a 'thing' that can be stolen or gifted or possessed, rather than a relational practice, a creative world-building process, a collective and social endeavour (Stevenson, 2012; Weeks, 2011: 22). At the same time, it is a discourse that misses human agency, insisting on victims that are truly objectified, eviscerated of will, empty ciphers.

This discourse cannot be countered simply by turning it on its head and celebrating the agency and resilience of those who find ways to pursue their own ends and maintain (or escape) social connections against all odds. The idea of a world in which intrepid subjects rescue abject objects has to be jettisoned without being replaced by the comforting certainty that 'heroic subalterns' (Brown, 2009) will seize the standard and lead the fight for rights and justice. To practice freedom, we have to somehow keep hold of the hope inspired by liberalism's statement of human liberty and equality, but attenuate it with both a recognition that liberalism itself is no guarantee of either equality or freedom, and that the ideal, independent liberal subject is a fiction. There are no persons who are not also things, and no human things who are not also persons. Therein lies the horror of transatlantic slavery, but also the potential for a better world, providing we can accept, and even celebrate, the fact of our inescapable (if fluctuating, variable and always ambivalent) dependence on Others, proximate and remote, kin and stranger.

The serious study of modern (by which I mean *transatlantic*) slavery could teach us much about contemporary political life in this regard. At least, it could providing we reflect on Vincent Brown's (2009: 1249) advice to slavery historians:

> If scholars were to emphasize the efforts of the enslaved more than the condition of slavery, we might at least tell richer stories about

how the endeavors of the weakest and most abject have at times reshaped the world. The history of their social and political lives lies between resistance and oblivion, not in the nature of their condition but in their continuous struggles to remake it. Those struggles are slavery's bequest to us.

# Notes

## 1 Imagining Modernity, Forgetting Slavery

1. The Protocol defines trafficking as:

   The recruitment, transportation, transfer, harbouring or receipt of persons, by means of threat or use of force or other forms of coercion, of abduction, of fraud, of deception, of the abuse of power or of a position of vulnerability or of the giving or receiving of payments or benefits to achieve the consent of a person having control over another person, for the purpose of exploitation. Exploitation shall include, at a minimum, the exploitation of the prostitution of others or other forms of sexual exploitation, forced labour or services, slavery or practices similar to slavery, servitude or the removal of organs.

   The Trafficking Protocol further provides that the consent of a VoT to the intended exploitation is irrelevant where any of the means set out above have been used.

## 2 Marking the Boundaries of Slavery

1. It refers to relations between creditor and debtor when the 'reasonably assessed' value of the labour/services provided by the debtor 'is not applied towards the liquidation of the debt or the length and nature of those services are not respectively limited and defined'.

## 3 Slavery and Wage Labour: Freedom and Its Doubles

1. I am grateful to Alf Gunvald Nilsen for drawing my attention to this point.

## 4 Mastery, Race and Nation: Prisons and Borders, Afterlives and Legacies of Transatlantic Slavery

1. This case involved the arrest of 117 enslaved and 11 free black men, charged with 'attempting to raise an Insurrection' (2009: 303). Denmark Vesey, the alleged leader of the plot, was said to speak several languages, and to have 'slaved in St. Domingo' before being resettled in Charleston by his master, a sea captain. The plot supposedly included a plan for the rebels to escape to

Haiti by sea following the 'insurrection', and Vesey thus 'embodied the radical promise of the Black Atlantic' (Wong, 2009: 184).

## 5 'Trafficking' as a Modern Slave Trade? Mobility, Slavery and Escape

1. I am grateful to Kyunghee Kook for making me think about this example.

# References

Acheson, J. (1981) 'Anthropology of fishing', *Annual Review of Anthropology*, 10, pp. 275–316.

Adams, J. (2007) *Wounds of Returning*. London and Durham, NC: University of North Carolina Press.

Africa4womensrights (2015) 'Nigeria', *Africa for Women's Rights*. http://www.africa4womensrights.org/public/Dossier_of_Claims/Nigeria-UK.pdf (accessed 17 March 2015).

Agamben, G. (1995) *Homo Sacer: Sovereign Power and the Bare Life*. Stanford, CA: Stanford University Press.

Aggleton, P. (ed.) (1999) *Men Who Sell Sex*. London: UCL.

Agustin, L. (2007) *Sex at the Margins*. London: Zed.

Ahmed, A. and Seshu, M. (2015) '"We have the right not to be 'rescued'..."': When anti-trafficking programs undermine the health and well-being of sex workers', in M. Dragiewicz (ed.) *Global Human Trafficking*. London: Routledge, pp. 169–180.

Albahari, M. (2006) 'Death and the modern state: Making borders and sovereignty at the southern edges of Europe', CCIS Working Paper 137, University of California, San Diego, May.

Alexander, M. (2010) *The New Jim Crow*. New York: The New Press.

Alpes, J. (2011) *Bushfalling: How Young Cameroonians Dare to Migrate*. Faculteit der Maatschappij en Gedragswetwnschappen.

Allain, J. (ed.) (2012) *The Legal Understanding of Slavery*. Oxford: Oxford University Press.

Allain, J. and Bales, K. (2012) 'Slavery and its definition', *Global Dialogue*, 14:2 (Summer/Autumn). http://www.worlddialogue.org/content.php?id=529 (accessed 10 March 2015).

Amnesty International (2014) 'Spain: Accountability urged for "appalling" migrant deaths in Ceuta', 14 February. http://www.amnesty.org/en/news/spain-accountability-urged-appalling-migrant-deaths-ceuta-2014-02-14 (accessed 10 March 2015).

Anderson, B. (2000) *Doing the Dirty Work*. London: Zed.

Anderson, B. (2013) *Us and Them: The Dangerous Politics of Immigration Control*. Oxford: Oxford University Press.

Anderson, B. and O'Connell Davidson, J. (2003) 'Is Trafficking in Human Beings Demand Driven? A multi-country pilot study'. *IOM Migration Research Series*, No. 15. Geneva: IOM.

Anderson, B. and Rogaly, B. (2005) *Free Market, Forced Labour?* London: TUC.

Anderson, B., Sharma, N. and Wright, C. (2011) 'Editorial: Why no borders?' *Refuge*, 26:2, pp. 5–18.

Andersson, R. (2014a) *Illegality, Inc.* Oakland, CA: University of California Press.

Andersson, R. (2014b) 'Mare Nostrum and migrant deaths: The humanitarian paradox at Europe's frontiers', *OpenDemocracy*, 30 October. https://

www.opendemocracy.net/5050/ruben-andersson/mare-nostrum-and-migrant
-deaths-humanitarian-paradox-at-europe's-frontiers-0.

Andrijasevic, R. (2006) 'Lampedusa in focus: Migrants caught between the Libyan desert and the deep sea', *Feminist Review*, 82:1, pp. 119–124.

Andrijasevic, R. (2007) 'Beautiful dead bodies: Gender, migration and representation in anti-trafficking campaigns', *Feminist Review*, 86, pp. 24–44.

Andrijasevic, R. (2010) *Migration, Agency and Citizenship in Sex Trafficking*. Houndmills: Palgrave Macmillan.

Anstruther, I. (1984) *The Scandal of the Andover Workhouse*. Gloucester: Alan Sutton.

Anti-Slavery Australia (2013) 'Forced Marriage'. http://www.antislavery.org.au/images/stories/5_-_What_is_Forced_Marriage.pdf.

Anti-Slavery International (2015) 'What is modern slavery?' http://www.antislavery.org/english/slavery_today/what_is_modern_slavery.aspx.

Aradau, C. (2004) 'The perverse politics of four-letter words: Risk and pity in the securitisation of human trafficking', *Millennium: Journal of International Studies*, 33:2, pp. 251–277.

Archard, D. (1993) *Children: Rights and childhood*. London: Routledge.

Ashworth, J. (1992) 'The relationship between capitalism and humanitarianism', in T. Bender (ed.) *The AntiSlavery Debate*. Berkeley, CA: University of California Press.

Aydelotte, F. (1913) 'Elizabethan Rogues and Vagabonds'. *Oxford Historical and Literary Studies*, Volume 1. Oxford: Clarendon Press.

Baboulias, Y. (2013) 'Greece's modern slavery: Lessons from Manolada', *New Statesman*, 19 April. http://www.newstatesman.com/austerity-and-its-discontents/2013/04/greeces-modern-slavery-lessons-manolada (accessed 8 March 2015).

Baines, D. and Sharma, N. (2002) 'Is citizenship a useful concept in social policy work? non-citizens: The case of migrant workers in Canada', *Studies in Political Economy*, 69, pp. 75–107.

Balch, O. (2013) 'Corporate initiative can play a major role in anti-trafficking movement', *Guardian*, 3 April. www.theguardian.com/global-development-professionals-network/2013/apr/03/human-trafficking-global-business-coalition.

Bales, K. (1999) *Disposable People: New Slavery in the Global Economy*. Berkeley, CA: University of California Press.

Bales, K. (2004) *New Slavery: A Reference Handbook*. Santa Barbara, CA: ABC-CLIO.

Bales, K. (2006) 'Testing a theory of modern slavery', *Free the Slaves*. https://www.freetheslaves.net/Document.Doc?id=14 (accessed 28 January 2015).

Bales, K. (2005) *Understanding Global Slavery*. Berkeley, CA: University of California Press.

Bales, K. (2007a) 'Defining and measuring modern slavery', *Free the Slaves*, https://www.freetheslaves.net/Document.Doc?id=21 (accessed 28 January 2015).

Bales, K. (2007b) 'Of human bondage', *Financial Times Magazine*, 16 March. http://www.ft.com/cms/s/0/4b75a5c8-d316-11db-829f-000b5df10621.html#axzz3638viyNC.

Bales, K. (2010) 'How to combat modern slavery', *TedX*. http://www.ted.com/talks/kevin_bales_how_to_combat_modern_slavery (accessed 15 February 2015).

Bales, K. (2012) 'Slavery in its contemporary manifestations', in J. Allain (ed.) *The Legal Understanding of Slavery*. Oxford: Oxford University Press.

Bales, K. (2013) 'Shining the light on modern slavery', *Huffington Post*, 17 October. http://www.huffingtonpost.co.uk/professor-kevin-bales/modern -slavery_b_4114123.html.

Bales, K. and Soodalter, R. (2009) *The Slave Next Door*. Berkeley, CA: University of California Press.

Ball, C. (2014) *Fifty Years in Chains, or the Life of an American Slave*. CreateSpace Independent Publishing Platform.

Barry, K. (1984) *Female Sexual Slavery*. New York: New York University Press.

Barry, K. (1995) *The Prostitution of Sexuality*. New York: New York University Press.

Bartley, P. (2000) *Prostitution: Prevention and Reform in England, 1860–1914*. London: Routledge.

Barzilay, A. (2012) 'Labor regulation as family regulation: Decent work and decent families', *Berkeley Journal of Employment and Labor Law*, 33:1, pp. 117–149.

Barzun, J. (1954) 'Introduction', *Flaubert: Dictionary of Accepted Ideas*. New York: New Directions.

Bastia, T. (2005) 'Child trafficking or teenage migration? Bolivian migrants in Argentina', *International Migration*, 43:4, pp. 57–89.

Batstone, D. (2007) *Not for Sale: The Return of the Global Slave Trade–and How We Can Fight It*. New York: Harper Collins.

BBC (2008) 'UN forum aims to end trafficking', *BBC News*, 21 February. http:// newsvote.bbc.co.uk/2/hi/europe/7242180.stm.

BBC (2013) 'Chris Grayling defends child smacking', *BBC News UK*, 3 February. http://www.bbc.co.uk/news/uk-21311916.

Beckles, H. (1987) *Black Rebellion in Barbados*. Bridgetown, Barbados: Carib Research & Publications.

Beckles, H. (1993) 'White women and slavery in the Caribbean', *History Workshop*, Colonial and Post-Colonial History (Autumn), 36, pp. 66–82.

Beckles, H. (1998) 'Taking liberties: Enslaved women and anti-slavery in the Caribbean', in C. Midgley (ed.) *Gender and Imperialism*. Manchester: Manchester University Press, pp. 137–160.

Behrmann, E. (2013) 'Gates helps Australia's richest man in bid to end slavery', *Bloomberg*, 15 April. http://www.bloomberg.com/news/2013-04-10/gates-helps -australia-s-richest-man-in-bid-to-end-slavery.html.

Bellagamba, A. (2015) 'The legacies of slavery in southern Senegal', *Beyond Trafficking and Slavery*, 29 April. https://www.opendemocracy.net/beyondslavery/ alice-bellagamba/legacies-of-slavery-in-southern-senegal.

Beneviste, E. (1969) *Le Vocabulaire des Institutions Indo-Europeenes*. Paris: Editions De Minuit. 2 vols.

Bernstein, E. (2007a) *Temporarily Yours: Intimacy, Authenticity, and the Commerce of Sex*. Chicago: University of Chicago Press.

Bernstein, E. (2007b) 'The sexual politics of the "new abolitionism."' *Differences: Journal of Feminist Cultural Studies*, special issue on God and Country, guest ed. Elizabeth Castelli, 18:3, pp. 128–151.

Best, J. (1993) *Threatened Children: Rhetoric and Concern about Child Victims*. Chicago: University of Chicago Press.

Best, S. (2004) *The Fugitive's Properties: Law and the Poetics of Possession*. Chicago: University of Chicago Press.

Bettelheim, B. (1978 [1976]) *The Uses of Enchantment: The Meaning and Importance of Fairy Tales*. London: Penguin.

Bhabha, J. and Zard, M. (2006) 'Smuggled or Trafficked?' *Forced Migration Review*, 25 May, pp. 6–8.

Bhambra, G. (2007) *Rethinking Modernity: Postcolonialism and the Sociological Imagination*. Basingstoke: Palgrave Macmillan.

Bibb, H. (2008) Narrative of the Life and Adventures of Henry Bibb an American Slave Written by Himself. Bibliobazaar Reproduction.

Black Lives Matter (2015) 'State of the black union', Black Lives Matter, http://blacklivesmatter.com/state-of-the-black-union/ (accessed 23 May 2015).

Blackburn, R. (1988) 'Slavery – its special features and social role', in L. Archer (ed.) *Slavery and Other Forms of Unfree Labour*. London: Routledge, pp. 262–279.

Blackburn, R. (2011) *The American Crucible: Slavery, Emancipation and Human Rights*. London: Verso.

Blackmon, D. (2008) *Slavery by Another Name*. New York: Doubleday.

Border Crossing Observatory (2015) Australian Border Deaths Database. http://artsonline.monash.edu.au/thebordercrossingobservatory/publications/australian-border-deaths-database/ (accessed 9 March 2015).

Bosworth, M. and Guild, M. (2008) 'Governing through migration control: Security and citizenship in Britain', *British Journal of Criminology*, 48:6, pp. 703–719.

Bourne, G. (1845) *A Condensed Anti-Slavery Bible Argument: By a Citizen of Virginia*. New York: S. W. Benedict. http://docsouth.unc.edu/church/bourne/bourne.html.

Brace, L. (2002) 'The tragedy of the freelance hustler: Hegel, gender and civil society', *Contemporary Political Theory*, 1, pp. 329–347.

Brace, L. (2004) *The Politics of Property: Freedom and Belonging*. Edinburgh: Edinburgh University Press.

Brace, L. (2007) 'The social contract', in G. Blakeley and V. Bryson (eds) *The Impact of Feminism on Political Concepts and Debates*. Manchester: Manchester University Press.

Brace, L. (2014) 'Bodies in abolition: Broken hearts and open wounds', *Citizenship Studies*, 18:5, pp. 485–498.

Brass, T. (1999) *Towards a Comparative Political Economy of Unfree Labour*. London: Frank Cass.

Brass, T. (2010) 'Capitalism, primitive accumulation and unfree labour', in H. Veltmeyer (ed.) *Imperialism, Crisis and Class Struggle: The Enduring Verities of Capitalism – Essays Presented to James Petras*. Leiden: Brill, pp. 67–149.

Braverman, H. (1974) *Labor and Monopoly Capital*. New York: Monthly Review Press.

Bravo, K. (2011) 'The role of the transatlantic slave trade in contemporary anti-human trafficking discourse', *Seattle Journal for Social Justice*, 9:2, pp. 555–597.

Breman, J. (2009) 'Myth of the global safety net', *New Left Review*, 59, pp. 29–36.

Breman, J. (2013) *At Work in the Informal Economy of India. A Perspective from the Bottom Up*. New Delhi: Oxford University Press.

Brennan, D. (2004) *What's Love Got to Do with It? Transnational Desires and Sex Tourism in the Dominican Republic*. London: Duke University Press.

Brown, V. (2009) 'Social death and political life in the study of slavery', *American Historical Review*, December, pp. 1231–1249.

Brown, W. (1847) 'Narrative of William W. Brown', *A Fugitive Slave*. Boston: Anti-Slavery Office. Kindle edition.

Brown, W. (2006) *Regulating Aversion: Tolerance in the Age of Identity and Empire*. Oxford: Princeton University Press.

Burnard, T. (2004) *Mastery, Tyranny, and Desire: Thomas Thistlewood and His Slaves in the Anglo Jamaican World*. Chapel Hill: University of North Carolina Press.

Busza, J., Castle, S. and Diarra, A. (2004) 'Trafficking and health', *British Medical Journal*, 328, pp. 1369–1371.

Butler, J. and Athanasiou, A. (2013) *Dispossession: The Performative in the Political*. Cambridge: Polity.

CAB (2007) 'Abuse of powers by bailiffs set to get much worse', *Citizens Advice Warns*. http://www.citizensadvice.org.uk/press_20070305.

Camp, S. (2004) *Closer to Freedom*. London and Durham, NC: University of North Carolina Press.

Campbell, G., Miers, S. and Miller, J. (2008) 'Strategies of women and constraints of enslavement in the modern Americas', in G. Campbell, S. Miers and J. Miller, (eds) *Women and Slavery*. Athens: Ohio University Press, pp. 1–26.

Carens, J. (1987) 'Aliens and citizens: The case for open borders', *The Review of Politics*, 49:2, pp. 251–273.

Carling, J. (2005) 'Trafficking in women from Nigeria to Europe', *Migration Information Source*. http://www.migrationinformation.org/Feature/display.cfm?ID= 318.

Carter, M. and Torabully, K. (2002) *Coolitude: An Anthology of the Indian Labour Diaspora*. London: Anthem Press.

Castles, S. and Kosack, G. (1973) *Immigrant Workers and Class Structure in Western Europe*. Oxford: Oxford University Press.

Caverno, A. (1992) 'Equality and difference: Amnesia in political thought', in G. Bock and S. James (eds) *Beyond Equality and Difference: Citizenship, Feminist Politics, Female Subjectivity*. London: Routledge.

Cesaire, A. (1972) *Discourse on Colonialism*. New York: Monthly Review Press.

Chakrabarty, D. (1992) 'Postcoloniality and the artifice of history: Who speaks for "Indian" pasts?' *Representations*, 37, pp. 1–27.

Chalabi, M. (2013) 'State-sponsored homophobia: mapping gay rights internationally', *Guardian*, 12 December. http://www.theguardian.com/news/data blog/2013/oct/15/state-sponsored-homophobia-gay-rights (accessed 8 March 2015).

Chapkis, W. (1997) *Live Sex Acts*. London: Routledge.

Cheng, S. (2010) *On the Move for Love: Migrant Entertainers and the U.S. Military in South Korea*. Philadelphia: University of Pennsylvania Press.

Chow, R. (1999) 'The politics of admittance: female sexual agency, miscegenation, and the formation of community in Frantz Fanon', in A. Alessandrini (ed.) *Frantz Fanon: Critical Perspectives*. London: Routledge.

Chu, J. (2010) *Cosmologies of Credit*. London: Duke University Press.

Chuang, J. (2013) 'Exploitation creep and the unmaking of human trafficking law', American University, *WCL Research Paper*. http://ssrn.com/abstract= 2315513.

Clark, N. (2013) *Detecting and Tackling Forced Labour in Europe*. New York: JRF. http://www.jrf.org.uk/publications/detecting-tackling-forced-labour-europe (accessed 10 March 2015).

CNN Freedom Project (2011a) 'Three voices how to end modern day slavery'. http://thecnnfreedomproject.blogs.cnn.com/2011/07/12/three-voices-how -to-end-modern-day-slavery/.

CNN Freedom Project (2011b) 'The Facts: Slavery, human trafficking definitions'. http://thecnnfreedomproject.blogs.cnn.com/2011/04/20/the-facts -slavery-human-trafficking-definitions/.

Cobden, J. (1854) *The White Slaves of England*. Auburn, NY: Miller, Orton & Mulligan.

Cohen, G. A. (1995) *Self-Ownership, Freedom and Equality*. Cambridge: Cambridge University Press.

Cohen, R. (1987) *The New Helots: Migrants in the International Division of Labour*. Aldershot: Gower.

Cohen, R. (2006) *Migration and Its Enemies: Global Capital, Migrant Labour and the Nation State*. Aldershot: Ashgate.

Coldham, P. (1992) *Emigrants in Chains*. London: Sutton.

Cole, J. and Booth, S. (2007) *Dirty Work: Immigrants in Domestic Service, Agriculture and Prostitution in Sicily*. New York: Lexington.

Collins, H. (1990) 'Independent contractors and the challenge of vertical disintegration to employment protection laws', *Oxford Journal of Legal Studies*, 10:3, pp. 353–380.

Constable, N. (2009) 'The commodification of intimacy: Marriage, sex and reproductive labor', *Annual Review of Anthropology*, 38, pp. 49–64.

Costello, C. and Freedman, M. (2014) (eds) *Migrants at Work*. Oxford: Oxford University Press.

Cottias, M. (2008) 'Free but minor: Slave women, citizenship, respectability, and social antagonism in the French Antilles, 1830–90', in G. Campbell, S. Miers and J. Miller (eds) *Women and Slavery*. Athens: Ohio University Press, pp. 186–107.

Craig, G., Gaus, A., Wilkinson, M., Skrivankova, K. and McQuade, A. (2007) *Contemporary Slavery in the UK: Overview and Key Issues*. New York: Joseph Rowntree Foundation.

Craven, P. and Hay, D. (1994) 'The criminalization of "free" labour: Master and servant in comparative perspective', in P. Lovejoy and N. Rogers (eds) *Unfree Labour in the Development of the Atlantic World*. London: Routledge.

Crawley, H. (2015) 'Europe's war on migrants', *Open Security*, 20 April. https: //opendemocracy.net/opensecurity/heaven-crawley/europe%27s-war-on -migrants.

Crowhurst (2012). 'Approaches to the regulation and governance of prostitution in contemporary Italy', *Sexuality Research and Social Policy*, 9:3, pp. 223–232.

Cruz, K. (2013) 'Unmanageable work, (un)liveable lives: The UK sex industry, labour rights and the welfare state', *Social and Legal Studies*, 22:4, pp. 465–488.

Cuentame (2012) 'Immigrants for sale'. https://www.youtube.com/watch?v= qJ20tIYirKg.

Cugoano, Q. (1999 [1787]) *Thoughts and Sentiments on the Evil of Slavery*. London: Penguin.

Cunliffe, M. (1979) *Chattel Slavery and Wage Slavery: The Anglo-American Context*. Athens: University of Georgia Press.

Datta, K., McIlwaine, C., Wills, J., Evans, Y., Herbert, J. and May, J. (2007) 'The new development finance or exploiting migrant labour? Remittance sending among low-paid migrant workers in London', *International Development Planning Review*, 29:1, pp. 43–67.

Davis, A. (2003) *Are Prisons Obsolete?* New York: Seven Stories Press.

Davis, A. (2014) 'From Michael Brown to Assata Shakur, the racist state of America persists', *Guardian*. http://www.theguardian.com/commentisfree/2014/nov/01/michael-brown-assata-shakur-racist-state-of-america.

Davis, D. (1975) *The Problem of Slavery in the Age of Revolution*. New York: Cornell University Press.

Davis, D. (2003) *Challenging the Boundaries of Slavery*. Cambridge, MA: Harvard University Press.

Day, S. (2007) *On the Game: Women and Sex Work*. London: Pluto.

Day, S. (2010) 'The re-emergence of trafficking: Sex work between slavery and freedom', *Journal of the Royal Anthropological Institute*, 16, pp. 816–834.

Dayan, C. (2010) *The Law Is a White Dog: How Legal Rituals Make and Unmake Persons*. Princeton: Princeton University Press,

Dayan, J. (1999) 'Poe, persons, and property', *American Literary History*, 12:3, pp. 405–425.

De Beauvoir, S. (1972) *The Second Sex*. London: Penguin.

De Genova, N. (2002) 'Migrant "illegality" and deportability in everyday life', *Annual Review of Anthropology*, 31, pp. 419–447.

De Lombard, J. (2012) *In the Shadow of the Gallows*. Philadelphia: University of Pennsylvania Press.

Diaz, M. (2006) 'Mining women, royal slaves: Copper mining in Colonial Cuba 1670–1780', in L. Mercier and J. Viskovatoff (eds) *Mining Women: Gender in the Development of a Global Industry, 1700–2000*. New York: Palgrave.

Dickinson, J. (1767–1768) *Farmer's Letters*, Reproduced on Web of English History. http://www.historyhome.co.uk/c-eight/america/farmer9.htm (accessed 25 January 2015).

Ditmore, M., Levy, A. and Wilman, A. (eds) (2010) *Sex Work Matters: Exploring Money, Power and Intimacy in the Sex Industry*. London: Zed.

Doezema, J. (2010) *Sex Slaves and Discourse Masters*. London: Zed.

Doherty, B. (2015a) 'Manus refugees fear being killed as they are forced into PNG community', 6 January. http://www.theguardian.com/australia-news/2015/jan/06/manus-detainees-recognised-as-refugees-will-be-forced-into-png-community.

Doherty, B. (2015b) 'Children in detention exposed to danger, Human Rights Commission finds', 11 February. http://www.theguardian.com/australia-news/2015/feb/11/children-in-detention-scathing-criticism-in-human-rights-commission-report.

Dolan, F. (1992) 'The subordinate('s) plot: Petty treason and the forms of domestic rebellion', *Shakespeare Quarterly*, 43:3, pp. 317–340.

Dottridge, M. (2014) 'How is the money to combat human trafficking spent?' *Anti-Trafficking Review*, 3, pp. 3–15.

Douglass, F. (1986) *Narrative of the Life of Frederick Douglass, An American Slave*. Harmondsworth: Penguin.

Doward, J. (2014) 'Qatar world cup: 400 Nepalese die on nation's building sites since bid won', *Observer*, 15 February. http://www.theguardian.com/football/2014/feb/16/qatar-world-cup-400-deaths-nepalese.

Drescher, S. (2012) 'From consensus to consensus: slavery in international law' in J. Allain (ed.) *The Legal Understanding of Slavery*. Oxford: Oxford University Press

Du Bois, W. E. B. (1966) *Black Reconstruction in America*. New York: Russell & Russell.

Durkheim, E. (1984) *The Division of Labor in Society*. New York: The Free Press.

Düvell, F. (2011) 'Paths into irregularity: the legal and political construction of irregular migration', *European Journal of Migration and Law*, 13, pp. 275–295.

Düvell, F. and Vollmer, B. (2011), *European Security Challenges. EU–US Immigration Systems*. Florence: European University Institute/Robert-Schuman Centre for Advanced Studies.

Dworkin, A. (1987) *Intercourse*. New York: Basic Books.

Dwyer, P., Lewis, H., Scullion, L. and Waite, L. (2011) *Forced Labour and UK Immigration Policy: Status Matters?* New York: Joseph Rowntree Foundation.

Eaton, R. (2006) 'Introduction', in I. Chatterjee and R. Eaton (eds) *Slavery and South Asian History*. Bloomington: Indiana University Press.

Edwards, L. (1998) 'The problem of dependency: African Americans, labor relations, and the law in the nineteenth-century South', *Agricultural History*, 72:2, pp. 313–340.

Edwards, L. (1999) 'Law, domestic violence, and the limits of patriarchal authority in the Antebellum South', *Journal of Southern History*, 65:4, pp. 733–770.

EJF (2012) *Sold to the Sea. Human Trafficking in Thailand's Fishing Industry*. London: EJ Foundation http://ejfoundation.org/sites/default/files/public/Sold _to_the_Sea_report_lo-res-v2.pdf.

Engels, F. (1973) *The Condition of the Working Class in England*. London: Lawrence & Wishart.

Equiano, O. (1999) *The Life of Olaudah Equiano, or Gustavus Vassa, the African*. Mineola, NY: Dover Publications.

Esping-Andersen, G. (1990) *The Three Worlds of Welfare Capitalism*. Cambridge: Polity.

Esson, J. (2015) 'Better off at home? Rethinking responses to trafficked West African footballers in Europe', *Journal of Ethnic and Migration Studies*, 41:3, pp. 512–530.

Fairlie, S. (2009) 'A short history of enclosure in Britain', *The Land*, Issue 7. http://www.thelandmagazine.org.uk/articles/short-history-enclosure-britain.

Fannon, F. (1970) *Black Skin, White Masks*. London: Paladin.

Farris, S. (2015) 'Migrants' regular army of labour: gender dimensions of the impact of the global economic crisis on migrant labor in Western Europe', *The Sociological Review*, 63:1, pp. 121–143.

FCO and Home Office (2013) 'Guidance on forced marriage', *Foreign & Common-Wealth Office and Home Office*. https://www.gov.uk/forced-marriage.

Federici, S. (2004) *Caliban and the Witch*. Brooklyn, NY: Autonomedia.

Feingold, D. (2010) 'Trafficking in numbers: The social construction of trafficking data', in P. Andreas and K. Greenhill (eds) *Sex, Drugs, and Body Counts*. Ithica: Cornell University Press.

Feltz, R. and Baksh, S. (2012) 'Business of detention' in J. Loyd, M. Mitchelson and A. Burridge (eds) *Beyond Cages and Walls: Prisons, Borders, and Global Crisis*. London: University of Georgia Press.

Fergus, C. (2013) *Revolutionary Emancipation: Slavery and Abolitionism in the British West Indies.* Baton Rouge: Louisiana State University Press.

Festa, L. (2010) 'Humanity without feathers', *Humanity: An International Journal of Human Rights*, 1:1, pp. 3–27.

Finley, M. (1964) 'Between slavery and freedom', *Comparative Studies in Society and History*, 6:3 (April), pp. 233–249.

Fleming, R. (1993) 'Happy endings? resisting women and the economy of love in day five of boccaccio's decameron', *Italica*, 70:1 (Spring), pp. 30–45.

Florida Department of Education (2013) 'Harriet Tubman Centennial Celebration'. http://www.fldoe.org/bii/curriculum/Social_Studies/tubman.asp.

Friedman, M. (1962) *Capitalism and Freedom*. Chicago: University of Chicago Press.

Fraser Institute (2012) 'What is artisanal and small-scale mining?' *Miningfacts.org*. http://www.miningfacts.org/Communities/What-is-Artisanal-and-Small-Scale-Mining/ (accessed 9 January 2015).

FTS (2013a) 'Child slavery, child labor and exploitation of children in mining communities Obuasi, Ghana', *Free the Slaves*. https://www.freetheslaves.net/document.doc?id=309.

FTS (2013b) 'Wives in slavery: Forced marriage in the Congo', *Free the Slaves*. http://ftsblog.net/wp-content/uploads/2013/06/FTS-ForcedMarriage-201306-V1-web.pdf.

FTS (2007–2014a) 'Modern slavery: Frequently asked questions', *Free the Slaves*. https://www.freetheslaves.net/faq.

FTS (2007–2014b) 'Glossary', *Free the Slaves*. https://www.freetheslaves.net/page.aspx?pid=305 (accessed 11 September 2014).

FTS (2014c) 'Survivor Stories', *Free the Slaves*. http://www.freetheslaves.net/survivor-stories-miguel-was-enslaved-in-floridas-orange-groves/ (accessed 11 September 2014).

Garcia-Moreno, C., Jansen, H., Ellsberg, M., Heise, L., Watts, C. and on behalf of the WHO Multi-country Study on Women's Health and Domestic Violence against Women Study Team (2006) 'Prevalence of intimate partner violence: Findings from the WHO multi-country study on women's health and domestic violence', *The Lancet*, 368:9543, pp. 1260–1269.

Geary, D. (2004) 'Brazilian slaves and European workers in the 18th and 19th century', *Mitteilungsblatt des Instituts fuer Soziale Bewegungen*. Bochum: Ruhr University.

Gilroy, P. (1993) *The Black Atlantic*. London: Verso.

Golash-Boza, T. (2012) *Due Process Denied*. London: Routledge.

Gomez, G. (2014) 'Family seeks answers in Jacksonville murders'. http://www.myfoxtampabay.com/story/26739297/2014/10/08/family-seeks-answers-in-jacksonville-murders.

Gould, S. (1996) *The Mismeasure of Man*. New York: W.W. Norton.

Gov.uk (2014) 'UK visa sponsorship for employers'. https://www.gov.uk/uk-visa-sponsorship-employers/your-responsibilities (accessed 16 March 2015).

Graeber, D. (2009) 'Debt, violence, and impersonal markets: Polanyian meditations', in C. Hann and K. Hart (eds) *Market and Society*. Cambridge: Cambridge University Press, pp. 106–132.

Graeber, D. (2011) *Debt: The First 5000 Years*. Brooklyn, NY: Melville House.

Grant, S. (2011) 'Immigration detention: Some issues of inequality', *The Equal Rights Review*, 7, pp. 69–82.

Grant, W. (2014) 'Las Patronas: The Mexican women helping migrants', *BBC News*, http://www.bbc.co.uk/news/world-latin-america-28193230.

Grayson, J. (2012) 'Britain as a private security state: First they came for the asylum seekers', *openDemocracy*, http://www.opendemocracy.net.

Greenberg, K. (1996) *Honor and Slavery*. Princeton, NJ: Princeton University Press.

Grier, B. (2004) 'Child labor and Africanist scholarship: A critical overview', *African Studies Review*, 47:2, pp. 1–25.

Grosz, E. (1994) *Volatile Bodies*. Bloomington: University of Indiana Press.

Grubb, F. (2000) 'The transatlantic market for British convict labor', *The Journal of Economic History*, 60:1, pp. 94–122.

Hadden, S. (2001) *Slave Patrols: Law and Violence in Virginia and the Carolinas*. Cambridge, MA: Harvard University Press.

Hairong, Y. (2008) *New Masters, New Servants: Migration, Development, and Women Workers in China*. London: Duke University Press.

Hall, C. (2002) *Civilising Subjects*. Cambridge: Polity.

Hall, C. (2003) 'The lords of humankind re-visited', *Bulletin of the School of Oriental and African Studies*, University of London, 66:3, pp. 472–485.

Hall, C. (2014) 'Macaulay's history of England: A book that shaped nation and empire', in A. Burton and I. Hofmeyr (eds) *Ten Books that Shaped the British Empire*. London: Duke University Press, pp. 71–89.

Hall, S., Critcher, C. and Jefferson, A. (1978) *Policing the Crisis: Mugging, the State, and Law and Order*. New York: Holmes & Meier.

Harris, K. (2013) 'Forced labour in the UK', *Guardian*, 20 November 20. http://www.theguardian.com/global-development/2013/nov/20/forced-labour-uk-escape-fear-polish-migrant (accessed 9 March 2015).

Hart, K. and Hann, C. (2009) 'Introduction: Learning from polanyi 1', in C. Hann and K. Hart (eds) *Market and Society*. Cambridge: Cambridge University Press, pp. 1–16.

Hartman, S. (1997) *Scenes of Subjection: Terror, Slavery and Self-Making in Nineteenth Century*. America. Oxford: Oxford University Press.

Hartman, S. (2007) *Lose Your Mother: A Journey along the Atlantic Slave Route*. New York: Farrar, Straus and Giroux.

Hartmann, H. (1997) 'The unhappy marriage of Marxism and feminism: Towards a more progressive union', in L. Nicholson (ed.) *The Second Wave: A Reader in Feminist Theory*. London: Routledge.

Harvey, D. (2007) *A Brief History of Neo Liberalism*. Oxford: Oxford University Press.

Hashim, I. and Thorsen, D. (2011) *Child Migration in Africa*. London: Zed.

Haskell, T. (1998) *Objectivity Is Not Neutrality*. Baltimore: John Hopkins University Press.

Hawksley, H. (2014) 'Punished by axe: Bonded labour in India's brick kilns', *BBC News*. http://www.bbc.co.uk/news/magazine-27486450 (accessed 28 January 2015).

Haynes, D. (2013) 'The celebrification of human trafficking, Part III'. http://traffickingroundtable.org/2013/05/celebrification-of-human-trafficking-part-iii/.

Henson, J. (2008) *Truth Stranger than Fiction: Father Henson's Story of his own Life.* New York: Barnes & Noble.

Heuman, G. (1986) *Out of the House of Bondage.* London: Frank Cass.

Hill, C. (1967) *Reformation to Industrial Revolution.* London: Weidenfeld and Nicolson.

Hill, D. (2011) 'Guest worker programs are no fix for our broken immigration system: Evidence from the Northern Mariana Islands', *New Mexico Law Review,* 41:Spring, pp. 131–191.

Hilson, G., Amankwah, R. and Ofori-Sarpong, G. (2013) 'Going for gold: Transitional livelihoods in Northern Ghana', *Journal of Modern African Studies,* 51:1, pp. 109–137.

Hilton, G. (1960) *The Truck System.* Cambridge: W. Heffer & Sons.

Hirsch, A. (2013) 'Niger to ban women and children travelling in Sahara after 92 perish', *Guardian,* 1 November. http://www.theguardian.com/world/2013/nov/01/niger-ban-women-children-sahara.

Hodal, K., Kelly, C. and Lawrence, F. (2014) 'Revealed: Asian slave labour producing prawns for supermarkets in US, UK', *Guardian,* 10 June. http://www.theguardian.com/global-development/2014/jun/10/supermarket-prawns-thailand-produced-slave-labour.

Hoff, J. (2007) 'American women and the lingering implications of coverture', *The Social Sciences Journal,* 44, pp. 41–55.

Hogan, L. (2014) 'The myth of "Irish Slaves" in the colonies', figshare. http://dx.doi.org/10.6084/m9.figshare.1250146 (accessed May 20, 2015).

Holmwood, J. and Bhambra, G. (2012) 'The attack on education as a social right', *South Atlantic Quarterly,* 111:2, pp. 392–401.

Home Office (2013) *Victims of Human Trafficking: Guidance for Frontline Staff.* London: Home Office. https://www.gov.uk/government/uploads/system/uploads/attachment_data/file/275239/Human_trafficking.pdf.

Home Office (2014) 'Ending violence against women and girls in the UK'. https://www.gov.uk/government/policies/ending-violence-against-women-and-girls-in-the-uk.

Honig, B. (2001) *Democracy and the Foreigner.* Princeton, NJ: Princeton University Press.

Howard, N. (2014) 'Teenage labor migration and antitrafficking policy in West Africa', *Annals of the American Academy of Political and Social Science,* 653:1, pp. 124–140.

Howard, N. and Morganti, S. (2015) '(Not!) child trafficking in Benin', in M. Dragiewicz (ed.) *Global Human Trafficking.* London: Routledge, pp. 91–104.

HRW (2005) *Maid to Order: Ending Abuses against Migrant Domestic Workers in Singapore.* http://www.hrw.org/reports/2005/singapore1205/index.htm.

HRW (2006) 'Building towers, cheating workers: Exploitation of migrant construction workers in the United Arab Emirates', *Human Rights Watch,* 18:8.

HRW (2010) 'Detained and at risk: sexual abuse and harassment in United States Immigration Detention'. http://www.hrw.org/sites/default/files/reports/us0810webwcover.pdf.

HRW (2014) 'Libya: Whipped, beaten and hung from trees', *Human Rights Watch.* http://www.hrw.org/news/2014/06/22/libya-whipped-beaten-and-hung-trees.

HRW (2015) 'UK: Amend modern slavery bill', *Human Rights Watch*. http://www.hrw.org/news/2015/02/22/uk-amend-modern-slavery-bill (accessed 15 March 2015).

HSTC (2005) 'Establishment of the Human Smuggling and Trafficking Center', Report to Congress. Human Smuggling and Trafficking Center. http://www.state.gov/documents/organization/49600.pdf.

Hughes, D. and Denisova, T. (2003) 'Trafficking in women from Ukraine', Final Report to the US Department of Justice. https://www.ncjrs.gov/pdffiles1/nij/grants/203275.pdf.

Hume, T. (2013) 'India, China, Pakistan, Nigeria on slavery's list of shame, says report', CNN, 18 October. http://edition.cnn.com/2013/10/17/world/global-slavery-index/index.html (accessed 20 May 2015).

Hunt, L. (1996) *The Invention of Pornography*. London: Zone Books.

Huong, L. (2010) 'A new portrait of indentured labour: Vietnamese labour migration to Malaysia', *Asian Journal of Social Science*, 38, pp. 880–896.

IFHR (2010) Women's Rights in the United Arab Emirates (UAE). Note submitted to the 45th Session of the Committee on the Elimination of Discrimination against Women (CEDAW) on the occasion of its first examination of the UAE. https://www.fidh.org/IMG/pdf/UAE_summaryreport_for_CEDAW.pdf.

IJM (2015) 'Gather. "Act. End slavery"', *Freedom Commons*. International Justice Mission. http://freedomcommons.ijm.org/issues/slavery.

ILO (2004) *Towards a Fair Deal for Migrant Workers in the Global Economy*. Geneva: International Labour Office.

ILO (2005) *A Global Alliance against Forced Labour*. Geneva: International Labour Office.

ILO (2011) 'Combating forced labour and trafficking of Indonesian migrant workers', *International Labour Organization*. http://www.ilo.org/jakarta/whatwedo/projects/WCMS_116048/lang–en/index.htm.

ILO (2013a) *Caught at Sea – Forced Labour and Trafficking in Fisheries*. Geneva: International Labour Office.

ILO (2013b) *Employment Practices and Working Conditions in Thailand's Fishing Sector*. Geneva: International Labour Office.

IOM (2014) *Fatal Journeys: Tracking Lives Lost during Migration*. Geneva: International Organization for Migration. http://publications.iom.int/bookstore/free/FatalJourneys_CountingtheUncounted.pdf (accessed 2 March 2014).

ITUC (2014) *The Case against Qatar*. Brussels: ITUC. http://www.ituc-csi.org/IMG/pdf/the_case_against_qatar_en_web170314.pdf.

Jacobs, H. (2000) *Incidents in the Life of a Slave Girl: Written by Herself*, ed. Jean Fagan Yellin. Cambridge, MA: Harvard University Press, 2000.

Jacobsen, C. and Stenvoll, D. (2010) 'Muslim women and foreign prostitutes: Victim discourse, subjectivity and governance', *Social Politics*, 17:3, pp. 270–294.

James, C. L. R. (2001) *The Black Jacobins*. London: Penguin.

James, J. (2005) *The New Abolitionists: (Neo)Slave Narratives and Contemporary Prison Writings*. Albany: State University of New York Press.

Jeffrey, L. and MacDonald, G. (2006) '"It's the money, honey": The economy of sex work in the Maritimes', *CRSA/RCSA*, 43:3, pp. 313–327.

Jeffreys, S. (1997) *The Idea of Prostitution*. Victoria: Spinfex.

Johnson, M. (2012) 'Freelancing in the Kingdom: Filipino migrant domestic workers crafting agency in Saudi Arabia', *Asian and Pacific Migration Journal*, 20:3–4, pp. 459–478.

Jones, M. (2003) 'Thailand's brothel busters', *Mother Jones*, November/December. http://www.motherjones.com/politics/2003/11/thailands-brothel-busters.

Jordan, D. and Walsh, M. (2007) *White Cargo*. New York: New York University Press.

Jordan, M. (2005) *The Great Abolition Sham*. Stroud: Sutton Publishing.

Kaiser, D. and Stannow, L. (2011) 'Immigrant detainees: The new sex abuse crisis', *New York Review*, 23 November. http://www.nybooks.com/blogs/nyrblog/2011/nov/23/immigrant-detainees-new-sex-abuse-crisis/.

Kant, I. (2009) *An Answer to the Question: What Is Enlightenment?* London: Penguin.

Kapur, R. (2005) 'Cross-border movements and the law: Renegotiating the boundaries of difference', in K. Kempadoo (ed.) *Trafficking and Prostitution Reconsidered*. London: Paradigm.

Kapur, R. (2013) 'Gender, sovereignty and the rise of a sexual security regime in international law and postcolonial India', *Melbourne Journal of International Law*, 14, pp. 1–29.

Kara, S. (2009) *Sex Trafficking: Inside the Business of Modern Slavery*. New York: Columbia University Press.

Kegan, C. (2011) *Experiences of Forced Labour among Chinese Migrant Workers*. London: Joseph Rowntree Foundation.

Kelly, P. (2008) *Lydia's Open Door: Inside Mexico's Most Modern Brothel*. London: University of California Press.

Kempadoo, K. (2004) *Sexing the Caribbean*. London: Routledge.

Kempadoo, K., Sanghera, J. and Pattanaik, B. (eds) (2005) *Trafficking and Prostitution Reconsidered*. London: Paradigm.

Kempadoo, K. (2015) 'The white man's burden revisited', *Beyond Slavery and Trafficking*, 11 January. https://www.opendemocracy.net/beyondslavery/kamala-kempadoo/white-man's-burden-revisited.

Keo, C. (2013) *Human Trafficking in Cambodia*. London: Routledge.

Kilgore, J. (2014) Tackling debtors' prisons: Reflecting on the death of Eileen DiNino' Truthout, 20 June. http://truth-out.org/news/item/24478-tackling-debtors-prisons-reflecting-on-the-death-of-eileen-dinino.

Klein, A. and Williams, L. (2012) 'Immigration detention in the community: Research on the experiences of migrants released from detention centres in the UK', *Population, Space and Place*, 18:6, pp. 741–753.

Knight, S. (2012) 'Debt-Bondage Slavery in India', *Global Dialogue*, 14:2. http://www.worlddialogue.org/content.php?id=535.

Koestler, A. (1964) *The Act of Creation*. New York: Penguin Books.

Kofman, E., Phizacklea, A., Raghuram, P. and Sales, R. (2000) *Gender and International Migration in Europe*. London: Routledge.

Kopytoff, I. (1982) 'Slavery', *Annual Review of Anthropology*, 11, pp. 207–230.

Kopytoff, I. (1986) 'The cultural biography of things: Commodification as process', in A. Appadurai (ed.) *The Social Life of Things*. Cambridge: Cambridge University Press, pp. 64–94.

Kopytoff, I. and Miers, S. (eds) (1977) *Slavery in Africa: Historical and Anthropological Perspectives*. Madison: University of Wisconsin Press

Kotiswaran, P. (2014a) 'Abject labors, informal markets: Revisiting the law's (Re)production boundary', *Employee Rights & Employment Law Journal*, 18:1, pp. 353–406.

Krabill, R. (2012) 'American sentimentalism and the production of global citizens', *Contexts*, 11:4, pp. 52–54.

Kristine, L. (2012) 'Photos that bear witness to modern slavery', *TEDx*, January. http://www.ted.com/talks/lisa_kristine_glimpses_of_modern_day_slavery (accessed 16 March 2015).

Lahiri-Dutt, K. (2006) "Gendered livelihoods in small mines and quarries in India: Living on the edge', Working Paper, Rajiv Gandhi Institute for Contemporary Studies, Australia South Asia Research Centre. http://www.indiaenvironmentportal.org.in/files/WP2006_08.pdf.

Lainez, N. (Forthcoming) 'Vietnamese sex workers and the constellation of debts: The limits of the anthropology of slavery', in L. Brace and J. O'Connell Davidson (eds) *Slaveries Old and New*. London: Proceedings of the British Academy.

Lake, M. (2014) '"The day will come": Charles H. Pearson's National Life and Character: A forecast', in A. Burton and I. Hofmeyr (eds) *Ten Books that Shaped the British Empire*. London: Duke University Press, pp. 90–111.

Lan, P. (2007) 'Legal servitude and free illegality: Migrant "guest" workers in Taiwan', in R. Parrenas and C. Lok (eds) *Asian Diasporas: New Formations, New Conceptions*. Stanford, CA: Stanford University Press, pp. 253–278.

Lebowitz, M. (2003) *Beyond Capital*. London: Palgrave Macmillan.

Leidholt, D. and Raymond, J. (eds) (1990) *The Sexual Liberals and the Attack on Feminism*. New York: Pergamon Press.

Leghtas, I. and Roberts, K. (2015) 'Modern slavery bill fails vulnerable women', *Beyond Slavery and Trafficking*, 16 March. https://www. opendemocracy.net/beyondslavery/izza-leghtas-kate-roberts/modern-slavery-bill-fails-vulnerable-women.

Lerche, J. (2007) 'A global alliance against forced labour? unfree labour, neo-liberal globalization and the international labour organization', *Journal of Agrarian Change*, 7:4, pp. 425–452.

Levi-Strauss, C. (1967) *Les Structures Elementaires de la Parente*. Paris: Mouton & Co.

Lijnders, L. and Robinson, S. (2013) 'From the horn of Africa to the middle East: Human trafficking of Eritrean asylum seekers across borders', *Anti-Trafficking Review*, 2, pp. 137–154.

Lindøe, P. (2007) 'Safe offshore workers and unsafe fishermen – a system failure?' *Policy and Practice in Health and Safety*, 2, pp. 25–39.

Lisborg, A. (2014) 'The good, the bad and the ugly: In the name of victim protection', in S. Yea (ed.) *Trafficking in Asia: Forcing Issues*. London: Routledge, pp. 19–34.

Lister, R. (1997) *Citizenship: Feminist Perspectives*. Houndmills: Macmillan.

Locke, J. (1993) *The Second Treatise on Civil Government*, in *Locke's Political Writings*. Ed. D. Wooton. London: Penguin.

Losurdo, D. (2011) *Liberalism: A Counter-History*. London: Verso.

Lott, T. (1998) 'Early enlightenment conceptions of the rights of slaves', in T. Lott (ed.) *Subjugation and Bondage*. New York: Rowman and Littlefield, pp. 99–130.

Lott, T. (1999) *The Invention of Race*. Oxford: Blackwell.
Loyd, J., Mitchelson, M. and Burridge, A. (2012) (eds) *Beyond Cages and Walls: Prisons, Borders, and Global Crisis*. London: University of Georgia Press.
Lubet, S. (2010) *Fugitive Justice: Runaways, Rescuers and Slavery on Trial*. Cambridge, MA: The Belknap Press of Harvard University Press.
Macpherson, C. B. (1962) *The Political Theory of Possessive Individualism*. Oxford: Oxford University Press.
Madziva, R. (2010) 'Living death: Separation in the UK', *Forced Migration Review*, 34.
Mahdavi, P. (2011) *Gridlock: Labor, Migration and Human Trafficking in Dubai*. Stanford, CA: Stanford University Press.
Malit, F. and Youha, A. (2013) 'Labor migration in the United Arab Emirates: challenges and responses', *MPI*. http://www.migrationpolicy.org/article/labor-migration-united-arab-emirates-challenges-and-responses/ (accessed 10 March 2015).
Malucelli, L. (2006) 'Gendered transitions: Made to prostitute, prostitute to maid', in C. Demaria and C. Wright (eds) *Post-Conflict Cultures: Rituals of Representation*. London: Zoilus.
Marden, R. (2009) '"That all men are created equal": "Rights talk" and exclusion in North America', in G. Bhambra and R. Shilliam (eds) *Silencing Human Rights*. Houndmills: Palgrave Macmillan, pp. 85–102.
Marriott, D. 2000: *On Black Men*. Edinburgh: Edinburgh University Press.
Marshall, P. and Thatun, S. (2005) 'Miles away: the trouble with prevention in the Greater Mekong Sub-region', in K. Kempadoo, J. Sanghera and B. Pattanaik (eds) *Trafficking and Prostitution Reconsidered*. London: Paradigm.
Marshall, T. (1964) *Class, Citizenship and Social Development*. Garden City, NY: Doubleday.
Martin, P. (2007) *The Economic Contribution of Migrant Workers to Thailand*. Bangkok: International Labour Office.
Marx, K. (1954) *Capital*, Volume 1. London: Lawrence & Wishart.
Marx, K. (1973) *Grundrisse*, trans. Martin Nicolaus, Middlesex: Penguin.
Marx, K. (1977) *Capital*, Volume 1, trans. Ben Fowkes. New York: Vintage.
Mason, I. (1893) *Life of Isaac Mason as a Slave*. Worcester, MA: Kindle edition.
Massey, D. (1993) 'Theories of international migration: A review and appraisal', *Population and Development Review*, 19:3, pp. 432–466.
Mauss, M. (2002) *The Gift*. London: Routledge.
May, T. (2013) 'Theresa May: The abhorrent evil of human trafficking taking place on London's streets', *Metro Blogs*. http://metro.co.uk/2013/10/14/theresa-may-the-evil-of-modern-day-slavery-taking-place-on-londons-streets-4144671/ (accessed 10 January 2015).
Maybin, S. (2014) 'Are murder laws sexist?', *BBC News*, 14 October. http://www.bbc.co.uk/news/magazine-29612916.
McClintock, A. (1995) *Imperial Leather: Race, Gender and Sexuality in the Colonial Contest*. London: Routledge.
McKeown, A. (2008) *Melancholy Order, Asian Migration and the Globalization of Borders*. New York: Columbia University Press.
McLynn, F. (1989) *Crime and Punishment in Eighteenth-Century England*. London: Routledge.
McVeigh, T. (2009) 'Debt chasers accused of bullying calls and threats', *The Observer*, Sunday 28 June.

Medhekar-Smith, A. (2003) 'Structural adjustment in sub-Saharan Ghana during the 1980s and its impact on the rural poor', in K. Roy (ed.) *Twentieth Century Development: Some Relevant Issues*. New York: Nova Science, pp. 153–174.

Meillassoux, C. (1991) *The Anthropology of Slavery*. London: Athlone.

Merry, S. (2012) 'Human rights monitoring and the question of indicators', in M. Goodale (ed.) *Human Rights at the Crossroads*. Oxford: Oxford University Press.

Mezzadri, S. (2015) 'Free to stitch, or starve: Capitalism and unfreedom in the global garment industry', *Beyond Trafficking and Slavery*. https://www.opendemocracy.net/beyondslavery/alessandra-mezzadri/free-to-stitch -or-starve-capitalism-and-unfreedom-in-global-garmen.

Mies, M. (1986) *Patriarchy and Accumulation on a World Scale*. London: Zed Books.

Miers, S. (1998) 'Slavery and the slave trade as international issues 1890–1939', *Slavery & Abolition*, 19:2, pp. 16–37.

Miers, S. (2004) 'Slavery: A question of definition', in G. Campbell (ed.) *The Structure of Slavery in Indian Ocean Africa and Asia*. London: Frank Cass, pp. 1–16.

Miles, R. (1987) *Capitalism and Unfree Labour*. London: Tavistock.

Miles, R. (1989) *Racism*. London: Routledge.

Miller, J. (2006) 'Slave trade: Combating human trafficking', *Harvard International Review*, 27:4, Winter 2006.

Mills, C. (1998) *The Racial Contract*. Incatha: Cornell University Press.

Mills, C. (2008) 'Racial liberalism', *PMLA*, pp. 1380–1397.

Mills, C. (2011) 'The political economy of personhood', *On the Human*. http://onthehuman.org/2011/04/political-economy-of-personhood/.

Moitt, B. (2008) 'Pricing freedom in the French Caribbean: Women, men, children and redemption from slavery in the 1840s', in G. Campbell, S. Miers and J. Miller (eds) *Women and Slavery*. Athens: Ohio University Press, pp. 155–171.

Molland, S. (2012) *The Perfect Business? Anti-Trafficking and the Sex Trade along the Mekong*. Honolulu: University of Hawai'i Press.

Mongia, R. (1999) 'Race, nationality, mobility: A history of the passport', *Public Culture*, 11:3, pp. 527–556.

Moore, S. (2013) 'Nigella Lawson pictures: if it's a "playful tiff", what does a serious one look like?' *Guardian*, 17 June. http://www.theguardian.com/commentisfree/2013/jun/17/nigella-lawson-pictures.

Moravcsik, J. (1998) 'Slavery and the ties that do not bind', in T. Lott (ed.) *Subjugation and Bondage*. Oxford: Rowman and Littlefield.

Mountz, A. (2012) 'Mapping remote detention: Dis/location through isolation', in J. Loyd, M. Mitchelson and A. Burridge (eds) *Beyond Cages and Walls: Prisons, Borders, and Global Crisis*. London: University of Georgia Press, pp. 91–104.

Musto, J. (2015) 'Domestic sex trafficking and the punitive side of anti-traffickin protection', Beyond Trafficking and Slavery, 27 January. https://opendemocracy.net/beyondslavery/jennifer-musto/domestic-sex-trafficking -and-punitive-side-of-antitrafficking-protectio.

Nah, A. (2012) 'Globalisation, sovereignty, and immigration control: The hierarchy of rights for migrant workers in Malaysia.' *Asian Journal of Social Science*, 40:4, pp. 486–508.

Nencel, L. (2001) *Ethnography and Prostitution in Peru*. London: Pluto.

Neumayer, E. (2006) 'Unequal access to foreign spaces: How states use visa restrictions to regulate mobility in a globalized world', *British Geography*, pp. 72–84.

News.com.au (2014) 'How Sandra became a modern day slave', 3 December. http://www.news.com.au/lifestyle/real-life/how-sandra-became-a-modern -day-slave-in-australia/story-fnixwvgh-1227142773890 (accessed 31 December 2014).

Nichols, T. (1980) *Capital and Labour*. London: Athelone Press.

Nichols, J. (2013) 'The line of liberty: Runaway slaves and fugitive peons in the Texas-Mexico Borderlands', *Western Historical Quarterly*, 44:(Winter), pp. 413–433.

Nilsen, A. (2012) 'Adivasi mobilization in contemporary India: Democratizing the local state?' *Critical Sociology*, pp. 1–19.

Nilsen, A. and Roy, S. (2015) 'Reconceptualizing subaltern politics in contemporary India', in A. Nilsen and S. Roy (eds) *Reconceptualising Subaltern Politics*. Oxford: Oxford University Press.

Northup, S. (2012) *Twelve Years a Slave*. London: Penguin.

Not for Sale (2015) http://notforsalecampaign.org.

Novak, D. (1978) *The Wheel of Servitude: Black Forced Labor after Slavery*. Lexington, KT: University Press of Kentucky.

Nyquist, M. (2013) *Arbitrary Rule: Slavery, Tyranny and the Power of Life and Death*. Chicago: University of Chicago Press.

Nzula, A., Potekhin, I. and Zusmanovich, A. (1979) *Forced Labour in Colonial Africa*. London: Zed.

Obama, B. (2012) 'Statement by the President on the Meeting of the Interagency Task Force to Monitor and Combat Trafficking in Persons', March 15. https://www.whitehouse.gov/the-press-office/2012/03/15/ statement-president-meeting-interagency-task-force-monitor-and-combat-tr/.

O'Brien, E. and Wilson, M. (2015) 'Clinton, Bush and Obama: Changing policy and rhetoric in the United States annual trafficking in persons report', in M. Dragiewicz (ed.) *Global Human Trafficking*. London: Routledge, pp. 123–137.

O'Connell Davidson, J. (1993) Privatisation and Employment Relations. London: Mansell.

O'Connell Davidson, J. (2005) *Children in the Global Sex Trade*. Cambridge: Polity.

O'Connell Davidson, J. (2006) 'Will the real sex slave please stand up?' *Feminist Review*, 83, pp. 4–22.

O'Connell Davidson, J. (2010) 'New slavery, old binaries: Human trafficking and the borders of "freedom"', *Global Networks*, 10:2, pp. 244–261.

O'Connell Davidson, J. (2011) 'Moving children: Child trafficking, child migration and child rights', *Critical Social Policy*, 31, pp. 454–477.

O'Connell Davidson, J. (2013) 'Troubling freedom: Migration, debt and modern slavery', *Migration Studies*, 1, pp. 1–20.

O'Connor, J. (1998) 'Social justice, social citizenship, and the welfare state, 1965–1995: Canada in comparative context', in R. Helmes-Hayes and J. Curtis (eds) *The Vertical Mosaic Revisited*. Toronto: University of Toronto Press.

Offe, C. (1984) *Contradictions of the Welfare State*. London: Hutchinson.

Ogden, A. (1858) *Reports of Cases Argued and Determined in the Supreme Court in Lousiiana*. New Orleans: Office of the Louisiana Courier.

O'Hara, M. (2014) '"Women will die" as legal aid becomes more difficult for victims of domestic abuse to get', *Guardian*, 10 September. http://www. theguardian.com/society/2014/sep/10/women-die-legal-aid-rules-domestic -violence-victims.

Okyere, S. (2012) 'Re-examining the education-child labour Nexus: The case of child miners at Kenyasi, Ghana', *Childhoods Today*, 6:1. http://www.childhoodstoday.org/article.php?id= 69.

Okyere, S. (2013) 'Are working children's rights and child labour abolition complementary or opposing realms?', *International Social Work*, 56:1, pp. 1–12.

O'Leary, A. (2008) 'Close encounters of the deadly kind: Gender, migration, and border (in)security', *Migration Letters*, 5:2, pp. 111–121.

OPHI (2010) *Country Briefing: Uzbekistan*. Oxford: Oxford Poverty and Human Development Initiative. http://www.ophi.org.uk/wp-content/uploads/Uzbekistan.pdf.

OSCE (2006) Handbook on Establishing Effective Labour Migration Policies in Countries of Origin and Destination. OSCE, IOM and ILO.

Oso, L. (2002) 'Colombian women, sex work and health in Galicia, Spain', *Research for Sex Work*, 5, pp. 10–12.

O'Toole, B. (2015) 'Thailand prisoner plan prompts protest', *Myanmar Times*, 19 January. http://www.mmtimes.com/index.php/national-news/12820-thailand-prisoner-plan-prompts-protest.html.

Painter, K. (1991) 'Wife rape in the United Kingdom', Paper presented at the American Society of Criminology, 50th Anniversary Meeting, 20–23 November, San Francisco. http://www.crim.cam.ac.uk/people/academic_research/kate_painter/wiferape.pdf.

Papadopoulos, D. (2012) 'Worlding justice/Commoning matter', *Occasion: Interdisciplinary Studies in the Humanities*, 3:1 (March), http://occasion.stanford.edu/node/79.

Papadopoulos, D., Stephenson, N. and Tsianos, V. (2008) *Escape Routes: Control and Subversion in the 21st Century*. London: Pluto.

Papadopoulos, T. (2005) *The Recommodification of European Labour: Theoretical and Empirical Explorations*. ERI Working Paper Series No. 3. University of Bath, European Research Institute.

Parekh, B. (1995) 'Liberalism and colonialism: A critique of Locke and Mill' in J. Nederveen and B. Parekh (eds) *The Decolonization of Imagination*. London: Zed.

Park, J. (2013) *Illegal Migrations and the Huckleberry Finn Problem*. Philadelphia, PA: Temple University Press.

Pateman, C. (1988) *The Sexual Contract*. Cambridge: Polity.

Pateman, C. (1992) 'Equality, difference, subordination: the politics of motherhood and women's citizenship' in G. Bock and P. Thane (eds) *Maternity and Gender Policies: Women and the Rise of the European Welfare States, 1880's–1950s*. London: Routledge.

Pateman, C. (1998) 'The patriarchal welfare state', in J. Landes (ed.) *Feminism: The Public and the Private*. Oxford: Oxford University Press, pp. 241–274.

Paton, D. (2001) 'Punishment, crime, and the bodies of slaves in eighteenth-century Jamaica', *Journal of Social History*, 34:4, pp. 923–954.

Paton, D. (2004) *No Bond but the Law*. Durham, NC and London: Duke University Press.

Patterson, O. (1982) *Slavery and Social Death*. Cambridge, MA: Harvard University Press.

Patterson, O. (1991) *Freedom*, Volume 1. London: I.B.Tauris.

Patterson, O. (2012) 'Trafficking, gender and slavery: Past and present' in J. Allain (ed.) *The Legal Understanding of Slavery*. Oxford: Oxford University Press.

Pattison, P. (2013) 'Revealed: Qatar's World Cup "slaves"', *Guardian*, 25 September. http://www.theguardian.com/world/2013/sep/25/revealed-qatars-world -cup-slaves.

Peck, G. (2000) *Reinventing Free Labor*. Cambridge: Cambridge University Press.

Pemunta, N. (2011) 'Challenging patriarchy: Trade, outward migration and the internationalization of commercial sex among Bayang and Ejagham women in Southwest Cameroon', *Health, Culture and Society*, 1:1, pp. 167–192.

Perelman, M. (2000) *The Invention of Capitalism*. London: Duke University Press.

Peters, A. (2013) '"Things that involve sex are just different": US Anti-Trafficking Law and Policy on the Books, in their minds, and in action', *Anthropological Quarterly*, 86:1, pp. 221–255.

Phillips, N. (2015) 'What has forced labour to do with poverty?', Beyond Trafficking and Slavery. https://www.opendemocracy.net/beyondslavery/nicola -phillips/what-has-forced-labour-to-do-with-poverty (accessed 17 February 2015).

Phizacklea, A. and Miles, R. (1980) *Labour and Racism*. London: Routledge.

Plant, R. (2008) 'Forced labor: Critical issues for US business leaders', Background paper prepared for conference on 'Engaging Business: Addressing Forced Labor', Atlanta, Georgia, 20 February. http://www.ilo.org/empent/areas/ business-helpdesk/tools-resources/WCMS_092176/lang–en/index.htm.

Polanyi, K. (2001) *The Great Transformation*. Boston: Beacon Press.

Potts, L. (1990) *The World Labour Market*. London: Zed.

Prakash, G. (1993) 'Terms of servitude: The colonial discourse on slavery and bondage in India', in M. Klein (ed.) *Breaking the Chains: Slavery, Bondage and Emancipation in Modern Africa and Asia*. Madison: University of Wisconsin Press.

Price, R. (1979) *Maroon Societies: Revel Slave Communities in the Americas*. Baltimore, MA: The Johns Hopkins University Press.

Price, R. (1986) *Labour and British Society: An Interpretive History 1780–1980*. London: Croom Helm.

Prince, M. (2004) *The History of Mary Prince*. Teddington: The Echo Library.

Prison Reform Trust (2013) 'Prison: The facts'. http://www.prisonreformtrust.org .uk/Portals/0/Documents/Prisonthefacts.pdf.

Prokhovnik, R. (1999) *Rational Woman: A Feminist Critique of Dichotomy*. London: Routledge.

Pupavac, V. (2015) 'Residual causes: Wilberforce and forced labour', *Beyond Trafficking and Slavery*. https://opendemocracy.net/beyondslavery/vanessa -pupavac/residual-causes-wilberforce-and-forced-labour.

Puwar, N. (2004) *Space Invaders: Gender, Race and Bodies out of Place*. Oxford: Berg.

Quintana, V. (2004) 'Why the Mexican rural sector can't take it anymore', in G. Gonzalez, R. Fernandez, V. Price, D. Smith and L. Trinh Vo (eds) *Labor Versus Empire: Race, Gender and Migration*. London: Routledge.

Quirk, J. (2011) *The Anti-Slavery Project*. Philadelphia: University of Pennsylvania Press.

Quirk, J. (2012) 'Defining slavery in all its forms: Historical inquiry as contemporary instruction', in J. Allain (ed.) *The Legal Understanding of Slavery*. Oxford: Oxford University Press.

Quirk, J. and O'Connell Davidson, J. (2015) 'Introduction: Moving beyond popular representations of trafficking and slavery', *Beyond Trafficking and Slavery*. https://www.opendemocracy.net/beyondslavery/joel-quirk-julia-o%27connell-davidson/introduction-moving-beyond-popular-representations (accessed 11 January 2015).

Radin, M. (1996) *Contested Commodities*. Cambridge, MA: Harvard University Press.

Rawlinson, K. (2014) 'Private firms "are using detained immigrants as cheap labour"', *Guardian*, 22 August. http://www.theguardian.com/uk-news/2014/aug/22/immigrants-cheap-labour-detention-centres-g4s-serco.

Reiman, J. (1987) 'Exploitation, force, and the moral assessment of capitalism: Thoughts on roemer and cohen', *Philosophy & Public Affairs*, 16:1, pp. 3–41.

Reisman, G. (2002) 'Some fundamental insights into the benevolent nature of capitalism'. http://www.capitalism.net/articles/Some%20Fundamental%20Insights%20Into%20the%20Benevolent%20Nature%20of%20Capitalism.html (accessed 14 March 2015).

Rich, A. (1980) 'Compulsory heterosexuality and lesbian existence', *Journal of Women's History*, 15:3, pp. 11–48.

Richardson, B. (2015) 'Still slaving over sugar', *Beyond Slavery and Trafficking*. https://www.opendemocracy.net/beyondslavery/ben-richardson/still-slaving-over-sugar (accessed 23 February 2015).

Robertson, S. (2002) 'Making right a girl's ruin: Working-class legal cultures and forced marriage in New York City, 1890–1950', *Journal of American Studies*, 36:2, pp. 199–230.

Robinson, J. (2006) *Economic Philosophy*. London: Transaction.

Rodger, J. (2008) *Criminalising Social Policy*. London: Routledge.

Rodney, W. (1989) *How Europe Underdeveloped Africa*. Nairobi: Heinemann Kenya.

Rogaly, B. (2008) 'Migrant workers in the ILO's global alliance against forced labour report: a critical appraisal', *Third World Quarterly*, 29:7, pp. 1431–1447.

Rogers, N. (1994) 'Vagrancy, impressments and the regulation of labour in eighteenth century Britain', in P. Lovejoy and N. Rogers (eds) *Unfree Labour in the Development of the Atlantic World*. London: Routledge.

Roper, M. (2003) *Narrative of My Escape from Slavery*. Mineola, NY: Dover.

Rosas, A. (2012). 'Some children left behind: Families in the age of deportation'. *Boom: A Journal of California*, 2:3, pp. 79–85.

Rosen, H. (2005) 'The rhetoric of miscegenation and the reconstruction of race: Debating marriage, sex, and citizenship in postemancipation Arkansas', in P. Scully and D. Paton (eds) *Gender and Slave Emancipation in the Atlantic World*. London: Duke University Press.

Roy, A. (2012) *The #GlobalPOV Project*: 'Who Sees Poverty?' http://www.youtube.com/watch?v=hrW8ier__4Q (accessed 8 February 2015).

Roy, S. (2013) 'Routine not exceptional', *Warscapes*. http://www.warscapes.com/opinion/routine-not-exceptional.

Rubin, G. (1997) 'The traffic in women: notes on the "political economy" of sex', in L. Nicholson (ed.) *The Second Wave: A Reader in Feminist Theory*. London: Routledge

Ruhmkorf, A. (2015) 'Global supply chains: the role of law', *Beyond Slavery and Trafficking*, 2 March. https://www.opendemocracy.net/beyondslavery/andreas-rühmkorf/global-supply-chains-role-of-law-role-for-law.

Ruhs, M. and Anderson, B. (2010) 'Semi-compliance and illegality in migrant labour markets: An analysis of migrants, employers and the state in the UK', *Population, Space and Place*, 16:3, pp. 195–211.

Rupprecht, A. (2007) 'Excessive memories: Slavery, insurance and resistance' *History Workshop Journal*, 64:1, pp. 6–28.

Samers, M. (2003) 'Invisible capitalism: Political economy and the regulation of undocumented immigration in France', *Economy and Society*, 32:4, pp. 555–583.

Sánchez-Eppler, K. (1988) 'Bodily bonds: The intersecting rhetorics of feminism and abolition', *Representations*, No. 24, Special Issue: America Reconstructed, 1840–1940, pp. 28–59.

Sánchez Taylor, J. (2001) 'Dollars are a girl's best friend? Female tourists' sexual behaviour in the Caribbean', *Sociology*, 35:3, pp. 749–764.

Sanders, T. (2005) *Sex Work: A Risky Business*. Cullompton: Willan.

Sassen, S. (2010) 'A savage sorting of winners and losers: Contemporary versions of primitive accumulation', *Globalizations*, 7:1, pp. 23–50.

Sayer, D. (1991) *Capitalism and Modernity: An Excursus on Marx and Weber*. London: Routledge.

Schilling, R. (1966) 'Trawler fishing: an extreme occupation', *Proceedings of the Royal Society of Medicine*, 59:5, pp. 405–441.

Schlosser, E. (2001) 'The chain never stops', *Mother Jones Magazine*, July/August Issue. http://www.d.umn.edu/~bmork/3945/3945meatpackingmotherjones.htm.

Scott, R. (2012) 'Under Color of Law: Siliadin v. France and the dynamics of enslavement in historical perspective' in J. Allain (ed.) *The Legal Understanding of Slavery*. Oxford: Oxford University Press.

Sexton, J. (2010) 'People-of-color-blindness: Notes on the afterlife of slavery', *Social Text* 28:2, pp. 31–56.

Sex Workers Project (2009) *The Use of Raids to Fight Trafficking in Persons*. http://sexworkersproject.org/downloads/swp-2009-raids-and-trafficking-exec-summary.pdf (accessed 16 March 2015).

Shah, A. (2006) 'The labour of love: Seasonal migration from Jharkhand to the brick kilns of other states in India', *Contributions to Indian Sociology*, 40:1, pp. 91–118.

Shah, S. (2014) *Street Corner Secrets: Sex, Work, and Migration in the City of Mumbai*. London: Duke University Press.

Sharma, N. (2003) 'Travel agency: A critique of anti-trafficking campaigns', *Refuge*, 21:3, pp. 53–65.

Sharma, N. (2006) *Home Economics: Nationalism and the Making of 'Migrant Workers' in Canada*. Toronto: University of Toronto Press.

Shilliam, R. (2012) 'Forget English freedom, remember Atlantic slavery: Common law, commercial law, and the significance of slavery for classical political economy', *New Political Economy*, 17:5, pp. 591–609.

Sichel, B. (1972) 'Karl Marx and the rights of man', *Philosophy and Phenomenological Research*, 32:3, pp. 355–360.

SIGI (2012) Social institutions and gender index. http://genderindex.org.

Skilbrei, M. and Tveit, M. (2007) 'Facing return: Perceptions of repatriation among Nigerian women in prostitution in Norway'. Report 555, Oslo: Fafo.

Skrivankova, K. (2010) *Between Decent Work and Forced Labour: Examining the Continuum of Exploitation*. New York: Joseph Rowntree Foundation.

Slater, D. (1998) 'Public/private', in C. Jenks (ed.) *Core Sociological Dichotomies*. London: Sage.

Smith, A. (1986) *The Wealth of Nations*. London: Penguin.

Smith, A. (1982) *Lectures on Jurisprudence*. Indianapolis: Liberty Classics.

Smith, C. (2006) 'The double indeterminacy of labour power: Labour effort and labour mobility', *Work, Employment & Society*, 20, pp. 389–402.

Soderlund, G. (2005) 'Running from the rescuers: New U.S. crusades against sex trafficking and the rhetoric of abolition', *NWSA Journal*, 17:3, pp. 64–87.

Soron, D. and Laxer, G. (2006) 'Thematic introduction: Decommodification, democracy and the battle for the commons', in G. Laxer and D. Soron (eds) *Not for Sale: Decommodifying Public Life*. Toronto: Broadview Press, pp.15–38.

Southern Poverty Law Center (2013) *Close to Slavery: Guestworker Programs in the United States*. Alabama: SPLC.

Standing, G. (2008) 'The ILO: An agency for globalization?', *Development & Change*, 39:3, pp. 355–384.

Standing, G. (2011) *The Precariat: The New Dangerous Class*. London: Bloomsbury Academic.

Stanley, A. (1998) *From Bondage to Contract*. Cambridge: Cambridge University Press.

Stanton, E. Cady (1887) *The Woman's Bible*. A Public Domain Book. Kindle Edition.

Steinfeld, R. (1991) *The Invention of Free Labor*. Chapel Hill, NJ: University of North Carolina Press.

Steinfeld, R. (2001) *Coercion, Contract and Free Labor in the Nineteenth Century*. Cambridge: Cambridge University Press.

Stevenson, N. (2012) *Freedom*. London: Routledge.

Stewart, J. (1998) 'The emergence of racial modernity and the rise of the white north', *Journal of the Early Republic*, 18:Summer, pp. 181–217.

Stewart, J. (2015) '"Using history to make slavery history": The African American past and the challenge of contemporary slavery', *Social Inclusion*, 3:1, pp. 125–135.

Still, W. (2007) *The Underground Railroad: Authentic Narratives and First-Hand Accounts*. Minneola, NY: Dover.

Stock, I. (2011) 'Gender and the dynamics of mobility: Reflections on African migrant mothers and "transit migration" in Morocco', *Ethnic and Racial Studies*. DOI:10.1080/01419870.2011.594175.

Stockl, H., Devries, K., Rotstein, A., Abrahams, N., Campell, J., Watts, C. and Garcia Moreno, C. (2013) 'The global prevalence of intimate partner homicide: A systematic review', *The Lancet*, 382:9895, pp. 7–13; September, pp. 859–865.

Sudbury, J. (2005a) 'Celling black bodies: Black women in the global prison industrial complex', *Feminist Review*, 80, pp. 162–179.

Sudbury, J. (ed.) (2005b) *Global Lockdown*. London: Taylor and Francis.

Sullivan, S. (2013) 'Ben Carson: Obamacare worst thing "since slavery"', *Washington Post*, 13 October. http://www.washingtonpost.com/blogs/post -politics/wp/2013/10/11/ben-carson-obamacare-worst-thing-since-slavery/.

Surtees, R. (2015) 'At sea: The trafficking of seafarers and fishers from Ukraine', in M. Dragiewicz (ed.) *Global Human Trafficking*. London: Routledge, pp. 57–75.

Szreter, S. (2005) 'Health and wealth', *History & Policy*, Paper 34. http://www
.historyandpolicy.org/papers/policy-paper-34.html.

Tabet, P. (2012) 'Through the looking-glass: Sexual-economic exchange', in *Chic, Cheque, Choc*. Berne: DDC-Commission Suisse pour l'UNESCO; Geneva: IHEID, pp. 39–51.

Taran, P. and Geonimi, E. (2003) *Perspectives on Labour Migration: Globalisation, Labour and Migration – Protection Is Paramount*. International Migration Programme, International Labour Organisation. www.ilo.org.

Testai, P. (2008) 'Debt as a route to modern slavery in the discourse on "Sex Trafficking": Myth or Reality?' *Human Security Journal/Revue de la Sécurité Humaine*, 6. http://www.humansecuritygateway.com/showRecord.php?RecordId= 21920 (accessed June 2012).

Testart, A. (2002) 'The extent and significance of debt slavery', *Revue Française de Sociologie*, 43:Supplement, pp. 173–204.

Thompson, E. P. (1963) *The Making of the English Working Classes*. London: Penguin.

Thompson, E. P. (1991) *Customs in Common*. London: Penguin.

Tiano, S. and Murphy-Aguilar, M. (eds) (2012) *Borderline Slavery*. Farnham: Ashgate.

Tinker, H. (1974) *A New System of Slavery: The Export of Indian Labour Overseas, 1830–1920*. London: Oxford University Press.

Titus, N. (2009) *The Amelioration and Abolition of Slavery in Trinidad, 1812–1834*. Bloomington, IN: AuthorHouse.

Townsend, M. (2013) 'Detainees at Yarl's Wood immigration centre "facing sexual abuse"', *Observer*, 14 September.

Treacher Kabesh, A. (2013) *Postcolonial Masculinities: Emotions, Histories and Ethics*. London: Ashgate.

Trodd, Z. (2013) 'Am I still not a man and a brother? Protest memory in contemporary antislavery visual culture', *Slavery & Abolition: A Journal of Slave and Post-Slave Studies*, 34:2, pp. 338–352.

TUC (2008) *Hard Work, Hidden Lives*. Commission on Vulnerable Employment Report. London: TUC.

Turley, D. (2000) *Slavery*. Oxford: Blackwell.

Turton, D. (2003) 'Conceptualising forced migration', RSC Working Paper No. 12. Oxford: Refugee Studies Centre.

Tushnet, M. (1981) *The American Law of Slavery 1810–1860*. Princeton, NJ: Princeton University Press.

Twelvetrees, H. (1863) *The Story of the Life of John Anderson, the Fugitive Slave*. London: W. Tweedie.

Tyler, R. (1972) 'Fugitive slaves in Mexico', *Journal of Negro History*, 57:1, pp. 1–12.

Uggen, C., Shannon, S. and Manza, J. (2012) 'State-level wstimates of felon disenfranchisement in the United States, 2010', *Sentencing Project*. http:// sentencingproject.org/doc/publications/fd_State_Level_Estimates_of_Felon _Disen_2010.pdf.

UN (1989) 'United Nations Convention on the Rights of the Child'. http://www
.ohchr.org/en/professionalinterest/pages/crc.aspx.

UN (2000) 'Protocol to prevent, suppress and punish trafficking in persons, especially women and children, supplementing the United Nations convention against transnational organized crime', *United Nations*. http://www.uncjin.

org/Documents/Conventions/dcatoc/final_documents_2/convention_%20traf_eng.pdf.

UN Data (2015) *Nigeria*. http://data.un.org/CountryProfile.aspx?crName=Nigeria (accessed 15 February 2015).

UNHCR (2015) 'Deported children face deadly new dangers on return to Honduras', *UNHCR News Stories*, 29 January. http://www.unhcr.org/54ca32d89.html (accessed 15 February 2015).

UNICEF (2014) 'Statistics and Monitoring'. http://www.unicef.org/statistics/ (accessed 25 January 2015).

UNITED (2012) 'United for Intercultural Action: European network against nationalism, racism and fascism, and in support of migrants and refugees'. www.unitedagainstracism.org.

Unmanned (2012) 'Unmanned Aerial Vehicles are Patrolling USA/Canadian Border', 30 April. http://www.unmanned.co.uk/unmanned-vehicles-news/unmanned-aerial-vehicles-uav-news/unmanned-aerial-vehicles-are-patrolling-usacanadian-border/ (accessed 9 March 2015).

UNOG (2014) 'Ratify treaty on migrant workers' rights, UN experts urge' states', United Nations Office at Geneva. https://www.unog.ch/80256EDD006B9C2E/(httpNewsByYear_en)/CE700AD7083D7E16C1257CB3004AA1BC?OpenDocument.

Urbina, I. (2014) 'Using jailed migrants as a pool of cheap labor', *New York Times*, 24 May. http://www.nytimes.com/2014/05/25/us/using-jailed-migrants-as-a-pool-of-cheap-labor.html?_r=3.

USI (2013) 'Understanding slavery initiative'. http://understandingslavery.com/index.php?option=com_content (accessed 12 December 2013).

Valverde, M. (1988) '"Giving the female a domestic turn": The social, legal and moral regulation of women's work in British cotton mills, 1820 – 1850', *Journal of Social History*, 21:4, pp. 619–634.

Vaughan, A. (1989) 'The origins debate: slavery and racism in seventeenth-century Virginia', *The Virginia Magazine of History and Biography*, 97: 3, pp. 311–354.

Viner, K. (2005) 'A year of killing', *Guardian*, 10 December. http://www.theguardian.com/uk/2005/dec/10/ukcrime.prisonsandprobation.

Wacquant, L. (2002) 'From slavery to mass incarceration', *New Left Review*, 13, pp. 41–60.

Waldstreicher, D. (2004) *Runaway America*. New York: Hill and Wang.

Walia, H. and Tagore, P. (2012) 'Prisoners of passage: Immigration detention in Canada', in Loyd, J., Mitchelson, M. and Burridge, A. (eds) *Beyond Cages and Walls: Prisons, Borders, and Global Crisis*. London: University of Georgia Press, pp. 74–90.

Walk Free (2014) 'The global slavery index'. http://www.globalslaveryindex.org.

Walzer, M. (1983) *Spheres of Justice: A Defence of Pluralism and Equality*. Oxford: Martin Robertson.

Ware, V. (1992) *Beyond the Pale: White Women, Racism and History*. London: Verso.

Webb, P. (1994) 'Guests of the crown: Convicts and liberated slaves on McCarthy Island, the Gambia', *Geographical Journal*, 160:2, pp. 136–142.

Webber, F. (2006) Asylum: from deterrence to criminalization. *European Race Bulletin*, No. 55. London: IRR.

Weeks, K. (2011) *The Problem with Work*. London: Duke University Press.

Weissbrodt, D. and Anti-Slavery International (2002) *Abolishing Slavery and Its Contemporary Form*. New York and Geneva: Office of the United Nations High Commissioner for Human Rights United Nations. http://www.ohchr.org/Documents/Publications/slaveryen.pdf.

Weitzer, R. (2007) 'The social construction of sex trafficking: ideology and institutionalization of a moral crusade', *Politics & Society*, 35, pp. 447–474.

Whitehead, A. and Hashim, I. (2005) *Children and Migration*. Background paper for DFID Migration Team. Unpublished.

Williams, E. (1964) *Capitalism and Slavery*. Chapel Hill: University of North Caroline Press.

Williams, E. (1970) *From Columbus to Castro: The History of the Caribbean 1492–1969*. London: Andre Deutsch.

Williams, P. (1997) *Seeing a Colour-Blind Future: The Paradox of Race*. London: Virago.

Wilshaw, R. (2015) 'What would loosen the roots of labour exploitation in supply chains?' *Beyond Trafficking and Slavery*. https://opendemocracy.net/beyondslavery/rachel-wilshaw/what-would-loosen-roots-of-labour-exploitation-in-supply-chains.

Wolfe, P. (2004) 'Race and citizenship', *OAH Magazine of History*, 18:5, pp. 66–71.

Wollstonecraft, M. (1975) *Maria: Or, The Wrongs of Woman*. New York: W. W. Norton.

Wollstonecraft, M. (2004) *A Vindication of the Rights of Woman*, ed. Miriam Brody Kramnick. Rev. edn. Harmondsworth: Penguin, 2004.

Wong, E. (2009) *Neither Fugitive Nor Free*. New York: New York University Press.

Wood, M. (2010) *The Horrible Gift of Freedom: Atlantic Slavery and the Representation of Emancipation*. London: University of Georgia Press.

Woods, T. (2013) 'Surrogate selves: Notes on anti-trafficking and anti-blackness', *Social Identities*, 19:1, pp. 120–134.

World Bank (2011) *Migration and Remittances Factbook 2011*. http://siteresources.worldbank.org/INTLAC/Resources/Factbook2011-Ebook.pdf.

Wu, B., Lan, G. and Sheehan, J. (2010) *Employment Conditions of Chinese Migrant Workers in the East Midlands*. Geneva: ILO.

Yang, A. (2003) 'Indian convict workers in Southeast Asia in the late eighteenth and early nineteenth centuries', *Journal of World History*, 14:2, pp. 179–208.

Yang, B. (2007) 'Life and death away from the Golden Land: The plight of Burmese migrant workers in Thailand', *Asian-Pacific Law and Policy Journal*, 8:2, pp. 485–535.

Yuval-Davis, N. (1997) *Gender and Nation*. London: Sage.

Zatz, T. (2008) 'Working at the boundaries of markets: Prison labor and the economic dimension of employment relationships', *Vanderbilt Law Review*, 61:3, pp. 857–958.

Zheng, T. (2009) *Red Lights: The Lives of Sex Workers in PostSocialist China*. Minneapolis: University of Minnesota Press.

# Index